Jacksons, Monk & Rowe and the Brodsky Quartet

The formative years

Jacksons, Monk & Rowe and the Brodsky Quartet

The formative years

Jacqueline Thomas

Copyright © 2022 Jacqueline Thomas

The moral right of the author has been asserted.

Apart from any fair dealing for the purposes of research or private study, or criticism or review, as permitted under the Copyright, Designs and Patents Act 1988, this publication may only be reproduced, stored or transmitted, in any form or by any means, with the prior permission in writing of the publishers, or in the case of reprographic reproduction in accordance with the terms of licences issued by the Copyright Licensing Agency. Enquiries concerning reproduction outside those terms should be sent to the publishers.

Matador
Unit E2 Airfield Business Park,
Harrison Road, Market Harborough,
Leicestershire. LE16 7UL
Tel: 0116 2792299
Email: books@troubador.co.uk
Web: www.troubador.co.uk/matador
Twitter: @matadorbooks

ISBN 978 1803133 096

British Library Cataloguing in Publication Data.
A catalogue record for this book is available from the British Library.

Printed and bound in the UK by TJ Books LTD, Padstow, Cornwall
Typeset in 12pt Bembo by Troubador Publishing Ltd, Leicester, UK

Matador is an imprint of Troubador Publishing Ltd

For Mam
4 December 1921–10 May 2021

About the author

Jacqueline Thomas was born in Middlesbrough, U.K. in 1961. A founder member of the Brodsky Quartet, she has been its cellist for fifty years, since the age of ten. The Quartet has built a stellar reputation through its global travels and huge discography, along the way collaborating with some of the most iconic names across all genres of music.

Aside from her performance schedule, she is a seasoned arranger and a compulsive inventor. She likes to design and realise property and home improvement projects, play golf, swim in the sea, watch football and enjoy glorious food and drink.

She lives in London with her husband Paul Cassidy, violist in the Brodsky Quartet. They have two grown-up daughters.

www.jacquelinethomas.org
www.brodskyquartet.com
www.facebook.com/thebrodskyquartet

Contents

Prelude	xi
1. The Big House on the Corner	1
2. Getting Going	8
3. El Sistema Original	15
4. Chamber Music	22
5. My Progress	32
6. Quartet Progress	42
7. Stepping Out	52
8. Dartington	60
Interlude I	70
9. Late Summer/New Term	80
10. Prejudice and Pride	87
11. Fame!	98
12. Pomp and Circumstance	106
13. Geeklemania	117
14. Concerts Galore!	129
15. La Fille Romantique et Révolutionnaire	140
16. End of childhood	149
17. Gap Year	160
18. Gap Year Continued	172
19. Student Life	181

20. Life on the Edge	191
21. Portsmouth	203
22. Post-Portsmatic Stress	211
23. Britten and Britain	222
24. Concours Français	230
Interlude II	238
25. Dissonance	246
26. Harmony	257
Postlude J,M&R signing off	266
Acknowledgements	272

Prelude

My life has been the Brodsky Quartet. From the age of ten to nearly sixty, as I am at the time of writing, it has been a constant presence. This is the story of how it all began, the formative years before we turned professional.

No other string quartet in the world was formed at such a young age and remained together into professional life. Whereas most musicians do start to learn to play from a very young age, chamber music is usually considered more suitable for older students. For us it was different; we seemed to know from the start that this was a serious undertaking and never once saw ourselves as just having fun. We were lucky enough to grow up in a part of the world where music lessons and instruments were free to any child wishing to take part, creating a rich environment of music-making for all ages. From this hotbed of opportunity, our group evolved and became the driving force of our young lives.

Along the way we encountered young musicians from an ever-widening clique of like-minded enthusiasts. Trips away to youth orchestras and national events brought us face-to-face with the competition and only served to increase fervour in our joint vocation.

The Cleveland Quartet, as we were in the beginning, became the Brodsky Quartet when we entered music college in Manchester. Here the group continued to dominate our studies and all our free time, performing and competing both at home and internationally.

In 1982 we had our first change of personnel – the violist, Alexander Robertson, left and was replaced by Paul Cassidy, who had been studying in London, graduating at the same time and therefore able to join us in Manchester.

At this point my memoir comes to an end, because Paul has just written a book covering the next forty years of the group's history. I was frankly surprised that these early years – and my journey within them – filled a book of their own, but then it is an unusual story: a classical string quartet being formed by children with the ambition to make it for life. Many times we are asked if it really started that young, if we are somehow exaggerating the story. We're not. As I wrote and the memories – as well as written and pictorial evidence – came flooding back to me, I too was surprised by just how true it is!

Though this book covers the first decade, there are flashbacks and -forwards to other moments in my story and the group's history: how my parents met, the provenance of my strange nickname (in the book's title), my early childhood within a big family and our crazy home. And moments in the story beyond this memoir. Paul and I got together, eventually marrying in 1990, and had two children, Holly and Celia, with whom we continued to travel the world for our work. Within the group, there were more changes of personnel along the way – my brother Michael left in 1998, Andrew Haveron and Daniel Rowland filled in the next 20 years, Gina McCormack was with us for only a very short time due to a personal crisis, and now we have welcomed in our new violinist, Krysia Osostowicz, with whom we hope to end our journey together… eventually.

In all this time, the three core members of the Quartet have remained the same, myself and Ian Belton ever since the beginning. My memoir aspires to paint a picture of the drive and passion behind this ever-so-long journey and the tenacity that finds us here to this day.

I started writing during the first pandemic lockdown of 2020. Here is how I began:

'I've just picked up my cello and played for the first time in almost four months. It's the one and only time in my exactly fifty years of playing this instrument that I have had a break of more than three weeks. Thank you Covid-19. My fingertips hurt and my stretch isn't what it was, but on the whole it was okay – now I need to rebuild my stamina to be back on top form for our return to work, whenever that may be.

'One of my musical heroes, Pablo Casals, wrote in his memoir of an accident in the mountains when he was at the peak of his career. As he lost his footing and went tumbling down a huge precipice, his immediate and glorious thought was, *Thank God, I'll never have to play the cello again!* The bittersweet tie we have to our instrument or our art, whatever it is, can often seem like a burden to those of us dedicated to a vocation. You never want to let it go, but given the opportunity for release by some other force, you'd take it... and then miss it like mad. I'm looking forward to getting back to work, but have enjoyed this enforced rest enormously.

'Sometimes along the way I've doubted my purpose and weathered many knocks to my self-belief, had an inkling to try a new career, or the urge to stay home with my young kids instead of traipsing around the world, my cumbersome companion by my side thwarting any pretence at grace and sophistication. But I always rekindled the energy to keep going, and I'm glad of it. I believe I hold the dubious honour of being unique in the world, as the only woman to have played in the same string quartet for fifty years!'

1

The Big House on the Corner

My family house is being sold and I'm visiting it for the last time. Sixty-five years of bustling comings and goings, five children at the time of moving here – three of us yet to be born – swelling its ranks as husbands and wives, grandchildren and great-grandchildren filled its four walls, then gradually diminishing till only my mother was left, and now she is too frail to remain here alone.

I was born here, in this grand Victorian pile on its corner plot that marks the start of Middlesbrough's more elegant neighbourhoods, a landmark house in the memories of many locals. The estate agents were chomping at the bit to view it, having always wondered what it would be like inside, and to be allowed to list it on their books. But even the most cunning agent-speak couldn't overlook the deceptive trick this house plays; it is the opposite of a Tardis. From the outside it looks huge, standing high by dint of a grand staircase to the raised ground floor, and is wrapped around by a luscious garden, hedge and tall trees. Great expanses of decorative brick and quoins adorn the front elevation, generous wrought-iron balconies and ornate arched windows promise a grandeur once inside.

But in truth this house is just a glorified two-up two-down back-to-back Victorian terrace. Configured as it is so bizarrely, it forms part of a block of four homes all adjoining and built, according to urban myth, by a father for himself and his three sons. Its design is decidedly strange. Two of the properties, including ours, have no back door and no back garden, and there were even secret passages in the attic rooms linking one house to the next.

Two-up two-down it may be, but the rooms on each level are huge, reached through long corridors and an Escheresque network of stairs. It is hard to imagine a more impractical house. The attic accommodation had once been servants' quarters – three small, dark rooms with two of them interconnected, meaning even generous estate agent propaganda would have to call it a 'four-slash-five-bedroom' house. So, for the young family who moved in all those years ago, there was already doubling up. By the time I came along we were sharing two or three to a room, the whole family of ten sharing one bathroom.

My parents had been wooed by its majestic size from the outside, my mother searching for a return to her semi-aristocratic Belgian roots and my father, who had just set up his own insurance business, perhaps keen to establish his local standing. Neither of them saw the house for what it was as they viewed it on the hottest summer's day of 1955 and took pleasure from the chill in the north-facing main room, never imagining the task ahead of keeping it warm in winter.

And now another buyer has fallen for its charms. We never expected the house to sell – no one had any faith it would pass the stringent demands of present-day sales procedure. With its ancient wiring, new fuse boxes being added to old crystal ones through the decades, it didn't even have a mains switch, so was irrevocably linked to the national grid, come what may. We were supplied with mains water via a long lead pipe, long-since illegal, and the leaky roof had been endlessly patched up over the years, cracks in all the ceilings threatening dangerous collapse at any moment. Yet here we are days away from completion, and the new residents are to be another family of seven, as were we when we took possession. Good luck to them!

As I enter, I sense the ghosts of my many arrivals: from school, from play, with friends – always welcome – to add to the numbers. School bags or cello in hand, then suitcases on holiday from college, home visits once I'd flown the nest, the last to leave.

The house has been mostly stripped out but here in the kitchen the solid oak draw-leaf table remains; having put in sixty-four years of tireless service it feels apt that this will be the last item to go. With both its leaves extended it filled the kitchen, where all meals were taken. There was no dining room. The other room on this floor was known as the Music Room, or indeed the Other Room, just as the kitchen became the Other Room if you were in the Music Room – a bit like the old days of television when there were only two channels and one would switch over to the Other Side.

This table I have sat on top of in many different guises. First I was Peter, lassoing the Wolf (my toy cat) with a piece of string, Prokofiev's classic work providing the soundtrack, me alone with my mother while all the others were out at school – a magical time for me. Later she found me cross-legged on this table, sewing by hand my latest dolls' clothes creations. She thought she'd seen a ghost as her grandfather and uncle had been tailors and it was their habit to sit cross-legged on the cutting table whilst working. She had never told me this – it must have been in my blood. Later still, I would lift a chair onto the table and climb up to practice my cello – one way to escape the chaos below. No one seemed to mind; they just walked around me. It was a good place to practise, detached from real life yet potentially always being heard, so a good performance was demanded. A precursor for life on my cello podium in the distant future.

Leaving the kitchen, I turn down the long L-shaped corridor, past where my brother's double bass would often lie, its spike threatening to snag the tights of passing teenage girls or draw blood from the shins of tearaway youngsters, past the rows of coat pegs, now empty, to the Music Room.

Here on the left was the upright piano where I played my first notes and tried to notate on a scrap of spare manuscript. I reckoned I'd penned the opening line of *God Save the Queen* but my dad's snigger when he looked over my shoulder and played what I'd written knocked me down a peg or two. (I thought it wasn't half bad, for a five-year-old with no training whatsoever.) In defiance I took a biro and scratched my name in the shiny varnish of the upturned lid: 'This piano belongs to Jacky Thomas', quite an audacious claim for the youngest of a large family of ivory tinklers. Everyone had a bash on those keys from time to time, but one sister, Joy, was particularly proficient and Dad could play anything by ear as long as it was in a key using mostly black notes. But it remained my piano for all to see, until we progressed to a baby grand, which stood pride of place in the large bay window overlooking the garden. (By now a bit older and wiser, I managed to resist the urge to repeat my engraving trick.) This alcove presented us with a stage of sorts, and we would stand around the piano as Dad played Schubert Lieder, all lustily singing along in English or badly pronounced German, depending on the edition he was using.

The house was always filled with music: practising for lessons, teens dreamily strumming guitars or smashing out rock music in the basement, records playing on every floor, from the huge mahogany radio set downstairs to the tinny portable up in the attic playing all types of music, classical and current. I can still picture the geometric of-their-time sleeve designs of each and every LP, still hear the moments in the music when a scratch would make the record jump or repeat the same bar over and over till someone gave the needle a helpful nudge. On a Saturday morning you could climb to the top of the house to hear *Children's Favourites* on the Light Programme while the older girls argued over what to wear for their weekly trip to town. Or twiddle the warmly lit dial of the radiogram down below, through its long list of mysterious stations, to the classical glories of 'The Third' (as Dad continued to call it long after it became known as Radio 3) or the plummy voices of The Home Service (Radio 4). I adopted my older siblings' sophisticated taste in pop music, so that The Who and The Beatles were as well known to primary school me as any teenager of the day.

We would sit around this table in the kitchen after Sunday lunch and sing along to strange songs from my dad's Cockney past, tunes that often had actions or even games attached. We'd line up by the cooker, in order of size, and go through the motions demanded by the dubious lyrics (acceptable back when they had been written, cringeworthy by today's standards) whose meanings were, and remain to this day, completely lost on me. 'Chinese cobblers, blacky man's eye, all round the merry-go-round, he winks his eye up to the sky and out goes [insert name of child here] with a big black eye.' Upon which cue you would leave the line and the song would start up again, eliminating each child in turn... till no one was left. I can't see how this was fun, unless I'm forgetting a crucial twist (quite likely, being the youngest, who always in a large family seem to be playing catch-up with the received wisdom of their elders).

Later, in the Music Room we would crowd around the television when anything we knew was being aired and sing along, including all the orchestral parts and harmonies, to such favourites as *Carmina Burana, Oliver!, Oh What a Lovely War!* and Handel's *Messiah*. Or play records of Belgian tunes sent over from our cousins in Brussels, trying to keep up in French though it wasn't spoken at home. Or dance wildly to the classical LPs, *Night on a Bare Mountain* or the *Polovtsian Dances*, flouncing around in a world of our own.

Even bedtime stories were set to music, Dad improvising with those lovely old Ladybird books, the rhyming couplets lending themselves perfectly to any number of musical settings. Thus, whenever I hear Haydn's *Emperor* Quartet (the theme adopted for Germany's National Anthem) I have in my head the heart-wrenching story of *Ginger's Adventures*, about a dog lost then gloriously re-found, which my dad delivered to that tune from beginning to end. The music lent the story even more pathos and many a tearful rendition was given and received.

But the house wasn't only filled with music; it was filled with every other kind of noise, all the time.

The sounds of warring teens, arguments over ownership of clothes, records, space; rows with parents over getting up too late, not helping enough, having a messy room; debates at mealtimes over current affairs or topics of interest, where the one with the loudest voice would invariably win; us marauding kids, using the house as a circuit for crazed races like Around the World in 80 Days – in the front door, round the corridor and out the French windows at breakneck speed; favourite games like running into the bathroom and slamming the door before a dart aimed from the landing above could find its target (you); climbing up to stand on the solid marble mantlepiece to jump off onto the sofa below, or the same game involving bunk beds and my cot; playing football on the front lawn, hitting tennis balls up against the huge expanse of windowless brickwork (just one of the architect's many bizarre decisions, whereby inclusion of a window could have offered sunlight to the chill Music Room – the upside, a stonking tennis wall); climbing (and falling from) the forty-foot trees, or crawling out of the attic dormer onto the perilously high roof to slide down the sloping bit onto the narrow ledge below; table tennis in the basement – hugely competitive tournaments involving the whole family and any willing hangers-on.

And animals... an endless menagerie of rabbits, guinea pigs, mice, gerbils, budgies; a one-footed pigeon (found injured in the garden and allowed to live in the kitchen – yes, the kitchen – for some considerable time); cats (one such three-legged)... and their kittens (all called Mimi); and most important of all, Conkey, a black-and-white Border collie, who suffered from the inevitable schizophrenia caused by having too many owners, none of whom knew how to handle a dog. He was mercilessly teased by some, provoking vicious growls and even bites, adding to the constant noise level as he yelped and roared, jumping up to catch the foot proffered provocatively through the staircase spindles and (usually) snatched away just in time. But he would take himself off for lone walks in the neighbourhood to escape the madness – and help boost the local mongrel population – and he lived for our weekly Sunday countryside excursions where he could play sheepdog to our flock of stupid sheep, keeping us in check as we rambled across moors and hills. To my delight, I had him all to myself in my last year at home, when everyone else had left, and was able to nurse him gently through his final days.

So as I make this final tour of the family home, all these scenes from my early childhood come to mind. Standing one last time in the Music Room, I recall how those crazed chaotic days were gradually replaced by a different kind of madness: instrument cases, music stands, sheet music littering the floor, sonorous melodies and crashing chords filling the air hour after hour, passionate exchanges and earnest endeavour, all in the name of this all-encompassing new obsession. Music, and more crucially chamber music, began to take over my daily life.

In this room half a century ago, the members of the Brodsky Quartet, then aged between ten and twelve, gave their debut performance.

2

Getting Going

Middlesbrough in the early seventies was experiencing a cultural renaissance. As in a handful of other regions, music lessons and instruments were available free of charge to all children, so there were no impediments to learning for those who felt the urge, or the parental push. But here there was something more happening, which led to a nationwide reputation as a hotbed of talent and achievement unexpected from what was ostensibly an industrial heartland. To this day, those I trained alongside are to be found throughout the music industry in many of the top jobs at international level. Where this fertile crop germinated is hard to say. Yes, there were key teachers and a passionate Music Adviser, as well as schools willing to nurture the emerging talent, but it seems to me not one element was behind the phenomenon: it was instead a lucky combination of many forces.

My own musical education began (barring claimed ownership of the family piano) in a most typical way: on the recorder. That blandest – in the wrong hands – of instruments, ubiquitous amongst primary school pupils and often providing the tuneless soundtrack for the throngs at home-time, walking whilst blowing without nuance or feeling, was nevertheless an excellent starting point for so many musical journeys. And the headmaster at my primary school knew it.

With this simple little instrument as his tool, he made sure each and every child who entered that school left with a basic ability to read music and a rich appreciation of the classical genre. As well as providing all comers with a recorder and tuition, each classroom was fitted with a loudspeaker high on the wall, from which would emanate his very own daily selection of orchestral greats. We would sit in silence and immerse ourselves in the rich tapestry of sounds filling the classroom, and indeed the whole school. There was something powerful in the knowledge that this was a joint experience throughout the building, a quasi-religious coming together. No one dared misbehave or interrupt the ritual; it was a cherished part of the routine and a wonderful way to start the school day. If only this enlightened approach could have been adopted into the curriculum nationwide, music might not be so undervalued as it has become in today's educational ethos. And mental health and wellbeing might be given an early boost.

I was reminded of the powerful influence of this daily routine when, in 2003, I and my colleagues in the Brodsky Quartet were preparing a schools project for the Contemporary Music Network. We had commissioned a new work for quartet and narrator – a kind of modern-day chamber version of *Peter and the Wolf* – and we needed an actor with musical skills to fill the role. A certain John Telfer was suggested, being highly recommended by the promoter, and we agreed on a date for our first meeting. We hit it off straight away with an easy rapport and the rehearsal was progressing well when we took a coffee break. Chatting about the sad state of music in general education, John proudly recounted the story of his own primary school, where the headmaster had piped classical music into the classrooms on a daily basis. "Wait, you can only mean Mr Starling!" I exclaimed. John's jaw hitting his chest told me that was exactly who he meant. With his dulcet thespian tones and received pronunciation, I had no idea he was a fellow North-Easterner and he hadn't realised the group hailed from his childhood town. The rehearsal dissolved into shared stories of home and nostalgia for those special moments of total immersion in the glorious classical playlist. (Later, and perhaps inspired by our joint experience, I devised a show called 'A Young Person's Guide to the String Quartet' in which John played a brilliantly hammy Papa Haydn and we his rebellious band of musicians, detailing the evolution of our art form.)

As is often the case, my childhood memories are accompanied by a musical soundtrack, which always comes to mind on the recounting of certain stories. One such event was my run-in with some metal railings, aged six, on the infant school steps. Being a bit of a loner, I was indulging in a melancholy rendition – only in my head of course – of *Land of Hope and Glory* whilst staring moodily into the distance, holding on to the railings as though trapped in some imaginary prison, probably pretending to be Joan of Arc (or some such character from my favourite annual, *Book of Heroines*.)

From one minute to the next, I was hurtled from historical dignity to infantile indignity as my head became irretrievably lodged between two of the cold iron uprights. A crowd formed quickly as the other children cottoned on to my plight, not sparing my blushes as they gigglingly sent for the teacher on playground duty. After what seemed like an eternity of painful pushing and pulling, someone had the bright idea of sending for the lollipop man. Somehow his long shiny white coat and huge beacon declaring 'STOP CHILDREN CROSSING' (whose lack of punctuation, negating its intended message, always annoyed me) doubled my sense of embarrassment and drew even more attention to the scene, so that by now the whole infant school was gathered to witness my eventual extrication, red-faced and sore around the ears.

I think of that moment every time I watch the flag-bearing throngs singing that famous anthem at the Last Night of the Proms...

Speaking of which, the BBC Symphony Orchestra has boasted several Middlesbrough-grown players, notably their principal cellist of many years, Susan Monks. Whilst the frivolity of this final concert of the world's greatest orchestral festival is being broadcast live to millions of viewers worldwide, spare a thought for the intensely skilful job at hand. There's a famous cello solo during one of the perennial favourites – some kind of folk song medley – during which the regular Promenaders adopt a faux-mournful expression and, dabbing white hankies, make great play of being moved to tears by the music. During this droll charade, the cellist on the spot must execute to perfection one of the most exposed and intricate solos in the orchestral repertoire. It sounds innocent enough, but is full of tricky leaps, each one of which must be tuned perfectly, and you just know the whole orchestra is holding its collective breath.

It would be great to think that this feat is appreciated by the frivolous crowd and the millions of viewers... but somehow you know it isn't. I've never seen Sue deliver it with anything less than consummate precision, but the look of single-minded concentration is one we musicians know only too well: she has completely blanked the TV cameras and the crowd around her with their chuckles and inappropriate honking horns, and is alone with her cello and her professionalism. Along the same lines, listen out for a stunningly beautiful cello solo next time you're at the movies – it will probably be Caroline Dale, another of our Middlesbrough alumni, top choice of Hans Zimmer et al for many of the most poignant moments on screen.

Back at the infant school, the sweet headmistress, Miss Ruddock, invited me into her office to recover from my ordeal. To me she always had a bit of a gypsy look about her, in long tiered skirts and floral blouses, seeming exotic and artistic. I was delighted a few years later to spot her in the viola section of the local amateur orchestra. Several of the school's teachers were keen amateur musicians and there was a great sense of the tables being turned when we young whippersnappers would come amongst them to boost the numbers or play concertos with them, their once terrifying persons – especially my fourth year junior teacher, Mr Knott – transformed into harmless innocents, ineptly struggling with the intricacies of their instruments and the orchestral score.

From the recorder I progressed to the piano, taking lessons with an aptly named local celebrity, Ella Pounder; her own playing was a touch heavy-handed, even by my inexperienced judgement. Not a slim woman, the reason for her generous size quickly became evident. Whilst I struggled with *Scenes at a Farm*, she grappled with a plateful of rich cream cakes, never once offering me even a bite, her instruction being barely discernible through full mouth, crumbs and cream falling onto the keys between my little fingers. But the piano wasn't the instrument for me; it was destined to take second place to another about to enter my life forever.

The way free instrumental tuition worked was this: once a year a letter would be sent home to parents offering the opportunity, and everyone who showed an interest was allowed to start. Simple. There was no aptitude test for the kids or means-testing of parents, just an unquestioned acceptance of all comers and no charge, whatever the family circumstances. Within my own family, the scheme had already put violins in the hands of three brothers and a sister, so when it came to my turn, my mum suggested the cello. I was delighted, having already fallen for the charms of my namesake Jacqueline du Pré, who had been making her infectious presence felt in the world for nearly a decade. My sharing her name completed the fit; it was meant to be.

There was one cello teacher in Middlesbrough at the time and she can claim a hand in the illustrious careers of many of today's high-flying cellists. As well as Sue and Caroline already mentioned, there was Ursula Smith (Zehetmair Quartet), Michal Kaznowski (Maggini Quartet), William Bruce (English National Opera), Ruth Alford (Age of Enlightenment Orchestra), Barbara Grunthal (BBC Philharmonic, Manchester Camerata), David Whittaker, Catriona Rooney and Lynda Perry (freelance players). All have a fond place in their hearts for this rather acerbic character with a no-nonsense approach and a tried-and-tested formula for nurturing talent. Her name was Kitty Peacock.

No other child in my school had picked the cello that year, so I was the lucky recipient of private lessons from the start. Being only eight and somewhat shy, I neglected to ask for clarity on the first task at hand. After a quick practical demonstration of what my new instrument could do, she drew a chart naming all the notes to be found in first position on each of the four strings. This might have been an obvious starting point for her, and no doubt worked for other kids, but I just saw a jumble of meaningless letters. I'm not sure I even played a note that day, but I was sent off with the task of learning the chart from memory and an instrument in an oversized canvas case bashing my shins as I walked home. It was small and rather characterful, well-used and with a warm – if scratched – varnish. I loved it because it was mine to take, but the novelty ended with carrying it home. With no clear sense of how to begin and the threat of the indecipherable chart to learn, I put the whole thing off until the day before my next lesson.

It was a Sunday, the garden was sunny and there was a great game in progress concerning mud and spades, when suddenly the realisation hit me that tomorrow was my lesson. I experienced my first sickening wrench to the stomach of neglected practice... the cross every musician must bear. In a panic I ran indoors, pulled my new instrument from its floppy case and attempted a few notes. I was encouraged by the rich sound I managed to produce, but my excitement was marred. I lay awake that night trying to memorise the letters on the dreaded chart, certain I would be tested on it straight away in my lesson, yet with no foundation as to how it worked or what it meant; it was a hopeless task.

As a peripatetic teacher, Kitty would find herself allocated odd corners of each school she visited based on whichever space was available, and so I found myself entering the hallowed ground of the junior school staff room just before morning break every Monday. As a result, my early memories of cello tuition are accompanied by the aroma of freshly brewing coffee and boiling milk. It was Kitty's job to prepare these in readiness for the staff's arrival, all eager for the caffeine kick they'd need to plough on with the school day. With only an old kettle, a wonky saucepan and a Primus stove, and health and safety standards a futuristic concept yet to be thrust on the world, Kitty would juggle pots and pans over an open gas flame in the hearth whilst I sawed away for her multi-tasking scrutiny. The milk never failed to boil over, initiating yelps and mutterings from her as she mopped up the grate, breaking the ice in many a lesson.

I actually think we bonded over this domestic scene and my love for the cello quickly blossomed. W. Squire's *Petite Marche* soon became my first performable repertoire and subsequently found its way onto the programme of family gatherings, and indelibly into my memory.

I never was tested on that chart – Kitty had forgotten all about it. Or maybe it was some clever power game she used to stamp her authority on new pupils. I must ask her one day.

3

El Sistema Original

Gustavo Dudamel and the Simón Bolívar Orchestra have long been turning heads across the globe following the fabulous success of an initiative bringing musical opportunity to Venezuelan kids of all ages: El Sistema. The transformative power of the project, started in 1975 by José Antonio Abreu, under the motto 'Music for Social Change', offered opportunity to thousands of young underprivileged and undervalued members of society, and has changed many lives forever. Kids are enlisted from a young age – learning as they go in the best way possible: surrounded by their peers – and stay with the System till they leave school. As it progressed, the original intake became so proficient that they eventually formed the SBO and have remained in the profession as a force to reckon with. It is seen as a unique model and has spawned many copycat projects worldwide. But this is just what we already had in Middlesbrough.

Edwin Raymond, a German-Jewish émigré, had begun to weave his magic in the sixties with the establishment of children's orchestras for all ages and an amateur orchestra and choral society for adults. Before this, there had been the Middlesbrough Junior Orchestra under the direction of Austin Melia, and a few noses were put out of joint by Raymond's arrival on the scene. But he had bigger ideas, encompassing a larger area and including more age groups. He was the driving force behind providing free tuition and loan of instruments to all, and his passionate belief in music-making at all levels was infectious and inspirational.

Early orchestral experiences were to be found in the Teesside Schools Orchestra, which met on Monday evenings, followed by the Training Orchestra. The adults' Symphony Orchestra met on Wednesdays, and the Holy Grail that was the Teesside Youth Orchestra got together on Friday nights. Whilst young people thronged to every rehearsal with enthusiasm and zeal, the adults' attendance figures (and ability levels) were sometimes thin on the ground, so kids would be enlisted to boost the numbers of the amateur orchestra. This led later to the formation of an additional entity, the Cleveland Philharmonic Orchestra, shrewdly made up of equal numbers from both demographics and therefore able to take the best from both worlds. Added to all this was the Choral Society, overseeing the International Eisteddfod Festival – which brought groups from all over the world to our little corner of England every two years – and his day job as head of the Music Service for the region; Edwin had his hands full.

My first orchestral experiences – very soon after I began cello lessons – came on Monday nights with the Schools Orchestra. Inevitably we had a basic repertoire and we can't have sounded that great. *March from Scipio* and Bizet's *Farandole* were scraped in a faltering manner; concerts were rare and to a limited audience of parents and teachers. The peripatetics drafted in to help with all these activities were as passionate as Edwin, giving up their evenings to the musical cause. One such, Mike Ingram, would take up the baton for the Beginners' Orchestra, and his pronunciation of these titles always comes to mind when I hear them even now. If the Handel was to be called for, he would tap his stand and declare grandly, "Oohkaay, Scipioooh" in a languid North-East drawl. Equally, the exotic title of Bizet's dance from L'Arlésienne Suite was given a caricaturist "Farandoooole", delivered in all seriousness.

In the wings were Keith Robson, the top violin teacher for the region – who, alongside Trevor Walshaw, also took the Training Orchestra – and other tutors, including of course Kitty Peacock, on hand to offer advice when needed.

Whilst the age of my fellow participants and our musical abilities lent the whole thing a slightly futile air (and I can sympathise now with my daughter who gave up after her first school orchestra rehearsal, preferring to stick to solo flute if this was the best she could expect from group activities), there was one event that captured all our imaginations and had us sitting straight in our chairs, all ears and attentiveness: a full-scale performance of Benjamin Britten's recently published masterpiece, *Noye's Fludde*. What a stroke of compositional genius, to insert a children's orchestra at the heart of an oratorio-scale work. What tender generosity of spirit to place professional musicians alongside beginners and make something that works, brilliantly. The lift it gave to us nine- and ten-year-olds, to be taking part in something that felt and sounded like real music on a grand scale, was invaluable.

To begin with, we were in the illustrious Town Hall and under the baton of the legendary Mr Raymond, a first for us all. Then we had our teachers joining forces to make up the solo quartet, as well as a proper recorder player (not the primary-school squawker we were used to hearing), representing the dove. Professional singers took the roles of Noye and Mrs Noye; trained boy and girl sopranos, their family. There was a team of percussionists of all ages, the adults on timpani, piano and glocks, the youngsters playing teacups, bells and whips. Meanwhile, we children of the string orchestra and recorder ensemble were able to create a tapestry of textures evoking the wind, the sea, raindrops then great storms, using open strings and simple techniques belying the overall effect. Massed school choirs in exotic costumes representing the animal kingdom and an adult congregation filled the town hall with iconic hymns, whilst the Voice of God bellowed beatifically over the whole.

The assemblage of this miracle play really was a miracle in my young life and its powerful impact has stayed with me forever. Many years later, for the fiftieth anniversary of the work, I was delighted to be able to take part, this time as quartet soloist, in two productions: one at Wimbledon Festival, which its enterprising director Anthony Wilkinson and I made into a beautiful film; the other in my home London borough of Haringey, where my own children were swept along with the six hundred other participants. Now when I play the solo quartet part, I never fail to be moved to tears in nostalgia and awe.

Middlesbrough Town Hall is a grand Victorian structure in the French Gothic style in the centre of town, and was the venue for every orchestral concert on offer. Local musicians of all ages regularly filled its stage, but there was also a steady stream of visiting orchestras from all over the world. The Newcastle-based Northern Sinfonia was our nearest professional orchestra, playing here at least six times a year, but all the regional and London orchestras would be sure to include us in their tour schedule and groups from Russia, Poland, Germany and many other countries followed suit. Capacity audiences flocked to a rich variety of orchestral concerts. I myself witnessed Campoli, Szering, Kyung-Wha Chung, André Previn, Michael Tilson-Thomas, coupled with the Israeli and Moscow Philharmonics, New York and London Symphonies and many more. Then it went through a period of decline; audience numbers fell and so it fell off the map of most touring orchestras. Even the Northern Sinfonia stopped coming.

When the Brodsky Quartet were touring Poland in the nineties, it was gratifying for me to see a huge old poster on the grand stairwell of the Warsaw Philharmonic Hall proudly announcing their resident orchestra's performance some twenty years earlier in Middlesbrough Town Hall. This was a sharp reminder of those days, and I felt a pang of sadness for lost glories. Even though I and many others knew that we had been a cultural hub to be proud of, a recent survey had awarded the town 'least desirable place to live in the UK'.

Even the name has a depressing sound to it. That 's' in the centre somehow brings it down; without it there could be a perkiness... but with the 's' and spoken in its regional accent, it sounds only downbeat. And to add insult to injury, the people of the region are nicknamed 'Smoggies'.

Local industry, which had for so long been supplying ships, steel and innovation to the world, was already in decline, unemployment and deprivation high. Another proud moment in my later life came when climbing the Sydney Harbour Bridge with my daughter Holly on a day off between concerts in the Opera House just across the water. The climb was fantastic. We had to wear harnesses and go through a short training session before it began, preparing us for the dangerous but spectacular ascent. Those girders were a formidable reminder of mankind's industry and engineering prowess, and as we climbed higher and higher, I imagined the gargantuan task of designing and forging every separate element and piecing it all together. Then, climbing through the underside of one such giant iron arm, I spotted three words soldered onto it that made my heart skip a beat: DORMAN LONG, MIDDLESBROUGH. A timely reminder of the glory days of industry for this town, which had so sadly waned and was now considered the arsehole of the country.

Yet here we had this thriving music scene with children of all ages being offered opportunities to play, or sing, in a wide variety of events, to compete in an assortment of festivals – each town in the vicinity had its own and the lists were always full – with adjudicators from the upper echelons of the profession. There was the biennial International Eisteddfod, second only to Llangollen in size and importance, with visiting dance troupes and choirs from all over the world. This event was so popular it had to be held in an enormous marquee, with an opening parade through the town, crowds cheering on the brightly costumed participants. My dad was chief steward one year, my sisters amongst the team of mini-skirt-uniformed ushers helping coordinate the hordes of dishy foreign visitors. Suddenly the house was full of the sounds of *Hava Nagila* and *Kalinka* as Gevatron or the Red Army Choir took to our turntable. The Eisteddfod even had a classical competitive strand, so we were later able to add it to our list of prize-winning opportunities.

Incredibly, Billingham – less than ten miles away – held its own International Folklore Festival with equally fervent participants arriving from all over the world, but especially from behind the Iron Curtain. (Though I didn't know it at the time, I suppose there was a sense of 'any excuse to get out'.) Billingham also created a futuristic Forum Arts Centre, complete with leisure facilities to be envied – an Olympic pool, a competitive-level ice rink, indoor tennis and bowls... and a theatre that would frequently host touring opera companies and chamber groups. The whole place was thriving. Having become hopelessly dated, its seventies' decor and building materials not fit to last, it has recently undergone a huge refurbishment, as has Middlesbrough Town Hall with its new neighbour, MIMA (the Institute of Modern Art), all making a concerted effort to return to their former importance as hubs of the community.

Along with the decline of industry and the closure of shipyards and mines, and to complete the image of being a nothing place, Margaret Thatcher later made sure that this thriving cultural scene, and especially the funding for free tuition, was ruthlessly axed. But against the odds the legacy has prevailed; Tees Valley Youth Orchestra, as it is now known, has just celebrated its fiftieth anniversary with an appearance at Carnegie Hall and a reunion concert at the Town Hall. And what a reunion it was. As well as all the cellists Kitty had nurtured, the TYO alumni from my era alone count amongst them Miranda Dale (Philharmonia), Angela Daly and Colin Twigg (City of Birmingham Symphony), Nigel Wareham (Bilbao Orkestra Sinfonikoa), Tony Robson and Matthew Truscott (Age of Enlightenment), Jan Kasnowski (various chamber groups and orchestras then ground-breaking teacher), John Kane (Bournemouth Symphony) and Eddie Jobson (Roxy Music, Jethro Tull and Yes).

It wasn't long before I was promoted from Monday night baby orchestra to the big boys and girls at the Friday night gathering of the Youth Orchestra. Here was my first taste of participation in real orchestral music and the incredible thrill to be involved in the creation of such an overwhelming sound: Symphonies by Tchaikovsky, Brahms, Schubert; Overtures and Concertos with visiting soloists and those from within our ranks, soon to be my own self. But within this new environment would emerge something altogether more intimate, more autonomous and, above all, not offered as part of the service. We discovered it for ourselves and ran with it... it was all-consuming and intoxicating. The String Quartet.

4

Chamber Music

Almost as soon as I could play a few notes on the cello, I began to think of composing for it, and my creative muse was led to the chamber music side of things. My nearest sibling in age, Michael, who had taken up the violin two years earlier and was already striding ahead, was the obvious victim for my first opus. A duet for violin and cello entitled *Sunday Morning*, it was a series of contrary motion scales and broken chords, never straying from the safety of C Major. Opening with a strident theme played in octaves, it ended with descending scales reminiscent of church bells.

As we drove to the Billingham Forum Arts Festival to offer it up in the 'Children's Original Composition' section, it was as yet untitled. Mam quickly thought up the obvious one and scrawled it at the top of the page in her distinctly adult handwriting, much to my horror. No matter, the content was clearly that of a child, as testified by the rounded crotchets and quavers with their heavy, awkward tails. It won first prize. Quite possibly it was the only entry, I don't remember. I was delighted anyway and felt more than vindicated for my *National Anthem* failure.

Perhaps because my dad drilled into his daughters that women lacked the creativity of men, had never and would never equal the genius of the great composers, I was discouraged from continuing in this trajectory. The boys were encouraged in their efforts and have all grown up with the ability and self-belief to write and perform a wide range of music. Does this back up Dad's argument or simply prove that conditioning is more powerful than we realise? Is it nature or (lack of) nurture? (I suppose the wealth of brilliant and unfettered female composers and singer-songwriters gracing 21st century concert halls answers that.) My older sisters would argue the case angrily whenever it arose, but I was too young to involve myself in dinner-time debates. Such can be the power of parental negativity that I suppose it found its way into my subconscious. Anyway, there was plenty of new music awaiting me, so I didn't need to try writing it myself.

Dad, who had played the violin as a young man, found himself inspired to take it up again; his love of the string quartet was inspiration enough to spur him urgently but falteringly through the Grade exams, while his young offspring sailed through them with precocious and annoying ease. In the UK we have a progress assessment system from Grade I (beginners) to VIII (conservatoire entry level); beyond Grade V, theory tests are introduced as an added hoop to jump through.

Even though she was completely untrained in music and could barely sing, let alone play an instrument, Mam's musical knowledge was extensive and her passion for it immense, especially for her beloved opera. It was she who put us through our paces when further progress in the practical exams demanded theoretical proficiency and certificates to prove it.

Music is a complex language with rules as imperative as any spoken tongue; learning to speak without a basic understanding of grammar and spelling leads to a poor delivery. Equally, gifted children can only go so far leaning on their talent before they will come unstuck on some basic knowledge they've missed out on. For this we have music theory – the written assimilation of the intricate workings of keys, time signatures, rhythms and so much more. Every child must learn to know without thinking that, for example, four flats at the start of the stave means they'll have to flatten B, E, A and D until further notice, and that they're playing in A flat major or F minor; the enharmonic use of accidentals, where a note can sound the same but be written differently according to the key – so a B♭ can become an A# and it has to be right; the difference between an augmented second and a minor third, which sound identical; the names *acciaccatura* and hemidemisemiquaver. While other kids are happy to sing along to Julie Andrews' *Do-Re-Mi*, we must learn the proper names of the scale and rattle them off by rote: *Tonic, Supertonic, Mediant, Subdominant, Dominant, Submediant, Subtonic!* All this is no mean feat and there is so much more to learn; a Pass in Grade V Theory was an unavoidable hurdle and Mam was our exclusive coach.

    I don't know how she did it, with no training of her own. She always loved puzzles, so must have approached it from a purely logical perspective. She came up with little acronyms, so we'd remember how to order the sharps and flats, how key relations worked and so on. To this day, when faced with a key signature of several sharps I mentally clock her brilliantly quirky aide-memoire, Fat Cats Get Drowned After Each Breakfast, meaning that F, C, G, D, A, E and B must be sharpened in that sequence.

    The number of sharps designated to the sharp major key signatures – being G, D, A, E, B and F sharp – are identified for me as: Graham Devlin (my first heart-throb in infant school), Alun Evans (footballer), Billy Fury (Mersey Beat singer-songwriter.) So, one sharp is G major (Graham), two sharps D major (Devlin) and so on. And this could be reversed for the flat keys. Genius! (I remember the day she asked us for names to create these acronyms, the four of us sitting around the kitchen table. I obviously provided the first, Mike, who was a keen footballer, thought up the second, then we were struggling til our sister Silvia popped her head round the door and provided the perfect BF combination.)

The pass mark for theory exams was sixty-six out of ninety-nine. I, the baby aged ten, proudly carried the interfamily top mark somewhere in the eighties, while dad got an average seventy-something and Mike scraped in with sixty-six, much to everyone's amusement – why get more than the bare minimum?!

My early efforts in group playing were little string trios by Pleyel and the like, with Dad and Mike my playing partners. Or we would team up with sister Janet for an early classical string quartet, she transcribing the viola part to play it on the violin. She also wrote out little duets we could play together, to suit our abilities. But we were soon to be inspired by a higher level of this art form. As well as the visiting orchestras to Middlesbrough, we were blessed with a thriving Chamber Music Society and frequent appearances by a host of exotic groups – the Hungarian Quartet playing Bartók, the Smetana playing Janáček – and, though I wasn't yet attending these concerts, the in-house LP collection started to swell as my elders' tastes became more eclectic.

So it was that one of the first proper quartets I became aware of was Bartók's 5th. It was mind-blowing. The madness and fervour pouring forth from the speakers in the Music Room, stringed instruments playing in a way I could barely imagine possible, madly complicated rhythms and chords, soaring lyricism and unearthly virtuosity within a completely new language. The way four players can have individual lines in cannon, but the collective aural effect is another thing altogether, like some kind of illusional puzzle. We would sit around the record player in awe as the final movement unfolded in frantic scales and runs, contrary motion and every which way, building to a frenzied climax. Then, suddenly, dissolving into a little nursery rhyme, out of tune and faltering, like four beginners had suddenly arrived to take over the performance, and we dissolved into hysterical laughter, before the madness once more took hold and propelled us towards the final triumphant notes.

As orchestra nights became more and more the highlight of my week, the carrot at the end of five days' tedious schooling, our big corner house became a hub for kids to congregate both before and after the rehearsal. Two such became regular participants and shared our fascination with this extraordinary music: Ian Belton and Alexander Robertson. At ten or eleven, our idea of a fun get-together was to sit around listening to these crazy outlandish recordings, jumping the needle ahead to our favourite bits, even trying to play along with the record. If there was a bigger gathering, we'd put on records like *Rhapsody in Blue* or *West Side Story* and make up 'modern dance' steps, or take out our instruments and have a 'jam', or we might just as likely hit the front lawn for a game of football, or the basement for table tennis. But more and more, the pull of this quartet thing won the day, and we four found ourselves forming a bond and becoming addicted to the format.

Our early repertoire was purloined from Dad's limited collection of sheet music, mostly the great classics – Haydn, Mozart, Beethoven and Schubert. These were of course exciting works to grapple with and we always kept them to hand, but we very quickly started sending away for more unusual works, inspired by the recordings and concerts we were now exposed to. Shostakovich No.11 was one such, and I still have my first copy of this work in which I have put a fingering number on every single note, including the repeated ones. (String players will know that this kind of excessive self-direction is entirely unnecessary and indicative of a fervour bordering on obsession). His 3rd Quartet was another early favourite, as was Prokofiev's 2nd, though both works had to wait a few years for us to tackle all the movements. Sometimes the language was wildly beyond our intellectual understanding, but we were able to copy what we heard and make a pretty good fist of it.

The day Ian and Mike went off to Newcastle to audition for a new violin teacher and returned, having visited the big city's more sophisticated music shop, Windows, with parts and score for Bartók No.5 was a momentous day indeed. Those magical and mysterious sounds we'd been listening to were suddenly there on the page, but it didn't make things all that much easier. The opening strident bars were fine – rhythmic unison gave us each an anchor to the whole – but once they were over and the music launched into that apparent free-for-all jazz jam, our individual abilities struggled with the complicated finger patterns and virtuosic bow techniques. Our mantra was to keep going at all costs, and it helped create a lifelong ability to keep up and stick together through any difficulty. The rhythm came first, notes later (in this case, much later!). The pocket score for this incredible work was equally fascinating, visually compelling as it was, based on hidden mathematics and symmetry. We would frantically peruse it as the record played; in the fast movements, pages needing to be whipped over quicker than our little hands could keep up with, the corners well-thumbed with our repeated essays into its treasures – till our dog Conkey got hold of it and carried it off down the road on one of his amorous encounters, no doubt trying to impress his latest conquest. Ian found it in a hedge a few days later, chewed and soggy, but still usable.

That these four kids with this shared passion lived within a radius of a few hundred yards is perhaps unusual. But there were more of us – all the Youth Orchestra members had this enthusiasm for the music; the highlight of everyone's week was Friday night. Perhaps having this self-satisfied precocious string quartet emerge from within the ranks inspired a more driven and ambitious whole than was the norm. We would arrive early for rehearsal so that we could practise (show off) in the hall as others were pouring in and setting up. It even spawned other groupings, who we would compete with in the local festivals, but we considered ourselves the real deal, ahead of all comers.

When I arrived on the Friday night scene, Ian Belton had recently made the local paper as leader of the Junior Strings, so was close to celebrity status. In his two-tone purple loons and tight knitted tank top, his David Cassidy-style glossy brown hair brushing long shirt collars, he was a vision of seventies' chic. Legend had it that his piano playing was as good as his violin, and his rugby and football were equally accomplished. It was quite a coup when he started turning up with the rest of us after orchestra. Alexander Robertson was altogether more of a geek, with excitable enthusiasm and an almost spectrum-scale understanding of the music. His violin playing was technically dubious but totally wired, his piano skills had been largely self-taught but were none the worse for it; he was a brilliant artist who could draw or paint anything with ease. His dark swarthy looks came from his Maltese mother, a devout Catholic who boasted several priests amongst her siblings, his creative eye from his dad, an art teacher who hailed from Scotland. Ian's parents were schoolteachers from County Durham, his dad a physics teacher with a determined logic and dry wit, which decidedly found their way into Ian's DNA. Neither set of parents contained an ounce of musical heritage, yet they produced these brilliant young talents.

Michael, of course, had come from where I came from, so we already had a close musical bond nurtured in that crazy family of singers, players and shriekers. We had a homespun rivalry that probably served to propel our learning more speedily than average, and once the quartet was up and running we had a shared passion. Though I looked up to him as my older brother, my drive was no less ambitious. I would eagerly chair decisions on which pieces we were going to learn or buy next and write them excitedly in my diary, as another girl might write about the latest popstar poster or teen magazine on sale. From the beginning, commitment was worn like a badge of honour. One day when

Ian cut short a rehearsal on his parents' orders, for homework or some other tedious duty, Mike was to be seen lifting the back of his bike off the ground, Ian frantically pedalling in mid-air, the two of them caught in this slapstick – but at the time oh-so-heartfelt – conflict of interest.

Most string quartets designate a player to each role, which remains fixed: Violin 1, Violin 2, Viola and Cello. We saw it differently. In the early days, the three boys all played violin and viola and rotated as necessary, taking particular pieces for each position. But before long, Alex decided the viola was his instrument and stuck solely to it, leaving the other two to swap equally between 1st and 2nd Violin. This democratic approach created in us a fervent belief that the string quartet is an instrument in and of itself, with one voice and no leader, only a succession of leading lines with subsidiary and harmonising roles being shared between the remaining players, whoever they may be.

Our first performance in the famous Music Room of my family home, to a small, select audience of parents, siblings and a teacher or two, was probably a few movements from Beethoven opus18 no.5 or Mozart G Major, Haydn *Lark* and maybe a bit of Shostakovich. Being all from the small enclave of Linthorpe, that was the first name we adopted for our inaugural showcase concert, but it quickly sounded too parochial for a group of grand international ambition.

The arrival of that Bartók No.5 score and the words emblazoned on its cover provided us with our next bright idea in the search for a name, the Hungarian word for 'string quartet': *Vonósnégyes*. This was just the kind of exotic title we were after and it had the added bonus of being cleverly tautologous – so we would be, literally, The String Quartet String Quartet. Our first outing at the Middlesbrough Festival Chamber Music Class soon put paid to this precocious piece of pubescent pretentiousness as the poor announcer tripped over the correct pronunciation (insisted on by us) – 'Vonooshnaygash' – and Mr Raymond subsequently asserted that if we didn't choose a different name, he wouldn't allow us to play at the St Barnabas' Church Prizewinners' Concert. This kind of threat to our worldwide trajectory was hard to ignore; a new name was needed.

Although its identity to outsiders is inextricably linked to the iron and steel and chemical industries, Middlesbrough's geographical setting belies this drab reputation. The town is on the doorstep of some of the country's most beautiful scenery: the North York Moors, the Yorkshire Dales, quaint fishing villages with mighty cliffs and rugged, scarred beaches, all within a short drive of home. Long rambles around Goathland or Richmond, or days by the sea in Whitby or Robin Hood's Bay, could be rounded off with pub meals in the most idyllic surroundings, or some of the best dripping-fried fish and chips you'll ever taste, eaten from the paper with a pint of Old Peculier on the beach as the sun sets behind you, throwing a shimmering light onto the North Sea. Even closer to home, just a ten-minute drive or an hour's bike ride for us kids, Kildale, Stokesley or Great Ayton, the charming villages at the foot of the Cleveland Hills, the Anglo-Saxon and Norse settlements with their strange pronunciations, Chop Gate (Chop-Yat) or Staithes (Steers). Many long days could be spent making dens in the high bracken and ferns or swimming in lakes and rivers, showering in freezing waterfalls; or climbing stiles over drystone walls through romantic farms with their solid stone farmhouses and bleating sheep, James Herriotesque characters with gruff, no-nonsense voices giving short shrift to attempted conversation.

In the search for a new name for the group, this rich playground became our focus. 'Cleveland' seemed more cosmopolitan and spoke more truly of these roots. Middlesbrough had been in the North Riding of Yorkshire but was now in the County Borough of Teesside. Whereas the upper reaches of this river fall through the idyllic scenery of the Upper Tees Valley, the lower waters conjure up images of industry and shipping with its great steel bridges, including the iconic – and frankly, weird – Transporter Bridge, which literally transports vehicles and pedestrians in a basket over the water in the most desolate part of town, seeming to go from nowhere to nowhere. The shipping had come with the arrival of the Stockton and Darlington Railway, with the river as its focus. Industry was everywhere and Teesside had the wrong flavour for our artistic endeavours.

Our choice of name seemed to be legitimised when the area received its new status as Cleveland County, linking it more fittingly with its rural surroundings. With our eye on the future, having already decided this was for life, we became the Cleveland String Quartet and the regional coat-of-arms motto fitted us perfectly: *Erimus* – We Shall Be.

5

My Progress

My days at primary school came to an end. Those comforting traditions of morning music, hymns in the assembly hall, recorder group and choir at lunchtime, Christmas nativities in winter and country dancing on the school field in summer – in those crisp little white blouses and dirndl skirts brought out for the occasion – skipping and elastics, marbles and tag in the playground; all were destined for the memory banks of childhood nostalgia, along with the pounds, shillings and pence we had just waved goodbye to in favour of the new decimalisation, to the accompaniment of The Scaffold and their clever songs, teaching us how to make the switch and calculate the differences. *Sixpence is two-and-a-half new pence* and *use your old pennies in sixpenny lots* – the power of music as an aide-memoire is testified to this day by the indelible imprint of the little songs onto my cerebellum...

But truthfully, these innocent pleasures and carefree days had already begun to fade with the retirement of Mr Starling and the arrival of the new head, Mr Mizon. Suddenly the *Pastoral Symphony* became *The Sorcerer's Apprentice*. A terrifyingly tall figure with a Hitler moustache, sleek black hair and... a wooden leg – yes indeed – which would swing out beside him as he walked, it being non-jointed and awkward, making his approach down the corridor all the more intimidating, he cancelled morning music and took to meting out punishment at morning assembly, caning boys and slippering girls in a public shaming, with the words 'this hurts me more than it hurts you' as his mantra. I was personally spared this particular horror, but there was a definite change to the atmosphere, well-timed with my own sense of moving on.

Having much older sisters who were fast developing into women in front of my eyes, I started to emulate their age group and give myself the airs of teendom. One day near the end of our final year, my close friend Pamela Baldwin and I were making a moody circuit of the playground, arms linked, gazing with derision at the lower classes busy in their childish games. Pamela was a bit of a fantasist – she had only one sister but had invented an older brother, whom she insisted was going out with current teen idol Lulu. (Not to be outdone, I rejoined that my sister was dating Donavan, though my dubious choice of namedrop let me down a bit, I dare say, he being decidedly Indie.)

Pamela was a fashion guru to me, always one step ahead with the latest trends. Besides a few home-sewn frocks, my wardrobe was dependent on the Belgian cousins' hand-me-downs – a most welcome parcel of unimaginable chic that arrived about once a year – or random items long-since discarded by the older girls. I scoured our attic for something I could pass off to match her most recent acquisition – a fab pair of bell-bottoms – and was delighted when she scrutinised my sister's old jodhpurs and asked "Are them your flares?", against all the odds clearly approving of the stand-ins, which, by their very design, couldn't be less suited to the job.

So, as we paraded the playground in faux-teen attitude, a group of girls approached and asked if we'd been to the swimming pool. We hadn't; I just hadn't had a bath for a week and it was starting to show. I replied with what I considered the ultimate in cool: "Nah, my hair's greasy", a phrase I had heard my sisters nonchalantly throw off. Pamela was furious we'd passed up an opportunity to brag – only the fourth years got to go to the swimming baths in town – and I, too late, realised idolatry of my older sisters was probably for my private appreciation only.

As we shuffled around the dance floor to Donny Osmond's *Puppy Love* at the Leavers' Ball, dressed in long cardigans tied at the waist with gold chains, I felt an inexorable melancholy for this old-style Victorian seat of learning and mixed emotions about my young experiences, and was ready to move on to a new life.

Upon receiving a letter of invitation to my allocated secondary school, I was horrified to find it was none of my siblings' *alma maters*. A new campus of two comprehensive schools had been built on the outskirts of town and I was to be amongst the first intake to remain for five years under one roof. My initial horror was quickly replaced with a more considered realisation that this was actually an advantage: with no preconceived prejudices or annoyingly hard acts to follow, I would be anonymous and there on my own terms.

Hustler was a huge school with an eight-class intake, brand new up-to-date facilities in purpose-built blocks, with four local factories as House names: Ashmore, Cummings, Dorman and Hunter. Although there was a school orchestra and various in-house musical activities on offer, I quickly decided that the broad demographic of pupils would not allow such highbrow pastimes to go unpunished, so I kept a low profile, managing to hide from even my class music teacher until well into my third year that I was in any way linked to the aesthetically sophisticated world of the cello or the string quartet.

This was a scary place where girls from the rougher parts of town would be likely to explode into vicious scraps, with hair-yanking being the more mild-mannered of their sparring techniques. These figures of formidable ferociousness would parade in packs, black flared skirts beneath school blazers giving way to impossibly huge platform shoes, thin ankles threatening to snap under the wedges' weight, their gruff dialect exaggeratedly pronounced to enhance the fear factor.

'Ow, yow!' (translation: 'Hey, you there!') being yelled at any given moment in the playground would provoke panicked glances by all in the vicinity, followed by sighs of relief at not being the addressee of such a greeting. Being from London and Brussels parental stock, the Middlesbrough accent hadn't been naturally acquired at home, so those of us who failed to adopt it were left with a decidedly posh-sounding voice. (It's all relative, of course – I'm easily identified as a Northerner to outsiders.)

Week One provided a memorable faux-pas that very nearly landed me the wrong end of a clenched nail-polished fist. When joining a bottleneck mob waiting to enter the science block, I felt a shove from behind and indignantly declared "Stop it, right!" in a pathetic attempt at assertive aggression. Surrounded by sniggers of derision, my new-found friends nearly ditched me there and then, as a faceless voice from the crowd mimicked my little outburst to perfection. It was a near miss and I decided I'd have to be more careful in future.

I was indeed something of a geeky misfit; I had this other life going on outside of school and all my focus and energy was on that. I enjoyed the education I was receiving and did well in most subjects, especially Music – to the amazement of the class teacher and to my amusement as I continued to keep her in the dark about my twilighting activities – but my heart lay elsewhere.

I had another close shave with the Cool Police when in English class we were asked to write an essay about our teen idol. I had recently received a landmark present on my sister Silvia's return from London: my first set of the Bach Cello Suites sheet music. I didn't know of the works or their importance in the repertoire of my chosen instrument, so I came to them completely fresh. It was an amazing voyage of discovery, to work my way through these masterworks at my own pace and gradually allow their magic to find its way into my being, as it still does to this day.

Shortly afterwards, I bought myself the iconic recording by Pablo Casals and immediately became enthralled with his story, his religious fervour for music, especially Bach, and not least his cute face and adorable pipe. He was in his nineties and living in self-imposed exile from the evils of Franco's fascist regime. Leafing through the autobiography I'd also saved up to buy, I was intrigued by the tale of his discovering the Bach Suites in a Barcelona backstreet bookstore when he was about my age. And how, late in life, he'd married a much younger and seriously hot Puerto Rican brunette, whose stylish photos I envied almost as much as her husband's facility on the cello.

Whatever madness persuaded me to cite this musical icon as my hero for the essay set by our teacher that day, I don't know. But there I was again, reading out my efforts to the whole class and laying myself open to the voracious appetite of the pack when faced with a rogue element. It wasn't just that I admired this weird old classical music guy; I also used the essay to poo-poo the inferior tastes of my peers, admiring as they did the current crop of pop stars and bands. I don't know why I did this – I was a keen follower of pop with an eclectic taste, built through my older siblings' record collection of Beatles, Stones, Dylan, The Who, Franklin, Procul Harem et al, and my own emerging appreciation for the seventies' icons, Bowie, Armatrading, Queen, 10cc... But somehow it fitted with my remit to big-up Casals and all he stood for as against the ephemeral culture of pop. I was promptly renamed Pablo by my perplexed but indulgently patient friends, and was never allowed to forget it.

My cello lessons with Kitty had moved to Saturday mornings at her house, which suited me fine for the purposes of keeping up my incognito double life. I had a new piano teacher, the adorable and diminutive Jean White, who indulged my decided preference for the cello but helped me in my stumbling efforts to maintain a moderate level on the all-important second-study instrument. I had progressed from my first scruffy cello to a shiny new one, which looked spanking but had no sound whatsoever. It quickly became clear that the free instruments available from the council were no longer good enough for the level I'd reached.

One day my parents returned from a trip to London with a cello of my very own – they'd gone to the Philips sale and found one they liked the look of. It was slightly smaller than average and described as a 'Lady's Cello'; it seemed meant to be. They bid and won it for £100 and brought it home to me, hoping I'd like it. I of course did. It had a rather elegant shape and an unusually long scroll, giving it a haughty air; it had extra-curvaceous F-holes and a lovely golden varnish with just the right amount of scratches and dents to look properly aged. And it was mine.

Mam put the icing on the cake by making a beautiful black canvas case, which we decorated together in a bright red trim; because the cello had been bought at sale, it didn't come with a case. And because of its unusually long scroll, a standard one didn't fit properly. She must have gone to a lot of trouble, first creating a prototype using an old sheet, then sewing at the machine all that cumbersome fabric. What an astonishing effort, along with all her daily chores…

Orchestra and Quartet were tripping along as usual and I was starting to play more and more demanding music, as well as tearing through the Grade exams at top speed. At this point Kitty suggested it might be time to move on to a teacher who could take me to the next stage, always aware as she was that the needs of her students should come before any sense of her own ego. Her speciality was beginners, and I had reached the end of that road.

Her usual recommendation to more promising students was the great Florence Hooton, who taught at the Royal Academy of Music. I would have to enrol for Junior Academy and commit to weekly trips to London every Friday night in time for a full Saturday of activities. This was my first moment of realisation that the Quartet had to come first in my life, and even Friday night orchestra was a weekly part of my routine I wasn't willing to forgo.

So I refused that route and opted for lessons with a newcomer to the area with promising credentials and a growing reputation as a soloist, Arnold Allum. He introduced me to my first concerto repertoire through Boccherini and Saint-Saëns, and in fact was himself invited to perform the latter with the adults' Symphony Orchestra soon after I'd started learning it. As was often the case, we youngsters were drafted in to boost the numbers and I found myself sitting at the back of the cello section for the first play-through without our soloist, in preparation for his arrival the following week. This routine of rehearsing the orchestra sans-soloist was normal procedure but it was new and troubling to me. From the dramatic opening chord there was a terrible void where the solo cello should have been and I could hear every note of it in my head.

After a few minutes of what seemed to me a farcical exercise, I burst forth with the solo line, much to the amazement and entertainment of all around me, including my dad in the violas and brother Pete in the bass section. Mr Raymond, with an amused smile, invited me to join him in front of the orchestra and I completed my ad hoc performance as well as I could, having not yet learnt the last movement.

This kind of unabashed precociousness was a trait I would take a couple more years to shake off and it must have been seriously annoying. Not long afterwards, I was in the audience for a performance of the Dvorak Concerto and, having devoured my recording but not yet learnt the notes, I affected to mime every bit of it from my seat in the balcony. Even at eleven, I don't know why this spontaneous air-cello performance seemed in any way appropriate behaviour and I must have narrowly avoided a slap to the back of the head by fellow audience members. The memory makes me cringe...

My lessons with AA didn't last long. He soon decided this wasn't a place he wanted to settle – hardly surprising as he'd chosen the most dreary enclave to live in. My Monday night winter drives through the Wilton chemical works to his house in Redcar made me depressed and scared, shimmering lights and live flames pouring out of the immense factory structures. (This industrial sprawl was the inspiration behind two dystopian worlds of fiction; Aldous Huxley's *Brave New World* and Ridley Scott's *Blade Runner*.) I would gaze out of the passenger window in awe and dread, imagining I was lost in that great maze of tracks and lanes, wishing I was back home, as Dad drove me inexorably towards my lesson. It wasn't a good association. No wonder he didn't stick it – I could well imagine AA might have landed himself *in* AA if he'd stayed a day longer.

In a tiny village up in the Northumbrian borders, a rambling stone mansion nestled amongst the rugged tundra and windswept elements. Music was always to be heard pouring forth from its many mullioned windows and a series of eccentric-looking characters would arrive to take up residence, frequently doubling the population of the village to a heady forty-something people. This was Edrom House, Duns, the unlikely setting for the grandly named International Cello Centre, brainchild of the formidable cellist Jane Cowan, with John Gwilt her partner in crime. I knew of it through a cellist friend from Richmond, Andrew Wardale, who sometimes made it across to Middlesbrough for Wednesday night orchestra, his dad being one of the amateur regulars. Andrew was a student at the ICC and urged me to give it a go; Mam dutifully made the phone call and Dad drove me the hour or so up the A1 for my audition.

But again, my reticence to prioritise my own playing over the pull of the Quartet made it a non-starter. It was a boarding school and I couldn't imagine being away from my colleagues, even at that age, for weeks at a time. (The inevitable homesickness was of course another consideration.) I did however spend a memorable day amongst the Centre's residents, with their odd routines and ways – they spoke a different language each day at mealtimes, and lessons were un-timetabled and could be sprung on you at any time by the lady of the house, who would hover outside the door of your practice room and suddenly burst in, bellowing musical criticism or technical instruction. At the communal lunch table I was aware of one particularly characterful kid, a couple of years older than me, who had entered wearing a geekily belted gabardine and wellies. He had wildly curly dark hair that hung low over his eyes, an engaging and cheeky smile, and a quirky sense of humour. Looking back many years later, I realised that this must have been Steven Isserlis, the school's most distinguished alumnus.

Having reluctantly turned down the invitation that followed to study at the ICC I followed another suggestion of Andrew's, that of a teacher in Richmond, his home town. So began the unlikely tutelage for the next couple of years under a certain Dr A.J. Bull, an eccentric, extremely tall, adorable English gentleman with a very loud voice and infectious laugh, whose other job was parish church organist. He must have been well into his seventies when I went to him in his tall Georgian house on Frenchgate, a cobbled hillside street near the centre of this idyllic market town on the edge of the Yorkshire Dales. I'd always loved visiting Richmond on family outings, and the idea of it becoming a regular Saturday morning trek was irresistible.

I delighted in the diminutive Georgian Theatre and the half-timbered hostelries, the market square and churches and the sweeping views over Swaledale.

Even though I was a lover of architecture, it was a strange credential on which to base one's choice of cello teacher; though he came recommended, his provenance as a cellist was entirely irrelevant to me. Maybe it was the memory of those dreary drives through the chemical works that made this old-world idyll seem so inviting. I adored the TV series that was playing at the time, *All Creatures Great and Small*, and could make-believe I was visiting James Herriot and co whenever we set off in the car. I imagine Dad didn't mind too much either, as chauffeuring me here would allow him an hour every week in pursuit of one of his favourite vices; browsing old secondhand bookshops.

Dr Bull took me all the way through to Grade VII and we had a lot of fun in the process. I even got to play in the Georgian Theatre as he held his student concerts there, so Andrew and I and a few others were able to share performances, and eventually, as A.J. was the founder of Swaledale Festival, the Cleveland String Quartet played one of its first proper recitals on that tiny stage.

6

Quartet Progress

Rewinding to our first triumphant appearance in the Music Room, barring family and friends soirées like this, concert opportunities for the Quartet were few and far between. We would occasionally be invited to share the bill with a local choir, or play in a mixed-bag concert involving other kids, but we had neither the repertoire nor the kudos to fill a proper recital. Therefore our outings were usually in a competitive capacity as we trawled all the local music festivals in search of prizes, recognition, glory… and discovery by some top agent or other.

Our one and only appearance as the Vonósnégyes String Quartet had been at the Middlesbrough Festival, where our pretentious choice of name, the announcer's embarrassment at having to pronounce it and our choice of repertoire did little to endear us to the adjudicator. The time limit of five minutes per candidate precluded much of the proper string quartet output, yet we selected one of Beethoven's greatest large-scale opening movements, that of opus 59 no.1, the first Rasumovsky. As the clock ticked past the allotted time and we were only just delving into the depths of the development section, the adjudicator started shuffling papers and his assistant, no doubt happy to take revenge on these four self-important upstarts responsible for her earlier tongue-tied mortification, rang a little bell to indicate that our time was up. Indignant that anyone would dare to interrupt the flow of this giant of the quartet repertoire, or indeed feel able to stop it before hearing every glorious note, we ploughed on, eventually petering out one by one as the increasingly feverish bell-ringing began to drown our efforts.

I don't think we won that particular class but we weren't put off – our next competitive outing was with the Variations Movement of the same composer's A Major opus18 no.5. This time, leaving out the repeats, we were able to just about stay within the prescribed time limit and manage to not annoy anyone, but I'm not sure we carried off the trophy.

No one tells youngsters how to negotiate the tricky path of striving for greatness whilst maintaining some level of humility, but it is certainly a lesson we could have benefitted from. The main trick is to avoid the Great Masters, as adult professionals will almost always feel a sense of protectiveness for the music and umbrage that mere whippersnappers feel entitled to tackle it.

In an effort to escape our growing reputation for aiming above our station, we headed further afield to the Harrogate Music Festival, where, being all of fifty miles away, we were assured total anonymity. And yet here again we refused to learn from past mistakes and offered as our entry the great man's Cavatina from his opus130, a movement so revered in the classical music world that it was chosen to represent mankind's highest achievement in a time capsule sent into outer space for future beings to find after Earth's inevitable annihilation. In his summing up, the adjudicator declared that we were too young to understand, and therefore attempt to perform, late Beethoven. To our horror and indignation, we were beaten into second place by a recorder ensemble playing a medley from *South Pacific*.

Undeterred by these annoying impediments to our trajectory of world domination, we ploughed on with our daily and intense rehearsals. These sessions had been taken extremely seriously from the start and the process in no way belied our pre-teenage demographic.

Except when it did.

There would be plenty of mirth and mucking on, usually on a geeky level, so that a fine joke would be, for example, emphasising the wrong beat in the bar for an entire movement, or playing in 3/4 when the dictated time signature was 6/8, or vice versa, making for a lopsided version of what the composer had intended.

Another favourite joke of mine was to create an interrupted cadence where a perfect one was intended. The notes in the upper parts remain the same, but I found that by going up a tone instead of down fifth, my part could single-handedly and unilaterally derail the finality of an ending – turning a musical full stop into a question mark – and make everyone laugh into the bargain.

If anyone made a slight mistake in a phrase, everyone who played that phrase thereafter would answer with the same slip-up – a game all pros like to play from time to time in rehearsal, but which we took to an extreme, even allowing it to enter into performances so that we'd be suppressing fits of the giggles on stage. On one occasion, we were playing Borodin's famous *Notturno* for the residents of an old people's home. In the final passage, a heart-wrenching little motif made up from the main theme gets passed around the group a number of times, starting with the cello. I tripped on the grace notes in a rather comical way and the other three in turn replicated it exactly, but with increasingly wide intervals between the notes.

This doesn't necessarily sound that funny, but when you realise what's happening and each successive player delivers on the joke to perfection, guffaws are exploding through clenched lips, tears running down cheeks. We had to excuse ourselves to our elderly and mostly oblivious audience in case any had taken offence. The situation wasn't helped when, during the next number – which was me playing the Swan with Ian at the piano – the other two somehow found their way up to the gantry above and laid face down to gaze over our performance, pulling crazy faces and even dropping stuff onto the stage around us.

All this frivolity was only natural to ones so young, but it also helped to train us into being alert at all times, not stuck in our parts or obsessed with our own technical struggles. One always had to have an ear on every other part, and this is the mantra every musician learns in order to achieve convincing and meaningful interpretations. So even without knowing it, we were preparing ourselves for an understanding of our craft that would find its way into our very beings forever after.

The serious side of rehearsals was, meanwhile, very serious. We slaved at rhythmic unity and matched intonation, appropriate vibrato or bow stroke, tempo and attack of articulation, balance and ensemble. None of it was easy as our technical abilities weren't sufficiently honed to even compare certain approaches, but we somehow managed to discuss them anyway. So in the way of Venezuela's Sistema, our progress was music-led, peer-driven and natural.

I remember rehearsing for hours the syncopated passage in the final movement of Beethoven's opus 59 no.1, where in pairs we play the same dotted rhythm but a quaver apart, so that those off the beat have a hugely difficult task to perform. We worked and worked at it and found tricks to facilitate the process, which I find still come in handy to this day. The sheet music we had was an old volume from Dad's collection, with the dots of a dotted rhythm often being placed after the bar-line following the note, in the space as it were. It looked so strange and isn't a method used in today's editions, although Henle have recently readopted it for total fidelity to the manuscript. These old editions also tended to notate high cello lines in the treble clef at an octave above the intended pitch, but how was I to know this? I would grapple with ridiculously high solo lines for a while, only to breathe a sigh of relief when by listening to a recording I had it confirmed that the lower octave was the composer's intention.

If we struggled with the notation of a rhythm, we might rewrite it in a way we could more easily understand, sticking bits of manuscript paper over the original. Thus a fiendishly difficult passage in Bartók No.5, with frequent time-signature changes, was re-notated in a regular metre. The aural effect was the same but, by dint of our nifty rewrite, we managed to not fall apart in its execution.

Equally, if we struggled with certain chords due to small hands or compromised ability, we might distribute the notes differently to facilitate the composer's wishes. These changes remain even now in some of our music parts, and one has to remember to remove the Tipp-Ex from time to time to check the original. It is usually better and more playable than we once thought!

When I was twelve, a schoolfriend gave me a diary for Christmas, a little flip-page A5 volume with colourful 1970s' designs on its cover. It had little space for writing more than just appointments, but I was inspired to start recording my life from that moment. The following year I bought myself a proper grown-up desk diary so as to have more space for the recording of crucially significant detail – 'Got up, had breakfast, went to school' being a typical opening gambit. But even my desk diary wasn't big enough and those all-important weekend days, having half the allocated size of the weekdays, had to have extra bits sellotaped on for all the unmissable events and youthful emotions. Eventually I progressed to open sheet volumes so as to be completely unfettered by the prescribed format of the standard diary. These journals were my daily companions for five years.

I was amazed and delighted to come across the diaries during the pre-sale sorting of my mother's house contents. I had presumed them lost to me forever, but there they were in the basement, buried in a heap of old school books and junk. I pored over them with a real sense of friends-reunited and, though mostly full of useless detail (I list any number of favourite outfits worn for each and every occasion, many home-made by myself or Mam; always record the menu at tea-time and never fail to note the taking of a nice hot bath, once the older siblings had left home and I was free to indulge in more than one a week) they have been a useful reference for the musical memoirs here documented. I love reading that on returning from school I would grab a glass of milk and four Ginger Nuts and sit down to watch some iconic seventies' TV like *Barbapapa*, *Wacky Races* or *Lizzie Dripping*, then launch into a rehearsal of sublime aesthetic involvement in Schubert G major or Dvorak *American*. It's a fabulous reminder that we were indeed children, and this self-disciplined activity was perhaps a tad unusual.

We had no lessons as a group, preferring to discover it all for ourselves. There was no push by parents, even though mine insisted on accompanying us to every competitive outing and getting upset on our behalf by ignorant non-recognition of our brilliance. (This carried on well into our twenties and became a serious bone of contention.) Anyway, we could hardly complain, as the parental taxi was often our only available form of transport.

Even our separate lives held no sway when a rehearsal was called. According to my diary, we didn't seem to have timetabled them at all – if Ian and Alex turned up, there might be a rehearsal and it might last several hours, or not. We might be congregating with three of us then find out our fourth was in Newcastle visiting family, or had homework to do. We rarely communicated properly – it was simply understood that every evening and weekend was fair game to be a rehearsal slot. If we weren't all there, table tennis easily and happily filled the time, or a jam involving piano and whichever instruments were present, or we just went back to homework or whatever we had been doing. Living a five-minute walk from each other meant that little or no inconvenience was caused by arrangements changing or literally not existing.

A couple of diary entries from the time give a good flavour of our typical routine:

> When I got home from school I practised the cello for ages then had tea. Ian had a piano lesson he had to practice for tomorrow so we couldn't have a quartet practice. God, what will happen on Saturday? I hope it will be alright.
>
> Ian and Al came so we practised Prok last mov brilliantly then the Beethoven 130 all the way through. Great!
>
> I was in a bad mood but the Prok went fabulously and my solo was superb so I was in a good mood.
>
> In the Borodin we played like professional grown-ups!!

As time went on, Ian's dad's garage was commandeered as an alternative venue. Even though my siblings had mostly left home, it became clear that we couldn't demand the use of one of only two rooms on the ground floor of the Big House on the Corner for hours at a time, chiefly because it also contained the telly. (My parents didn't mind, especially Dad, who claimed to hate television and was completely delighted that he'd spawned half of a string quartet amongst his progeny. But my sister had made her case by removing the TV to her bedroom and putting a lock on the door, so that we had to get permission to watch our favourite programmes.) So the garage attached to Ian's more conventional three-bedroom semi on Emerson Avenue started to come into play. Though the walls were lined with Edwin's perfectly organised tools and gadgets, the space was neat and clean and provided a private studio where we could immerse ourselves thoroughly without interruption. Much later we used this early set-up as a publicity strapline: 'The Garage Band of Classical Music!'

Ian's house was quiet – he only had one sibling, Judith, and she was usually busy studying or practising the violin in her bedroom, out of the way. His parents were mild-mannered and undemonstrative, and there was a pervading sense of calm. The kitchen was clean and uncluttered and often filled with the sublime smell of Enid's homemade bread. There was a generous garden out the back with a greenhouse full of carefully tended vegetables, the lawn was neat and the flowerbeds orderly – it was the antithesis of my own rambling and chaotic house. I was mortified when one day I decided it was a good idea to throw a glass marble up in the air and try to catch it, only my inaccuracy and clumsiness at throwing of any kind meant the projectile veered off to one side and came to land on the floor of the greenhouse, making a spectacular mess of one of the glass panes en route.

Edwin was quietly amused and bemused at my stupidity and teased me about it for years after. Ian wasn't so clever himself. One day in my garden I was wielding a tennis racquet and he saw fit to chuck me a ball. I, imagining it was a tennis ball, dutifully held the racquet in front of my face to let the ball bounce back to him. The painful clunk as it instead came back to meet my forehead told me that Ian had actually launched a stray boule that had been lying forgotten since the lawn had doubled as a Provençale boulodrome the previous summer. Ian was in turn mortified and we were quits!

Alex had two younger brothers, one with severe autism who found gatherings challenging, so we rarely rehearsed at his house. Chez Robertson had a bohemian quality and was rather scruffy, a bit like ours. There was always a piece of art on the go by any one of the boys or Alec, their dad, so it had a creative feel, but the overriding atmosphere came from the many crucifixes and Our Lady statuettes on display. I had never been in the home of a Catholic family before, and I found the devotional fervour quite intimidating, though they couldn't have been sweeter people: Rose was gentle and kind and infinitely patient with her youngest and the challenges of his condition.

Being Catholic, Alex had made his way up through a different set of schools to the rest of us, and was currently enjoying the excellent education provided by a dynamic and brilliant music teacher at St George's & St Mary's. The school frequently staged brilliant productions of shows and musicals, polished to an unusually high standard, including a fabulous *West Side Story*, in which Alex took to drum kit in a pared-down version of the orchestral forces. He really could turn his hand to anything.

Many of his co-students were to be found in our Youth Orchestra, mostly of Irish Catholic heritage as there had been a huge migration here during the industrial boom years, second only to that to Liverpool. These bright young kids with their sing-song names and friendly natures filled the ranks with smiles and enthusiasm, and it was only later in my life, when I got to know their ancestral homeland more intimately, that I understood where they all got their sunny personalities. Angie Daly, Carole Greenan, Paul Doherty, Catriona Rooney, Liz Geraghty… descendants of a musical heritage way out west.

Maybe we as a group can take some credit for the phenomenon of so many professional musicians coming out of the area. For our friends of the TYO to have as their core this totally driven band of four was perhaps an irresistibly infectious incentive to seriousness. It's hard to imagine a time when there weren't young string quartets popping up from every music school, but when we started out it was simply unheard of. Kids learnt their instrument, played in orchestras and eventually went to music college, where they finally got to play in smaller groups if they wanted to. It wasn't even compulsory, so little was chamber music respected as a legitimate learning tool, let alone an essential part of any musical education, as I believe it to be.

We were so dismissive of this obsession with the solo trajectory of most music-educational thinking that we pompously declared, in our very first newspaper interview for the local rag, *The Evening Gazette*, 'If we don't make it as a quartet, we can always fall back on being soloists!'

7

Stepping Out

Horizons were opening beyond the confines of our area. An annual orchestral course on Tyneside drew the more promising members of Teesside Youth Orchestra to join forces with their counterparts from County Durham, Sunderland and Newcastle, to form the Northern Junior Philharmonic Orchestra. Having progressed to violin tuition with the Northern Sinfonia's leader, Barry Wilde, Mike and Ian had already been travelling to Newcastle regularly for their lessons and had joined NJPO the year before. Now it was my turn.

The residential course was held in Sunderland that year and was my first taste of boarding away from my parents. At twelve, I was one of the youngest participants and was about to experience the powerful effects of proper orchestral playing for the first time. Edwin Raymond had been careful not to overtask his young players of the TYO with anything too demanding, avoiding the huge symphonic works and selecting carefully the more playable ones, especially aware of the physical limitations of immature wind players. So I was about to witness my first Mahler Symphony – No.1, no less – from right within its ranks.

As that magical opening unfolded, with the eerie sustained high harmonic in the violins, I gazed around me in awe as one after another the wind section uttered bird calls, fragments of themes, quirky cuckoos in hesitant imitation, distant hunting horns and far-off trumpet fanfares... *How do they know when to play?* I asked myself. They seemed completely assured and confident and yet the whole thing had an exploratory, even improvised, feel to it.

I'd never been amongst orchestral players who'd actually practised their individual parts in advance, or even listened to recordings in preparation for coming together under a conductor. At TYO it was learn-as-you-go, warts and all, and it must have been a real slog for our long-suffering conductor to pull together over successive Friday nights. Here we had the towering figure of Norman Del Mar with all his experience, know-how and wit, putting us through our paces with consummate charm and assurance. It was a whole new experience.

As the cellos made their grumbling first entry right at the bottom of the instrument, I was completely unprepared, still in my dream state as the bar lines flew past in an unregistered meter. I had to jump to it to be with my section as we began our chromatic climb, drawing the forces together for the long build, cuckoo-calls ever more frantic, to eventually release into that carefree theme straight from the Austrian mountains, all cowbells and Alpine horns. I felt transported and elated.

The week-long course flew by in a whirl of rehearsals, tutors' concerts and walks to the sea, witnessing in awe a Yard of Ale competition at the bar and taking part in a memorable performance on tuned beer bottles, led by the Cleveland String Quartet, of Brahms' *Lullaby*. Being my first time away from home and used to only one weekly bath, I forgot to wash my hair and must have looked a sight. Eventually the lovely Barbara White, my piano teacher's daughter, who was a co-cellist, took me in hand and gently suggested a visit to her room so she could wash it for me over the sink. We just made it in time as the orchestra buses were leaving for Newcastle City Hall, grand venue for our end-of-course concert.

Back in Middlesbrough, Quartet rehearsals carried on apace and with increased fervour. The annual festivals had come round again – in the violin class, Ian winning one age group, Mike another, then Alex, and so on. Then they'd all be teamed up for duet classes and win those too: Bach or Vivaldi doubles, Bartók duos and so on, Ian and Mike, Ian and sister Judith, Mike and Alex, Joe Kane and Alex, co-students at the Catholic school; in the viola class, Alex versus Angie Daly and the Aldren brothers. In the cello section there was a solid field for every age group, almost all pupils of Kitty, at least fifteen in each class. I would alternate with my friends from orchestra to pick up the trophies on offer in rotation.

Then one day we all became aware of some new kids on the block: three sisters, two of whom were string players, tiny like miniature dolls. The cellist, at six or seven already possessing a rich and mature sound, sat on a little three-legged stool carried to the stage by her mum, as her feet wouldn't reach the ground on a normal chair; the violinist, who couldn't have been much more than three, had piercing brown eyes and would stare directly out at the audience as she gave a perfect rendition by memory of the prescribed work. They created quite a stir. They were the Dale sisters, Miranda and Caroline, with Susan, a flautist, making up the trio.

The string-playing tots were both too young to represent any real threat to our dominance, but eventually Caroline and I built a healthy rivalry as we alternated for supremacy in the Under-16s and Open Classes. She followed Kitty's advice on the Florence Hooton route, taking her to Junior Academy and therefore out of TYO circles. She went on to become the first String Category winner of BBC Young Musician of the Year, in-demand soloist, and eventually that sumptuous sound on movie soundtracks, including the cello voice of Jacqueline du Pré in the film *Hilary and Jackie*.

Miranda eventually led the TYO and was still there when I returned in my mid-twenties as guest soloist in the Dvorak Concerto; duetting with her soaring violin solo in those gorgeous closing pages increased my sense of nostalgia for the old days. She has a career in the Philharmonia Orchestra, is Principal 2nd Violin with the Britten Sinfonia and lives a stone's throw from me in London, where my daughter babysits her kids.

The Quartet would carry off most of the prizes in the chamber classes – it was a very small field and we'd wisely stopped submitting Beethoven – and there was even a Family Class which we Thomases frequented.

Now, Dad had bravely kept up his climb through the Grades and was enjoying his chamber music evenings with amateur orchestra friends and often with us kids, but his playing was prone to going into panic mode when under the spotlight and, to our amusement, this often led to a certain amount of dribbling onto his instrument as concentration on the task at hand took away awareness of all else.

Chamber music with him always involved an awful lot of catch-up and indulgence; he thought he had a sense of rhythm but he really just had a bunch of clever kids who could follow his every move. We did him no favours; when he was back with his less-accommodating friends they would have heated debates about who had gone wrong and derailed the play-through of whichever quartet they were currently battling with. Dad couldn't understand why he never seemed to have these problems when playing with us youngsters, and poor Joy, faced with fiendish piano parts in Beethoven or Schubert Trios, would be his go-to scapegoat if she couldn't fit in all the notes and follow him at the same time!

One year, for the Family Class we decided to submit the Rossini String Sonata, with Mike and Dad on violins, me on cello and Pete on double bass. The last movement is a set of Variations, including a notoriously difficult one starring the 2nd Violin – running non-stop demisemiquavers, totally exposed while the rest of the group plays a simple accompaniment.

Dad would struggle with his solo at the best of times; once in front of an audience, all bets were off. His foot started to bang the floor uncontrollably; his jaw, seeming to follow the patterns made by his madly tripping fingers, went into similar spasms of activity, while a long stream of dribble began to run down his chin and onto his precious Hopf. Meanwhile, the sound that came out bore no resemblance whatsoever to the composer's intentions, his bow barely making contact as it bounced several inches above the strings at a speed roughly double the one prescribed.

The adjudicator was dropping lower and lower in his seat in an effort to suppress his laughter, and eventually gave up altogether, tears streaming down his cheeks as Dad reached the finishing post of his ordeal in the spotlight. As the movement ended, the whole audience stood and cheered, probably out of relief as much as sympathy for this poor man, an intelligent and successful local businessman descended into inadvertent comedic farce, a caricature of the amateur player, surrounded by the easy talent of his own kids. As I said, amateur music-making really is a leveller.

Touring professionals must have had a pleasant surprise when their schedule brought them to our neck of the woods. So often the demographic of chamber music audiences is the mild-mannered retired generation, come to appreciate this more specialist genre in later life as chicks flew the nest and they regained control of their leisure time and radio sets. They say our audience is ageing, but I say it's always been that way, and they're still there! And I am humbled by the tenacity of audiences who bother to come out, in all weathers, despite an ever-growing number of reasons not to, to hear and support the live music that we and so many others feel compelled to continue performing.

The army of volunteers who keep local music clubs afloat are a formidable bunch. They devise tours, booking the players, dealing with agents, coordinating programmes, finding – or providing in their own homes – accommodation and making sumptuous high teas for the gap between rehearsal and concert, when they become the audience along with a small group of quietly appreciative like-minded enthusiasts. Every touring string quartet has been there and knows what to expect.

Except when they get to Middlesbrough.

We four and our friends from TYO attended every concert on offer and brought down the audience's average age by some decades. What a pleasant surprise it must have been for these road-weary and possibly jaded players to step out onto the stage to cheers even before they'd begun, ovations and foot-stamping afterwards, then autograph-hunting groupies at the stage door.

> Billingham for Tel Aviv String Quartet. Mozart Beethoven which were both absolutely superb! The cellist is amazing - superb, second violin a genius (typical second violin!) Magnificent violist - incredible! Then they played Bartók 1 which was so superb!
>
> What professionalism it is! We cheared and cheared! [sic.] I've got the cellist's autograph. And some of his bow hair!

Sometimes we even knew the performers, if they'd been tutors on a course for instance, and then we revelled in chummy repartee like old pros. We'd attend any concert on offer, as far afield as Billingham or Stockton, sometimes walking the few miles home if the last bus had left or if we were still buzzing and needed to cool off. Those night walks along the A19 past the furnaces of ICI and over Newport Bridge, looking down into the dark waters of the Tees, singing at the tops of our voices whichever Bartók, Janáček or Schubert quartet we'd just been enthralled by... magic.

These weren't the kind of night-time rowdies the local inhabitants of Middlesbrough had grown accustomed to. One might often be woken from slumber by the thick vowels and sing-song, boisterous timbre of youths at pub turfing-out time; our house being the other end of the road from a huge establishment – the Linthorpe Hotel, or 'the Linny' – we were well used to it. Through the more genteel enclave I inhabited, the home-bound rabble would invariably break into song, but it was football chants not Janáček (though the two could easily be mistaken). The continuation of our Crescent was Linthorpe Road, the main thoroughfare into town but also the main route to Ayresome Park, home of The Boro: Middlesbrough FC.

It was a characterful ground with old-style seatless stands and a cheap section up top and open to the elements known as 'the Boys' End', much to my disgust as I was often to be found amongst the kids on its terraces and found the sexist assumption insulting. Even if I wasn't going to the match, which as I entered my teens became more often the case, there was a tremendous excitement on home match days.

Starting around midday, crowds would converge on our corner and make their way towards the ground, just a few hundred yards away. Gradually their numbers built until the roads were filled, and cars had to patiently wait for a route through. By three the streets were empty, and there would be a collective holding of breath for the roar emanating from the stadium as the first home goal found the back of the visitors' net. We could even hear the 'ooh's following missed chances or shouts of disdain as the referee made a bad decision to the detriment of the Boro. Then the roads were once again filled with a heaving mass of bodies, and if we'd won the excitement was worn proud on the passing faces.

My diary entries would often include match day results, especially if some of us had made it to the match so we couldn't rehearse. (I was thrilled years later to discover that Shostakovich's diaries were also peppered with football minutiae from fixtures in Russia, though he would go into rather more technical detail about tactical intricacies and the like, and didn't tend to describe what he wore to matches.)

After the crowds had died down we'd go indoors to watch *Final Score* followed by *Pink Panther* or *Doctor Who*; it being Saturday, we were allowed to have our tea in front of the telly. Then if the evening was light, a game of football, or if not, a Quartet practice.

Sundays were for country walks and homework, but there was always the chance of a rehearsal. Then the evenings could be filled with any number of cultured offerings on the BBC – programmes that would now be demoted to obscure channels or the middle of the night back then found their way onto prime-time television.

As well as highly esoteric things like The Fires of London playing Peter Maxwell Davies' latest oeuvre, there might be Jacqueline du Pré and cohorts Zukerman, Perlman et al, in the famous Trout Quintet documentary. A Shostakovich Symphony could easily fill the whole of Sunday evening's schedule and it was thrilling to know some of the players on screen from amongst our teachers or courses we might have attended. *André Previn's Music Night* even made it onto Saturday Night Primetime, such was the acceptance of classical music as an important part of life.

These glimpses into a whole musical world we felt destined to become a part of were tantalising. It was time to explore.

8

Dartington

In the summer of 1974 we made our first foray as a group into the wider world by enrolling for a week's tuition at Dartington International Summer School in Devon. We had no idea what to expect but the roll-call of professionals was impressive, from Sándor Végh to Joan Dickson, the Dartington String Quartet… and intriguingly, the Cleveland Quartet. We weren't sure how another group felt entitled to use our name, but we were willing to discuss it. This said, our main aim was to spend time immersing ourselves in our art with no external distractions – no school, no homework, no orchestra: just us four and a load of music.

The long drive south – my parents had enrolled too, so we had built-in transport – was exciting. Once we'd passed Exeter and left the A road we traversed increasingly stunning scenery, the narrow lanes running between high hedges, forming veritable tunnels of verdant splendour. Tiny thatched pubs and ancient bridges decorated the winding route through the Dart Valley until finally we found the long driveway leading to Dartington Hall.

The first time I walked through the covered archway into that courtyard comes back to me every time I have since. There is a hush that descends as you emerge into the light, blinking at the sight before you. A magnificent cypress tree takes pride of place near the entrance, so your view of the whole is at first obscured. Then you walk round the circular path, made up of great flagstones interspersed with perfectly ordered cobbles, and the scene unfolds before you. Characterful three-storey accommodation with charming roof-dormers lines the perimeter, stone mullions and ancient leaded glass twinkling in the sunlight, little staircases leading to who-knows-where, till you reach the majestic structure at the far end – a huge banqueting hall festooned with mediaeval tapestries, towering point-arched windows, an impressive cantilevered roof, a minstrel's gallery at one end and a dais at the other: the Great Hall.

I was bewitched. Life within the confines of this place was secluded and cloistered, making for a sense of privilege, of heightened sensory experience; all the more so as it was the first time we'd been able to exclusively concentrate on our purpose in life for any length of time. Our accommodation – the boys in one dorm, me in another with my parents – was in another old building, a short but magical walk through golden fields with far-reaching views over the valley. An ancient steam train would pass by, chugging and puffing a smoke trail and hooting its old-fashioned whistle as we made our way to rehearsals, classes and concerts aplenty.

Further exploration brought us out of the courtyard to acres of resplendent gardens and woods, including a tiltyard with dizzying perspective across its length and breadth and perilously steep sloping sides to roll down with gay abandon. The ruined remains of an abbey and a tumbledown old church, hidden stone benches amongst the trees and hedges, endless English borders all immaculately tended and, most enchanting of all, tiny thatched cottages straight out of a children's book of fairy tales, which were actually practice rooms or study spaces. Even though our surrounding countryside at home was stunning, I'd never seen anything like this: a place of such peaceful and remote beauty, no cars or traffic, no signs really of modern life in any form, where music was the main agenda. We were eager to get to work.

Our tutor was the adorable Michael Evans, cellist with the Dartington String Quartet. He was delighted to find that such a young group had arrived pre-formed and with every intention of making it our priority. So often, especially back then, experts in chamber music find themselves an afterthought in the education process, having to contend with young players who've never tried to play in groups and who simply want to shine, with no awareness of their colleagues, before returning to the pressing issue of individual tuition. Michael's experience in a real quartet and his passion for the art form inspired us even more, as he took us through our repertoire with constructive criticism and consummate encouragement, his sing-song Welsh lilt always gentle and kind.

We had experienced a bitter disappointment earlier that summer when trying our hand at a national competition in London. We'd been thrilled to progress through the preliminary rounds in Newcastle to reach the finals and compete amongst twenty nationwide groups. The *Evening Gazette* heralded our departure with a photo and short feature; we were feeling confident of meeting with recognition and accolades. None came. Here at Dartington, we were determined to find out why, and Mr Evans helped heal our wounds with a healthy disregard for the inconsistencies and vagaries of competitive music. He was all about the pure joy of it.

Word got around that there was this ambitious young group on campus, and we were invited to play in a masterclass setting to the great Sándor Végh. His was a name we knew as one of the great chamber musicians on the planet, formerly of the

Hungarian Quartet, with whom he'd premiered our beloved Bartók 5, and we were more than a little intimidated as we entered his voluminous presence, all Viennese gesture and triple chins.

The art of giving good masterclass is to entertain the audience – sometimes at the expense of the blushing student – as much as to impart wisdom, and Végh had it off to a T. He was amused by our seriousness and indulgent with our efforts, but wanted to stamp his ego on proceedings. We brought him Mozart's glorious E flat Major Quartet and gave what we considered to be a good, if nervous, performance of the first movement. He didn't patronise us – he delved into the musical content and technical intricacies as thoroughly as if he were teaching graduate students at Julliard, and one particular phrase was picked out for examination.

The violins had to repeat the phrase between them and Végh tore it apart, analysing their efforts in minute detail and offering demonstrations to ram his point home, always preceded by a loud grunt, almost singing and growling rolled into one, speaking morphing into playing, as he put his violin to his enormous wobbling chins. This affectation became known to us in later years as a favourite of classical giants to portray a sense of being elsewhere, artistically distracted, but this was the first time we'd witnessed it and we were open-mouthed in appreciation of the weirdness.

Luckily a fit of the giggles was avoided and I even ingratiated myself to the great man later in the movement when it was my turn to play the offending phrase, which I instantly dispatched as per his preference and with ease. He had been about to stop us so he could instruct me as he had the fiddles, but instead he laughed and congratulated my resourcefulness, complimenting me for the entertainment of the spectators. "Ah, bravo! She is queeck!" he exclaimed in his exaggerated Austro-Hungarian drawl, rolling his eyes at the ladies on the front row. I was mightily chuffed.

My dad was enrolled to take part in amateur chamber music with the host of other adults who, over the years, have kept this venerable old institution afloat with their fees and donations. He was a very sociable man, always happy to enter into conversation with strangers, so he quickly made friends amongst his fellow players, including a sweet old gentleman and pianist known as Colonel Solly. Through him I was introduced to the lyrical joys of the Dvorak Piano Quintet, one of his favourite works, for whom he was in search of playing partners in crime. Dad quickly commandeered a quartet from amongst the string players he'd already befriended, and they met for the arranged play-through with me in tow as their audience.

The Dvorak is a deceptive work – all happiness and charm yet fiendishly difficult and not necessarily suited to the level of playing here assembled. The poor cellist was struggling from the off and I, hovering behind her, would point to the page every time she got lost, showing her where to play. But even when she found her place, she was unable to rejoin proceedings, unfamiliar with this romantic nationalist genre where the cello is utilised to its full potential, more than just the simple bass line she had been accustomed to in her limited early classical repertoire to date.

Within minutes I had unashamedly wheedled my way into her seat and taken over the part, never to relinquish it back to her. I found the music intoxicating and revelled in the pure charm of its harmonic language. My poor counterpart retreated to the shadows and eventually left us to it – no one even noticed she'd gone.

The precocious kid had done it again, though this time it was worse than the Saint-Saëns Concerto episode, being actually at the expense of another's feelings. I blush when I think of that day – and whenever I play this wonderful piece – though I was vindicated when the sweet Colonel congratulated me and said she had no business putting herself forward if she couldn't make the grade.

So life at Dartington was full and varied, with more than just the musical saturation to entertain us. There were two open-air swimming pools, unheated and therefore not overly frequented, and we delighted in games of dare and bravado, often ending with a soaking, fully clothed. We left campus only once, driving through lovely Totnes to the gorgeous fishing port of Dartmouth, where I tasted my first Devon clotted cream ice cream – oh, heaven in a cone. But as with all havens away from real life, we had already become institutionalised in our cocooned existence and were happy to return to its safe confines, and confine the car to the car park for the rest of our stay.

During the course of our time there, I discovered a little music shop tucked away in one of the outbuildings, where I bought my first set of Beethoven Cello Sonatas. It was one of the proper Bärenreiter editions with the blue cover, and I felt I'd gone up a level in musical seriousness. I also had an individual masterclass with Joan Dickson, the boys played to Végh, and we continued our daily sessions with Mr Evans, but we didn't come into contact with our namesakes of the Cleveland Quartet until, following one of their concerts in the Great Hall, we went backstage to congratulate them and introduce ourselves, using our group's title.

Their educated dulcet American response was gracious and polite – amused laughter and shaking hands – but it became clear they were as entitled to the name as we were, hailing as they did from Cleveland, Ohio. Our Cleveland was the original, we pointed out. But they had formed three years before us, so they'd got in first. We suggested they use the extra tag, Ohio, in future, in case they should be mistaken for their young namesakes, but they said 'no, you're alright thanks, we'll risk it'. Much hilarity all round.

These heady, rarefied days came to an end all too soon and we solemnly vowed to return every year, so much had we enjoyed the experience. But other pulls were destined to get in the way of that promise and following summers passed by with a giant Dartington-sized hole in them.

On the final day we were invited to feature as the last act in the Students' Concert, playing a movement from Prokofiev's 2nd Quartet to much acclaim. It was the first time of many that we would perform on the ancient polished oak boards of that famous stage, but the next time we did we were ten years older and we were being paid for the pleasure! (Though any musician who's appeared at Dartington will understand that as a loose term…)

It was also the first of many such post-concert parties in the White Hart, where a little too much drink was imbibed by my older colleagues, a forerunner of years ahead as we took this wonderful place back into our hearts in 1984 and continued to return every one of the fifteen subsequent years. My parents made a habit of coming along too, which was a nice way to spend time together as our schedule became increasingly busy. Mam even joined the choir and performed her first ever concert, aged sixty-something, on that same stage in whichever oratorio made up the final night's concert that year; Dad continued to join in with the amateur groups and they would often sign up for our coaching sessions.

On one occasion some time in the mid-eighties, they'd booked me for a class in that residential building across the fields, scene of my Dvorak Piano Quintet faux-pas. It was a horrible day worthy of any West Country Gothic horror novel; torrential rain lashed the windows. I was mid-lesson, imparting some pearl of wisdom to my captive audience, when Mam burst through the door soaked to the skin and looking pretty distressed. Instead of stopping to attend to her obvious plight, I continued in my self-important task while she stood waiting to be noticed. But I was one of the 'professionals' trying to do a job and didn't want my mum entering the room to cramp my style. The poor thing had been searching for us and got caught in the downpour, and we all just ignored her. She had forgotten I wasn't just her daughter; I was there working. I was conflicted by the wish to run to her aid and the need to maintain my dignity. It's a delicate balance to strike, as I would later find with my own daughters.

Another year, we shared the stage with Dad as he took part in a sponsored play devised by us, raising funds for the ever-struggling institution. The format was simple and popular; members of the public could pay £100 for the 'honour' of replacing one of us in their choice of work. He chose Schubert's famous 'Death and the Maiden' slow movement, usurping Ian's chair for the occasion. Again, the fine line between filial duty and professional swagger was a hard one to tread, as I felt his nervousness from across the stage and wanted to protect his vulnerability. He rose to the occasion, brilliantly upstaging us all when we came to take our bows, pushing past us like the fat lady on Morecambe and Wise, to the delight of the impromptu audience.

Dartington provided us with many lifelong friends over the years, among fellow performers and students too. We also invited colleagues to join us there as we became more a part of the planning process. In 1992, our twentieth anniversary year, we performed the entire Shostakovich Cycle and persuaded a certain Elvis Costello to join us in a special concert and to add his considerable experience to the team of visiting tutors on the songwriting course. He mingled with co-teachers John Woolrich et al with humility, delighting them with a lack of pretension his rockstar status could have afforded him. Together we gave the second ever performance of *The Juliet Letters*, which we had co-written over the preceding months and premiered just weeks before. It was still being tweaked and added to and it was here that a new encore – *The Favourite Hour* – was penned and premiered. The Juliet Letters had yet to be recorded, still a work-in-progress and very much an unknown quantity for us all, its impact on the disparate musical worlds we inhabited yet to be tested. It was a thrilling yet scary moment.

Joining forces with musicians from across the genre divide was still a risky and often frowned-upon activity, especially for classical musicians who might be accused of selling out. Yet we believed in this work with all the conviction the painstaking process of its creation engendered in us. And our loyal audience at Dartington took it to their hearts, embracing the sense of adventure and trailblazing bravura. There was one in the audience, my dad, who could claim a small part in the creative process; the quirky title of one of the songs was the nickname he'd given me as a child and which only he ever used. Jacksons, Monk and Rowe was introduced to the wider world.

*

In 2007 I was on the jury of the Banff Competition, where one of my fellow jurors happened to be the cellist Paul Katz, formerly of the Cleveland Quartet (Ohio!). He remembered well our coinciding at Dartington back in 1974 and we shared a laugh over the young group who claimed rights to the name already taken by his world-famous ensemble. We of course eventually gave in and later found a new name, in deference to their seniority and established position on the musical map.

Also at Banff and in a sweetly life-affirming moment, a young American group, the Attacca Quartet, took me aside after the competition to tell me that The Juliet Letters had been their guiding light through school and college, we their idols and living legends. It was so refreshing and consoling for me to know that all the stuffiness of former days, resistance to the unknown Other Genres, which causes such distrust in our world, simply didn't exist for these youngsters. They were open to all types of music and happy to admit it; our album was their road trip soundtrack as they toured the small music clubs of the

USA in a beaten-up Oldster. I was reminded of our young selves and greatly encouraged by the way things had moved on.

I next spotted the members of the Attacca in the film *A Late Quartet*, appearing in a cameo role as students in a masterclass with their cello guru, played by Christopher Walken. And who were Walken's character and quartet based on in the film? Paul Katz and the Cleveland Quartet!

Interlude I

Names and Nicknames - a journey back to the forties and beyond

When Francine Geneviève Andrée Jacqueline Philippart was approaching her eighteenth birthday, war broke out and her home city of Bruxelles was promptly occupied by the advancing forces of Nazi Germany. Her comfortable bourgeoisie life in one of the Saint Gilles district's elegant mansion houses, with her parents and younger sister and a live-in maid, came to an abrupt end.

Fanchon – as she was known at home – had been a feisty and rebellious child, sent to a convent school in an attempt to tame her, but she came out fighting and soon found a close group of like-minded artistic friends who spent the early war years dodging the authority of the parasites and cycling out to the countryside for camping trips, where she learned to trap, throttle and skin a rabbit before roasting it on a spit over open fires or taking it home to her grateful family. For this troupe of friends she would devise shows and plays, mostly comedy or translations of Shakespeare, and she had an image of her future-self as a creative writer. She had a boyfriend, indeed fiancé, who was training to be a doctor. A fine future would have been there for the taking, were it not for this war.

But university was a far-off dream. Work had to be sought, preferably with meals provided as food was so scarce. She lived easily amongst the German soldiers, who she found to be polite and respectful, especially towards a stunning blonde not afraid to speak her mind. She would take the train to Paris with her girlfriends and quite enjoyed the whole experience of being young and relatively free during these strange times, despite the hideous background of oppression and death.

When liberation came, she and her father headed straight to the huge edifice the Palais de Justice, where he happened to know all the best wines had been stashed by the Nazis, and they joined the other families privy to this insider knowledge, everyone carrying as much as they could manage in their looting frenzy. As the Allied troops marched into the capital, they were welcomed with open arms and a quantity of this excellent wine, whatever food was available and a warm bed for the night. Fanchon and her papa bonded over this exciting night of revelry, but their joy was short-lived when it became clear that the marching forces had missed their rendezvous and potentially helped derail the offensive on Arnhem, leaving the Airborne Regiment unsupported, sitting ducks. Many other factors contributed to this failed manoeuvre, but the loss of nearly two thousand British and Polish lives remained on the collective conscience of Fanchon and other Belgian and Dutch civilians, whose innocent welcome parades had had such devastating consequences.

A year later, the war in Europe finally over, Fanchon felt it her duty to help in the aftermath of six years of chaos and signed up with UNRRA, the United Nations Relief and Rehabilitation Administration. She was sent to Normandy for training, given a uniform and briefed in the delicate job of dealing with displaced persons and traumatised victims of the war. She and many like-minded young people, in their smart uniforms, formed a jolly troop with optimism for the future and an enthusiasm for change.

Following bootcamp, they were sent in the back of huge army trucks across the wreckage of battlefields, on broken roads through flattened towns, to Northern Germany, a long and arduous journey for even the fittest amongst them. Once there, Francine was shown into a huge assembly hall and directed to a dais at the far end, where stood a man in British Army uniform. He was to be her boss in her role as translator and secretary. With her good but charmingly accented English and his dapper and thoroughly British manner, they hit it off immediately.

Alfred James Thomas grew up in the Thameside enclave of Bermondsey, the eldest of five children. The cramped Victorian terrace where they lived and his father's job as tenant publican, whilst providing him with happy childhood memories of singing around the pub piano and mudlarking on the riverbank, made for a frugal lifestyle with low prospects for the future. But Alf was ambitious and hard-working. He learnt to play piano and violin by ear and built up a cultural appreciation for music and the arts. He found a decent blue-collar job and studied at night school for the Matriculation Certificate, passing with flying colours. When war came, his Reserved Occupation gave him an out for a few years, but when he was eventually called up, this self-betterment, along with an acquired elocution, was rewarded with the honour of officer status.

He was sent with the King's Royal Rifle Corps to a training camp near York, where he got his first taste of the glorious Yorkshire countryside later to become home. He joined the D-Day offensive a couple of weeks in, landing at Arromanches; the action had moved further into France by now but was still very much ongoing. His finest moment came when he had his eardrum blown out during a terrifying and brave moment of action: his much-diminished platoon had single-handedly ambushed a bunch of Germans who eventually fled, believing themselves to be under fire from a much greater force.

Shipped back to London with his injuries, he was faced with the ruination of his family home, bombed out during the Blitz. When the war ended, Tommy (as he had become known) received a promotion and took up a new post as Town Major in the small North German town of Ratzeburg. Here he was briefed with the overwhelming role of coordinating housing and transport for thousands of refugees, soldiers and medics, all the detritus of Europe's long struggle. Shortly into this daunting task, his day was lifted dramatically by the arrival of a beautiful new assistant, a young Belgian, fresh-faced and ingénue... The team immediately dubbed her Baby.

Tommy and Baby fell into an easy rapport. He invited her up to his quarters to listen to his gramophone, intending to impress her with his cultural knowledge and maybe something more. He instead was seriously impressed when this young woman was able to not only identify the Beethoven Violin Concerto but could also name the soloist as Jascha Heifetz. He had no idea she would know anything about music, let alone possess such in-depth knowledge. It just happened to be one of a handful of 78s her parents owned and which she had loved to listen to back home. Their relationship blossomed over the following months as they partied amongst the officers of the newly designated sectors of the various conquerors of Germany. Mad New Year's Eve parties in the Russian Zone, vodka flowing and anaesthetising the bodies which then flung themselves into the flowing waters of the Rhine, breaking the ice in a crazed drink-inspired attempt to swim across it. Weekends in Hamburg where the only remaining hotel was the iconic Art Deco wonder, The Atlantic, still standing firm amongst the devastation of the surrounding rubble which that city had become.

A quick informal wedding led to the arrival of a daughter, whom they named Joy to reflect their own. After a hasty visit to Bruxelles to introduce the baby and new husband, mother and daughter left for England whilst Tommy tied up his job in Germany, to join them later. Fanchon's parents were sad to see her depart to a life abroad, but they recognised the couple were happy and accepted the situation. "Why do you call her Baby?" teased the new mother-in-law. "She's our baby!" Whether or not this claim became an issue is unclear, but Baby got an alternative tag – Funny Face – and the two later adopted a new unisex name for each other, Shaby (pronounced like lay-by), or sometimes simply Darling, or 'Yoo-hoo!', and continued their long life together without ever addressing each other by their proper names.

Baby/Shaby/Funny Face and baby, now nicknamed Pussy, waited in Dover for Tommy/Shaby to return. Long letters between the couple were infused with unintentional double entendre, Fanchon declaring that Pussy was missing him and was dying to be kissed again. Once reunited, they made their way to London to meet Tommy's family in Bermondsey's Luftwaffe-redesigned landscape, then on to the Midlands following an offer of work plus accommodation in one of the many post-war prefabs and converted Nissen huts springing up like mushrooms across the country. Again, Tommy's work involved him in the rehabilitation of refugees and displaced persons, and he befriended a group of immigrant musicians, who called themselves the Latvian String Quartet, arranging concert opportunities for them in his spare time.

By the time baby number two was due, Tommy had become best of friends with this playful foursome and they spent the night wetting the baby's head to strains of Beethoven Quartets, whilst Baby laboured under the strain of the baby's head's delivery. She was in no mood to receive the news later that night that the new baby boy would be named Arvid, in honour of the Latvians' first violinist. They compromised and made it his middle name, along with Fanchon's own maiden name. Poor Peter faced the long hard road ahead of school days owning up to two most embarrassing middle names – Arvid Philippart. Given this indignity, he escaped the added complication of the now all-but-compulsory nickname.

There followed a move north, Tommy answering a job opportunity in Billingham to run a social club with an almost musical name. Perhaps he had visions of retaining his ad hoc status as entrepreneur to another set of rarefied artists, creating his own Sinfonia and concerts to match. But his cultural bubble was burst; the *Synthonia* Club got its exotic-sounding name from an agricultural fertiliser, being a contraction of 'synthetic ammonia', a product manufactured by the nearby ICI chemical plant, with which the decidedly un-musically motivated club was affiliated.

This job also came with prefab housing, only marginally better than the glorified tent they were given in Stafford, and along came three little maids in quick succession, though thankfully no one thought of calling them Yum-Yum, Peep-Bo or Pitti-Sing. Janet (a nod to Charlotte Bronte), Silvia (an homage to Schubert) and Josephine (no, not Napoleon's sweetheart, she was actually named after Fanchon's paternal granny), soon made up an inseparable trio who later, and with little imagination, were dubbed 'The Girls'. For nicknames they got Gravy (due to liking the stuff), Billy (derived from Silly Billy) and Pobby (after Edward Lear's toe-impaired Pobble).

Shortly following the birth of Pobby it became evident that a new home was needed. Tommy had moved into business and was busy setting up his own insurance brokers in nearby Middlesbrough. Wandering the genteel streets of Linthorpe village whilst waiting for Gravy to complete her ballet class, they spotted a 'For Sale' sign on a majestic corner house and fell in love. Francine had delusions of returning to the grandeur of her own upbringing in a house she finally recognised as such. They just about had the money for a deposit and took out a private mortgage with the vendor.

The rambling house was quite a handful and meant that Fanchon never achieved the luxury and glamour she had maybe envisaged in the move. Cleaning and laundry were a constant grind, a sink and mangle in the basement her only tools against a daily mountain of nappies and clothes. She had been forced to learn to cook the minute she moved to England, something she'd never had to do before, barring the odd al fresco skinned rabbit. Now she produced three meals a day for a growing army of children, coping with being a foreigner amongst the drawling tones of the North East accent when shopping for war-reduced groceries, and tailoring her menus to the very British tastes of her London-bred breadwinner. She must have yearned for the smell of garlic or herbs, which were a staple in Belgium but unheard of in post-war Middlesbrough. No matter, she mastered the suet pastry, puddings and pies, Sunday roasts plus trimmings... but slipped in her own favourites... Pain Perdu (French toast, literally 'lost bread') and Tête de Veau (brains on toast with a squeeze of lemon), happily renamed pamper-doo and tett-devoo by her oblivious children.

Shaby was the kind of Englishman who might make the effort to learn a few words in a foreign language but would doggedly speak them in an English accent; he considered any attempt at correct pronunciation to be insufferably pretentious. So there was certainly no question of a bilingual household – Shaby had to make all the effort, and though she tried to stick to English with them, the children grew up with a strangely hybrid vocabulary and diction. She was their Mama and he their Dada, but as the children mixed more with local kids, these were given a lazy Northern drawl far from the sweet French inflection she was used to... Daader and Maamer didn't sound quite right.

Equally, saying pipi and caca instead of wee and poo, along with some embarrassing mispronunciations of common words, like pollissman and kalle-y-dosscop, landed them in the firing line for some vicious teasing by school chums. On top of all this, Fanchon had to grapple with the pitfalls of improving her language skills in the company of children and would drop inappropriate words into polite conversation, perhaps declaring something to be crappy, or misguidedly using "Ow do?' as a greeting. Eventually, Dada and Mama became Dad and Mam to blend with local custom; bit by bit the Belgian-ness was being lost, along with the bourgeois upbringing, as they settled into life amongst the Smoggies.

She did manage to hire a home-help – poor Marie didn't know what hit her – by the time another trilogy of babies had arrived. First two boys, Christopher and Michael, giving Peter the much-needed balance of male company, albeit belatedly as he was by now approaching his teens. They were nicknamed respectively Barley Boy or Conkey (which name eventually transferred to the dog) and Leno or Dilo, interchangeable at whim (or sometimes Weetabix due to the boy's limited palate).

Finally, and apparently unexpectedly (though birth control appears to have been of minimal importance), arrived a little girl called Jacqueline, the baby of the family complete; five girls and three boys. (At this point, Tommy took matters into his own hands, so to speak, and bought some condoms.) This young trio was, again unimaginatively, dubbed 'The Little Ones' and in due course the youngest received her own nicknaming tag.

Next to Tommy's office in the centre of Middlesbrough, in a grand Victorian square of townhouses converted to offices, was a firm of solicitors, a group of colleagues who all gave their name to the business. The first name vaguely resembling that of the baby of the family triggered the obvious choice of nickname, but for added quirkiness the other partners were also named, including the pluralising of the first name due to it representing a set of siblings. Probably the longest – and strangest – nickname ever given to a child, she became known as Jacksons, Monk and Rowe.

Tommy would return from work at six on the dot, sometimes greeted by the young legal-team-namesake waiting for him at the gate on a little wooden chair. On seeing her he would grab both her hands and dance a little jig, singing: "Jacksons, Monk and Rowe, Jacksons, Monk and Rowe, We will go rejoicing, Jacksons, Monk and Rowe!" to the tune of *Bringing in the Sheaves*, all the while the loose change in his pockets providing a jolly background jingle. Or later, in a more peaceful mood before bedtime, he might sing the words "Oh my lovely Jacksons, Monk and Rowe" to the tune of Schumann's *Kreisleriana No.2*.

Thus were the Thomases of Linthorpe established. It was a nice story that kept the children amused in its occasional tellings as they grew up in the Big House on the Corner. But some began to feel that things didn't quite add up. Why did their parents speak so rarely about those early times of courtship? And why did they never celebrate, or even put a date on, their wedding anniversary?

Thirty years later the shocking truth finally emerged; Tommy had been married with a child back in England when he met and fell in love with Baby. His choice was clear – abandonment or duty. He chose the former and he and Baby lived with the guilt of it for many years, keeping this half-brother a secret from all those that followed until they were well into adulthood. It was a tragic and unnecessary mistake, though perhaps understandable when seen through the skewed-reality lens of wartime life.

As soon as the Thomases of Linthorpe were introduced to their new brother, the bonding that should have happened decades earlier was allowed to blossom, and sibling friendships forged that helped abate the sense of anger and shame for Alan's sad loss. He was, and remains, entirely forgiving.

Incidentally, this revelation, whilst shocking and welcome all at once, had the unfortunate effect of undermining the integrity of some song lyrics being penned at that exact time. Young

Jacksons now had gender-equal numbers of older siblings, so that 'Sisters four and brothers three', should have been 'Sisters four and brothers four'. But that doesn't rhyme with 'Hanging off the family tree'!

They're looking for you high and low, now there's nowhere for you to go. So you'll just have to come out and face the music, Jacksons, Monk and Rowe.

9

Late Summer/New Term

Following Dartington, late that same summer, I went with my mother to visit her sister in Bruxelles. We spent a few pleasant days being tourists in the city of her childhood and youth, and I learnt to appreciate the splendour of Art Nouveau and Fin de Siècle architecture. We went to the Congo Museum where I was hoodwinked into thinking their dubious activities down there had been anything but ignoble and self-serving; King Leopold's vanity-driven, misguided imitation of the French and British Empires, just as deadly to indigenous populations. (Tante Janine and Fanchon (Mam) seemed oblivious, loyal to their Homeland's integrity and entrenched in the propaganda still prevalent back then.)

My cousins and I bonded over mutual efforts to speak each other's language – and I again bemoaned the sad fact that my lot hadn't been brought up bilingually. It had always seemed a terrible waste to me that my siblings and I missed out on the one benefit of having a mum with a weird accent. For her it must also have been sad; I couldn't imagine having to speak to my babies and toddlers in a foreign language. However good a linguist Mam was, it must have been hard for her as a young mum, and unrewarding.

Perhaps because of this monolingual upbringing, I have never properly acknowledged the other half of my heritage. I considered myself English with a Belgian mother, rather than half-English, half-Belgian. It is only recently – thanks to my husband's encouragement – that I have embraced my true identity and make sure to announce it at every opportunity. Audiences in that tiny country are always sweetly gratified to hear that one of us is one of them, even though they have a rich heritage of musicians, especially string players, as part of their history. The Conservatoire Royal de Bruxelles has enjoyed a long line of great teachers, and of course hosts the famous Queen Elisabeth Competition. Walking past the impressive building whilst sightseeing as a child, I made a vow to come and play here one day. Twenty-one years later, between rehearsal and concert, I was perched on the choir steps of that staggered stage, breastfeeding my firstborn.

If nothing else, my adoration of the *Tintin* comic strip books is testament to the true roots binding me. We had the full set growing up and I could recite many of them from memory. They were a favourite go-to on sick days off school, comfort food for the poorly brain. The huge mural of the Boy Reporter arriving at Marlinspike Station that greets Eurostar passengers at Brussels-Midi always gives me a pleasant sense of returning home, even though I've never lived there. I didn't know my Belgian grandparents; they had both died by the time I was one, at which point the annual family holidays to Coq-sur-Mer ceased.

Up until then, Mam would take the boat train with her many children and spend the entire summer holiday at this chic beach resort, staying in a quirky villa near the seafront, second home of her parents. My grandfather had been responsible for the development of the small resort into a gem of the Belle Époque style. He designed the layout and sold plots of land to the in-set from Bruxelles and Bruges, whilst careful to retain an unpretentious, relaxed atmosphere. The rule was 'there are no rules': houses must all be different and, above all, characterful. I love that. But he had high standards and disallowed anything 'trop haut, trop rapproché, de mauvais goût' (too high, too close together, in bad taste). So great villas were springing up in floral-bordered avenues, all around a central park with tennis courts and bowling greens, restaurants selling moules frites lining the esplanade.

My mum had been a child when the place was created so she became the model for advertising photos, splendid in her 1930s' swimsuit, digging great holes on the endless golden sandy beach. Here they would make flowers from crepe paper and sell them using seashells as currency, all the holiday children well versed in the protocol. Years later when she brought her own children here, and even when I brought my kids in 2001, chic little bathing-suited children tripped out of brightly painted beach huts and pedalled around the village on old-fashioned bikes, and there were those same crepe flowers still being peddled.

At one point my grandparents had a rather important guest renting the annexe next door; a certain Albert Einstein. My mum remembers him well and famously got into trouble for teasing the goat of his wife who grazed in the front garden. (The goat, not the wife.) She also recalls seeing crumpled papers covered with mathematical scribbles in the wastepaper basket in the great man's room. They could have been worth fishing out and keeping... but no one did. Hey-ho.

My bonding trip with Maman came to an end. Returning to London on the boat train, we had an appointment with another venue that was to become a huge part of my life in the following years. So far my visits to the capital had been limited to the suburbs for cousins' weddings, and I hadn't got to know it at all. Dad's parents were both gone by the time I was three, so the Bermondsey homestead wasn't a place I ever knew. Arriving that late summer afternoon and climbing the steps leading from the Royal College of Music, past the queuing Promenaders, I felt a frisson of excitement, on the brink of something that would become important to me.

The National Youth Orchestra of Great Britain was performing in the Proms at the Royal Albert Hall and Mike had been admitted into their hallowed ranks. This year they were to give the Proms Premiere of Shostakovich's 15th Symphony and I had been avidly listening to the recording as he prepared for the course.

Witnessing the performance from the RAH gods, up high in the perilously gradiented seats and looking out into the void of that immense space, I felt part of something huge. Sebastian Comberti was leading the cellos and made a great job of those soaring solos in the slow movement. He looked minute down there on the stage, surrounded by the assembled forces of these smartly dressed youngsters, and I was struck by his consummate professionalism. The familiar quotes of Rossini and Wagner that pepper the symphony with humour and pathos gave me a thrill, as if I was in on some secret cultural joke or political movement. As the work played out – those chattering percussion and celeste episodes, seemingly the toyshop gone feral in the hands of this conflicted and tortured soul – I beamed with knowledge and appreciation.

It would be another year before I stepped onto that stage for the first time, but then it would become a huge part of my youth, followed by a break of twenty-five years, at which point I'd be there breastfeeding my second baby on the choir steps of that staggered stage between rehearsal and concert! (Of a work written for the Brodsky Quartet by Paul McCartney.)

After the Prom, Mam and I took the night train back home. Snug in our sleeper compartment, I replayed those closing notes of the 15th Symphony over and over in my head. My drowsy brain started to confuse the clickety-clack of the train with the percussive chatter of Shostakovich. Whenever I hear that brilliant evocation, *Night Train* by Benjamin Britten, set to Auden's poem, I think of this night. Looking back, I realise I was witnessing the dying generation of the sleeper and mail trains and their diligent team of workers. As the sweet guard brought us a morning cuppa – yes, breakfast in bed was part of the service – the Cleveland Hills came into view.

I was ready for action again. When I arrived home, I called for a rehearsal...

> Last day of the holidays. Ian and Alex came and we had a most incredible practice. We played Borodin. Mr Marshall was watching and I played so well. I love the Borodin. We played Shostakovich and I remembered the Prom. Great!

Inspired by our Dartington experience, we were eager to get back to work. A spate of intense rehearsals, enthusiasm, dedication and ambition engulfed us once more.

> Played Schubert G major and it was brilliant. It is a great quartet. So lovely and quirky. Fantastic.

> Had a terrible headache and went for a walk. Then we had a four-hour quartet practice doing Prokofiev, Bartók, Beethoven F and Schubert G. We were exhausted.

> I had tea and then Ian came and we played three hours for Friday and then Alex came and we played the two Shostakovich - 7 and 11 and again 7 - for the 17th! Then we played Beethoven F major and we loved it and then we played MY Brahms and the others were as enthusiastic as me. It was just superb.

We had yet to perform to an audience in our own right. Sharing the bill playing bits of quartets was all very well, but it was time to grow up and devise a proper programme of entire works for a solo appearance. If opportunities weren't going to present themselves, we would have to create them. (And therein lies the First Lesson in The Holy Book of Chamber Music – no need to encourage these types 'cos they're so driven they'll organise their own concerts, play for nothing and thank you for the privilege. At thirteen that's fine, but it really shouldn't last into adulthood and yet sadly it often does.)

> We walked Ian home and talked about the kind of concert we want and then with Alex to his house talking about sponsors. We need concerts and money in order to give them. We will have a sponsored play definitely.

The search for sponsorship has been an endlessly frustrating dead-end street all our professional lives. It's just not a glamorous enough art form to entice big business in the way sport and even other musical forces seem to. (Imagine an art so lowly that, when asked to do a TV ad for Volvo, the Lindsay Quartet weren't even given a car to endorse. Despite the whole point of the ad being how a Volvo Estate easily accommodates an entire string quartet and all their gear, they had to use their own car!)

The idea of a sponsored play was one we were to come back to, but at this time we didn't get round to it as a veritable swathe of opportunities soon presented themselves:

> We have got two bookings - one recital in the autumn and part of a concert in June. Great!

Ian's Uncle Alan was a lecturer at Teesside Polytechnic, where occasionally concerts were arranged in a sizable hall boasting a good acoustic and a proper stage. He managed to get us onto the billing for a lunchtime slot that October and we feverishly set about publicising, deciding on the repertoire and getting down to some serious work. Having just been studying Prokofiev No.2 with Michael Evans, its inclusion was an obvious choice, but we still had a lot of work to do on the last movement. Dvorak *American* was a favourite of ours and we decided it would make a good pairing.

The college had a built-in audience but we wanted to make sure we reached all the local dignitaries, movers and shakers, opportunity-makers, so – according to my diary – Ian made invitations that we posted by hand and stuck in newsagents' windows.

Rehearsals were intense and we focused on the evasive art of performing in rehearsal, so that the concert situation wasn't a surprise. There was even a contingency to practise way faster than necessary so that it felt easier on the day, like runners training at altitude in preparation for the Olympics. In the event, the concert was a veritable triumph, as my diary entry from that day bears witness:

> I got up and had a lovely bath and got clean and put my long flowered dress on and played the cello and Ian and Alex came and we talked and prepared ourselves and caught the bus to the Teesside Polytechnic. We were directed to the main lecture theatre - cor! And we played in the great acoustics. We were prepared. Lots of people arrived and we played the Prokofiev so professionally and superb and MY CADENZA! And then we stopped and played Dvorak tremendously! It was quite amazing. We were superb. Everyone congratulated us fantastically and "I was So Loud!" We all walked home and suggested the quartet get a meal but it was too late and all the chip shops were closed so we all came back - loads of us - and ate Mam's lovely risotto and listened to Mr Marshall! Oh the recital was great. Thank you so much for such a good gift of Cello Playing.

10

Prejudice and Pride

That mention of my being 'So Loud' was telling. Some months before, I had suffered a serious set-back to my sense of belonging and self-esteem: one of the local music teachers was listening to a rehearsal of the Dvorak and saw fit to tell my colleagues that if things were going to get serious, they should look for a boy to play the cello instead of me.

> Baggy thinks I shouldn't be in the quartet - FUCK. (Ian stuck up for me like hell.)

I was absolutely devastated at the idea that anyone could think of me as anything but an integral part of the group. His argument was that I was too weak in the *pizzicato* accompaniment at the start of the last movement; I had yet to learn the crucial rule that *pizzicato* dynamics need to be taken with a pinch of salt, as plucking tends to project less readily than playing with the bow. So the *piano* indication that I dutifully followed made me too low in the balance, between the energetic chugging of the inner parts and the perky melody above. Once I'd dried my tears and the others had reassured me that I was going nowhere and that Baggy (his nickname) was a twat, I settled back down to the task of holding my own in a man's world.

They do say women have to be twice as good and try twice as hard to make it… I made that my mantra. Though it is tough to accept that a thirteen-year-old full of the excitement of this joint venture, one of the gang from the beginning, had to prove herself equal to the boys at such a young age. It stayed with me, that sense of Imposter Syndrome, and as I grew up I would always scrutinise mixed-gender groups and check that the girls were holding their own. It was a terrible legacy to be foisted with as I progressed, and with little reason. I just had to get my plucking act together and I was back on level terms, balance-wise. The moral high ground, though, was harder won; the boys certainly enjoyed teasing me about it when they wanted to see my face drop, threatening to ask David Beale – one of the TYO cellists – to take my place.

Why does a woman have to fight to be a part of a society she has helped to create? Baggy notwithstanding, I wonder if women are women's worst enemies. Throughout my young life I came again and again into contact with women detractors and nearly became one myself. The very essence of a string quartet was, in those days, four old men in penguin suits. I'd never heard of the Hollywood Quartet with the wonderful Eleanor Aller as cellist, and so I had no role model in my own world. Of the few groups I knew with female members, they tended to be on Second Violin or Viola, the men unwilling to relinquish the Primarius position or the solidity of the bass line to the 'weaker sex'. In the culture of the day, women would be unlikely to complain and would rarely form a group themselves to take back control.

An inbuilt distrust of female teachers had already formed within me. I was invited to play for Joy Hall in a series of masterclasses, but my diary records my reticence thus:

Should I do masterclass? Women teachers - yuck!

She had been a founder member of the Delmé Quartet ten years before we formed, and their only female, and their cellist! She had left the quartet by this time, and was offering to share her valuable experience with kids like me. Yet here I was, the product of a female pedagogue from the start, a quartet specialist and a huge fan of Jacqueline du Pré, refusing the opportunity. What was I thinking?

I must have been brainwashed by all the negativity surrounding me, starting at home with parents who undermined their daughters' potential with gender-based judgements and assertions, though they would swear they treated us all equally. The boys were encouraged, but not the girls; creativity was a male preserve. (Even though Mam had loved her own creative writing as a young woman, I don't recall her ever trying to defend her sex.)

Patriarchal society was entrenched in a belief born out of nothing less than a conspiracy of oppression: female writers of music and literature, as well as scientists and inventors, were kept down, forced to work under a pseudonym or sacrifice domestic normality for their art. I can't really blame my parents for their programming – it was endemic throughout the 'civilised' world. Dinner table debates on this point could be framed as lighthearted, teasing, but the damage can last... We eventually undermine ourselves, losing belief and confidence.

While we 'Little Ones' were still toddling around in nappies, one of our sisters, Janet, was herself in a string quartet, leading the local Youth Orchestra (the one in existence before Edwin's TYO) in which she frequently played solo roles. She also competed successfully in local festivals. When her group won, she recalls Dad quipping that they must have been up against the School for the Deaf – his idea of a joke. Why was there no pride in her achievements? She says my parents never came to support her efforts, never turned up at school concerts or the like. It could be argued that they had little ones at home to look after, but that wouldn't excuse both of them. And anyway, there was never any problem leaving us with older sisters for in-built childcare when needed.

Joy, a gifted pianist, was denied the lessons she deserved when her regular teacher became ill months before she was to take Grade VIII. Joy struggled through on her own, no one having the foresight or inclination to find her alternative tuition at this crucial time.

I had it easy compared to these two; it seems the Quartet gave me a passport to a bit more favour. But perhaps that was the height of it? My parents would never miss a performance or outing by the quartet, but failed to turn up when I was soloist in the Elgar Cello Concerto at a major German concert hall, aged just seventeen. (My two older brothers had chosen the non-classical route for their creative muse so usually missed out on parental patronage at their public appearances, despite their gender!)

In all these cases, circumstances unknown to their children will have been a contributing factor, but it is hard not to take it personally and even allow it to infiltrate our opinions of our own kind.

I later joined the National Youth Orchestra, whose female boss, Ivey Dickson, openly stated that boys only would be chosen as section leaders, and that even outside desk positions (i.e. at the edge of the stage) should be held by boys – for fear of putting the audience off, one can only surmise. Strange, then, that she also banned girls from wearing trousers. She had a terrible habit of judging the girls for the inevitable romances that would emerge in the ranks and if you were pretty, you could be sure of a snide sideways glance. "Either you are a musician or you wear nail polish!" she famously asserted to a friend of mine. I never wore the stuff and grew up believing that make-up was for commoners – a doctrine that fitted in with Dad's beliefs – and that any serious musician shouldn't be concerned with the fripperies of female prettiness.

As women in classical music, we had to play down our femininity to be taken seriously. We wore long dresses, mostly by Laura Ashley – demure florals and decidedly un-glamorous – but we didn't do anything nice with our hair, and our eyes and lips were as nude as the day we were born. The first time I shared the stage with a made-up woman it was the violist, Nobuko Imai. She was an incredible player and looked amazing in her crimson lipstick; and yet I honestly remember thinking, *How will she be taken seriously?* We all remember the uproar at Vanessa Mae's unashamedly sexy debut photoshoot. Her playing ability was immediately cast in doubt by press and public alike.

Ivey Dickson demoted me in my second year at NYO to the back desk of cellos. This followed a brilliant audition full of praise and encouragement, yet there I was, deflated and baffled. It only lasted for one course, one without concerts, so was clearly some kind of psychological power game... I was soon moved back up the ranks. Many, many years later she heard me with the Brodsky Quartet on Radio 3 – in Beethoven's *Serioso* opus 95 with its involved and perilous cello moments – and took the trouble to phone to congratulate me.

"I knew it was you," she purred in her softly spoken Scottish syllables. "I always thought you were a wonderful player, right from the beginning."

So why did she keep putting me down?

Back to the quartet and, to my unashamed schadenfreude, I wasn't the only one at the mercy of jealous and bitter teachers who wanted to bring us down a peg or two.

> Baggy said that Mike is immature in his playing – God – it's awful what silly people say.

Wisely spoken, kiddo! But true to my nature, even now if I'm not careful I will give more credence to the words of detractors than to those of encouragers. According to my diary, at this same time, adjudicator Maurice Jacobson had made special mention of my part in the group after one of our festival outings, speaking to my parents afterwards and suggesting I go further afield to find proper support for my talent. I, not my colleagues, was chosen to perform in the grand prizewinners' concert at the Town Hall to an audience of over a thousand. Yet I have no recollection of these accolades – my memory all these years has only held on to the negative comment of someone less qualified. So yes, we learn to put ourselves down before others do.

That autumn I made my concerto debut, under Edwin Raymond and the Symphony Orchestra, playing the Boccherini. As usual, Dad and Pete were in the orchestra, along with some of my old primary school teachers, and I felt proud and worthy of being there, holding my own. Looking back, it seems quite an achievement for a thirteen-year-old who'd only been playing for four years; I hope Baggy felt bad for trying to have me ejected from the Quartet!

I contacted him recently to ask why he had been so unfair towards me all those years ago. He was genuinely shocked to hear what was said to have come from his lips. It's true that it was only hearsay. And all this time…

Our triumphant lunchtime concert immediately led to a couple of invitations and we were starting to feel decidedly proper. A local enthusiast asked us to play at the nearby Leeds University Centre; being equidistant to all our homes, roughly one hundred yards away, an extremely 'neighbourhood gig'. We played Shostakovich and Beethoven (though I'm pretty sure it wouldn't have been a complete performance of the latter) and my diary entry excitedly announces that we were promised payment in kind, in the form of some new sheet music:

> She has offered to buy us a quartet or two! Great! But we don't know which to choose!

Well, it was a start.

Looking further through the tiny scribble of this diary, once I get past the endless waffle about who fancies whom, what I wore, being fat and lazy (This week will start again now and none of your horrible aimless days. How about a quartet practice or two! I love the CSQ!), I see that we did actually have a pretty big repertoire already, though not every movement of every piece necessarily. Rehearsals could be full and varied:

> After dinner I made cream horns and Mr Marshall was here. We had to play his bloody duet. Then Ian and Alex came and we practised doing Mozart G, Prokofiev, Dvorak - it was fantastic. Mr Marshall listened and was impressed. Then we mucked about and laughed and laughed and laughed.

Who is this Mr Marshall?

One day a man had appeared at our gate when we were all playing in the garden. He was dressed in a dark gabardine, belted at the waist, his old-fashioned twill trousers tight to his ankles with metal bicycle clips. He pushed his ancient bike as he walked up the path, taking exaggerated strides, lifting his knees at every step. It soon became evident from his thick spectacle lenses that he had severely impaired eyesight, so his lack of perspective made for this strangely mannered gait. His hair was slicked and oily and his face was lined with the sullen features of a dour Northerner.

This creepy-looking figure, caught watching us kids frolicking in the garden, might nowadays elicit a swift rebuttal as he's shown the gate. But this was the early seventies and manners came before suspicion, even if they had suspected anything, so far was it from anyone's imagining that...

Strangers would never be turned away. My dad would welcome all comers into the house to debate whatever politics or religion they were peddling door-to-door. He was himself a staunch socialist and was active on the canvassing trail, enlisting us all into envelope-stuffing and the like. He was a pacifist and an atheist who later became a Quaker, so he was happy to debate with any number of callers. But Mr Marshall wasn't here to exchange ideas, except maybe musical ones.

As it turned out, he was neither paedophile nor political posturer, simply an ex-musician in search of some company. It appeared he had been a cellist, and a good one by his own reckoning. He'd seen all the musical instruments coming and going through our gate day after day as he cycled to the village for his meagre bachelor groceries and had finally given in to curiosity.

Maybe he thought it was a music school of some sort, or perhaps he'd heard through the grapevine about this family and their many musical friends. He just wanted to be a part of it. So he was invited in, offered tea and biscuits, got his feet under the table and never looked back. He became a regular, only he usually chose weekday afternoons, so Dad, having initiated the acquaintance, was spared the inconvenience and it fell to the rest of us to entertain him.

In his rather acerbic, thick Middlesbrough accent he would preach to us about his favourite players of yore, Piatigorsky being his ultimate hero. But his pronouncements always seemed to be confrontational or aggressive, as if he had something to prove. And the Russian name lost all exotic flavour when delivered in his Mrs Tweedy-esque diction, as he pontificated on his favourite recordings, players and composers, with brusque disregard for anyone else's opinions. He would drawl on somewhat and, though politeness precluded withdrawing while he spoke, we nevertheless found it hard to stay focused. He might mention a piece of music saying, "D'you know it?" and, if you nodded unthinkingly, having drifted off into your own thoughts, he might suddenly challenge you – "Sing it then!" – catching you out in your pretence. (This barked order was then adopted as an in-phrase at home if anyone claimed to know anything at all, musical or otherwise, to our endless amusement.)

Returning from school, your heart would sink if you caught sight of this grim figure leaning on his bike at the bottom of the stairs to the house. There was no escape if he'd seen you, although we gradually began to realise that his abysmal eyesight often meant he hadn't and you could sneak off in the other direction and wait till he gave up and left. No one ever warned me not to let him into the house if I was on my own. We knew nothing about him but what he'd told us; we didn't know his first name, nor where he lived. It seems amazing now looking back on it, but I might be left there alone with him aged twelve or thirteen, playing my cello or having to listen to him droning on. We would sometimes invite him to listen to our quartet rehearsals, but it was never a very comfortable feeling. He didn't seem to be a tremendously kind man and would give guarded praise, even to ones so young. But I was touched to find that he had actually composed music, which we would try out (under sufferance) and that he took the trouble to make me sheet music of a piece I'd been admiring.

> Marshypants was here. He gave me the Rococo Variations that he had written out!
> Practised Rococo and Peacock with the record then Allemande. They were all superb!!!

He was probably a very lonely man for whom we offered some respite in his singleton existence. But he just became tiresome, turning up too often and not being pleasant enough to inspire a true welcome. My diary tells me that I overheard Mam giving him a telling-off. Maybe he'd been inappropriate with her? Eventually his visits grew more sporadic and one day he just stopped coming. We never found out what happened to him, but I hope he didn't die alone.

*

An invitation to play further afield – a shared concert in Durham – brought us into contact with a fantastic young pianist, William Fong, with whom we would go on to collaborate years later on various concert platforms. Of Chinese and French parents, very unusual in our neck of the woods, I was tickled to hear his mum ask him 'Tu veux faire pipi?' before he was due to play. She may have felt secure in the knowledge no-one would understand, but Mam and I had a little smile to ourselves. (I teased him about it when we, as much older professionals, would be about to go on stage together.) The concert obviously had me worried beforehand, but the work seems to have paid off:

> We have to really knuckle down for Saturday - it is important!

> Went to Durham. Got there and saw everyone. We played the Shostakovich beautifully and got lots of congratulations. It was great because Boro beat top of the league West Ham 3-nil. Hooray!

> I was sad, I am in a rut
> What shall I do? I wish I knew.
> I love my quartet like mad.
> I sewed my skirt and watched a bit of telly - Tortelier. (Cor-telly, eh?!) Oh, he made me feel great to be a cellist... cellos forever!

It wasn't all fun and happiness; never mind dealing with the prejudice of our detractors and nay-sayers, there seem to have been plenty of arguments and falling out within our ranks. Emotions ran high, as in all teenage kids, but despite everything we were immensely proud of our achievements and ambition.

My diary is filled with grand statements of lifelong devotion, which are so touching to read nearly fifty years later.

> Had a quartet practice. We played the Beethoven. It was really petty and we were being bitchy. We played the Schubert A minor - the same. Then I suggested the Borodin and from the start I was so emotionally moved that I felt like crying and I was playing so well. By this piece the quartet was brought together and I was playing with my whole heart and body. They were amazed and they played table tennis and I played the piano blues. Mike talked to me after and he said they are all amazed at me. This is me for the rest of my life - loving everyone and everything.

11

Fame!

I watched a North-Eastern music programme - great. We ought to get on that! declared my diary at the beginning of 1975. Ambition and drive had me constantly on the lookout for opportunity. I don't know what that programme might have been, but coincidentally we were just then offered our first TV appearance, causing immense excitement. Tyne Tees Television asked us to go up to their Newcastle Studios for an interview and short performance on their early evening magazine slot. We decided we'd play a bit of the Dvorak and beamed with importance on receiving written instructions; when to turn up and what to wear – 'not white shirts!' as they would play havoc with the new technicolour cameras, for some reason.

There seems to have been a fracas, as the appointed day clashed with some school exams I had. *How important can they be at thirteen?* I asked myself, trying to justify missing them altogether. But in the end I realised I could do the exams in the morning, dash home to a waiting taxi and bomb up the A19, arriving in plenty of time for the great TV debut. Showbusiness!

The Big House on the Corner.

The young family as was when they took possession.

With Dad and Mam.

The family complete, with our Belgian cousins either side of me and their mum, Tante Janine, centre back (Mam probably took the photo).

Alan around the time of reconnecting with Dad, shortly after I was born. It would be thirty years later that I found out I had another brother and the family really was complete.

Conkey.

My first public performance — a family concert in Northampton, 1970.

FESTIVAL CONCERT BY YOUNG MUSIC MAKERS

A STUDY in concentration is captured by our photographer as Ian Belton, of Teesside, led the junior strings orchestra in a festival in Middlesbrough Town Hall last night.

TWO HUNDRED schoolchildren from throughout the North-east and further afield took part in a junior string festival at Middlesbrough Town Hall last night.

The young musicians, all under 12, were conducted by David Martin, a celebrated violin soloist and professor at the Royal Academy of Music in London.

Ian and Mike at a junior strings event in the Town Hall.
We were all there but only those two made the papers!

Musical harmony

FOUR TEESSIDE teenagers will be carrying the hopes of Cleveland with them at the weekend when they travel to London in an attempt to play their way to a major musical prize.

Together they make up the Cleveland String Quartet.

The quartet, pictured above, is made up of (from left) Ian Belton, 15, of 28, Emerson Avenue, Alex Robertson, 15, of 10, Eastbourne Road, Jacqueline Thomas, 13, and her brother Michael, 14, of 2, The Crescent, Linthorpe, all of Middlesbrough.

All four are members of the Teesside Youth Orchestra and have been together as a quartet for two years.

Their music has earned them a place in the national finals of a chamber music competition in the National Festival of Music for Youth, which takes place at the Fairfield Halls in London at the weekend.

The quartet, which qualified for the finals through success in preliminary rounds held in Newcastle, will be competing for the major honours against 20 other ensembles.

Our first press exposure and the oldest existing photo of the group – two years in. On the steps of the Big House on the Corner. Evening Gazette, June 1974.

My first publicity shot, in the Music Room (Big House on the Corner).

First Cleveland Quartet publicity shot, outside the house next door (with rather more road than necessary!)

First visit to Dartington, 1974.

Next visit to Dartington, 1984.

Dad's 'Fat Lady Sings' moment, Dartington 1994.

Fanchon in the dunes at Coq sur Mer, posing for the holiday brochure.

Tommy and Baby around the time they met.

Their first home as a family.

Dad with Arvid & Co. – the Latvian String Quartet.

TYO. Ian leading, Alex and Mike either side of Edwin Raymond, me on second desk of cellos.

Edwin and the TYO at the Schools Prom, 1975 (Ian and Mike visible at back left, and that could be Alex wielding a trombone. I'm off-picture).

NYO at the Proms.
(Alex and Mike left, me centre.)

The twenty-strong NYO cello section (David Strange at centre in black jacket, me front row right.).

Setting sail for France.
(Ian, Alex and Mike at right.)

A few cello friends and me (centre) with the formidable Ivey Dickson.

■ BACK in the mid-70s, this group of pupils from Acklam's Hustler School would sit having their lunch and singing songs such as The Ballad of Casey Jones.
Those ex-pupils, including Hilary Davies, Nancy Borchard, Jill Bennett, Sara Scott, Allison

The Casey Jones Appreciation Society outside the Little Room, last day of school, from an Evening Gazette 'Where are they now?' feature.

At the school theatre, as Moloch the Wizard with the back-combed hair.

The first-prize trophy, etched with the full score of Britten's Young Person's Guide to the Orchestra.

Cleveland String Quartet
Middlesbrough
Third Quartet,
2nd and 3rd movements Shostakovich

The Cleveland String Quartet was formed five years ago by four members of the National Youth Orchestra, all from Middlesbrough. They receive no coaching as a quartet and therefore deal with all problems of interpretation themselves. Locally, they have made a name for themselves by winning major prizes at music festivals and giving recitals. They now have a large repertoire from Haydn to contemporary composers.

Shostakovich's Third Quartet, one of the finest in the cycle, was composed in 1946. The contemplative 2nd movement has an almost Mozartean grace and poignancy, sharply contrasted to the 3rd movement which recalls Shostakovich's war experiences with its ferocious hard-driven, march-like theme.

Cleveland String Quartet

CSQ at the National Festival of Music for Youth, 1977.

The offices of Jacksons, Monk & Rowe and Dad's Linthorpe Insurance Brokers at the centre of this handsome Victorian terrace, from an ad in 2019 for the sale of the whole row of eight four-storey properties, asking price £800k. What North-South divide??

Back cover for The Juliet Letters album.
J, M & R makes it onto the world stage!

Some old manuscripts – our Palm Court arrangements and more.

> 23rd April: Went to school and had the exams. Humanities was really good cos at first appearance you thought you couldn't do it but then you could. I kept mixing up my religions though. I came home and the others arrived. We got in the taxi and drove to Newcastle and arrived about 10 to 1. We went in. It's great. We had a lovely dinner and saw them rehearsing the first half. We got made up and had a tea break. Then they shot the first half and we watched from the controls. We saw the rehearsing and the shooting of the first bit of the 2nd half then we did ours. The rehearsal was a bit cronic [sic] and we had to cut the conversation cos of time. Then we shot it. It went really well. I don't know what I looked like though. Oh dear. Good atmosphere. Tony Basterville was the interviewer. We finished and me and Alex came home on the train when Ian and Mike went for their lesson with Barry Wilde.

Says it all really. I notice certain things never change: taxi laid on for arrival, public transport home... to this day BBC Portland Place's favourite tactic for the non-megastars they interview. And how many times has the 'conversation bit got cut' for classical musicians on TV. It's shameful – and so it was in that first appearance. But to be fair, the novelty of the piece was what we were doing, being the age we were, not what we might say. Though I bet there would have been a few cringingly arrogant quotes to amuse the viewers.

Returning to school the following day my friends were none the wiser about where I'd been, but as the transmission date drew nearer I thought I should warn them, in case they got a nasty surprise over their TV dinners. The big day arrived and my diary announced it in capitals across the top of the page.

THE CLEVELAND STRING QUARTET WERE ON TELEVISION. (THAT'S ME FOLKS!)

> After school I taped the NYO Easter concert off the radio then we watched us on telly! It was OK CHUM. It went miles better than we thought. It was fine. After tea we taped a great impro then a mixed noise.

(Not sure what that was but it sounds far-out.) I love the way I'm persuading myself – unconvincingly – that the transmission had been acceptable.

The next day school was full of it. Boys were coming up and singing 'You're a star, you're a star' (the signature tune of *New Faces*, ITV's current talent-spotting show) and asking pseudo-reverentially for my autograph. I showed admirable restraint and maturity in my response, feigning boredom with their games, as if appearing on TV was a regular part of my life and not worthy of comment.

> It was really peculiar when everyone was going on about the telly all the time. So unoriginal.

Now that we'd had our first fifteen minutes of fame (well, five actually) our ambitious trajectory persuaded us to have another bash at that competition we'd bombed in, the National Festival of Music for Youth. Mr Raymond had announced his intention to enter TYO in the Orchestral Category. This was meant to be: we could travel to Croydon's Fairfield Halls, do our bit of the competition then join up with the orchestra and kill two birds with one stone. The debate began about what to play. Yet again we failed to learn from past experience:

> Ian and Alex and me and Mike started the phone debate about Croydon. It ended with Beethoven as I feared, but I don't fear it now!

Wrong. You should have stuck to your guns, little me! Despite previously having our fingers burnt with competitive outings of Beethoven, it appears we plumped for op.18 no.5, the Variations movement... again. Having overcome my justifiable reservations, I was determined to make a go of it and tried to assert my authority in rehearsal.

> Sunday - we had a quartet practice. It was great. Really funny. I made sure about Beethoven being thoroughly looked at.

But dedication and seriousness can get boring sometimes so we made time for fun. In the process, we appear to have invented the frisbee (the trend hadn't reached Middlesbrough yet) by recommissioning some old camping gear from the basement.

> We played the Trout Quintet (Me Ali Alex Ian Jo and Mike a bit.) I love Schubert! Then we played a game with plastic plates going along the lawn in mid-air. Really great!!

That 'part of a concert in June' that had been so proudly catalogued as one of our 'two bookings' came around, and it seems we had been thinking a little more about presentation. The choice of new costume is very of its time and, though this predated *Saturday Night Fever* by a couple of years, might have been better suited to a flashing disco floor than the venue we were headed for that day.

> Friday June 6th
> Listened to Peacock Variations then Mike, Ian and Al got back from town. They had bought white ties and black shirts. Really smart. We left orchestra at the break and Mam and Dad took us to Redcar. It was on the pier ballroom and we had a walk on the beach while the choir sang. We came back for the interval and took our instruments backstage - talked about NFMY. We were all being beautiful to each other. We played

> absolutely perfectly and it has broken the chain of timidness - we are now a Great Quartet! We came home and listened to records with food.

(I bet it wasn't the Bee Gees.)

As the trip to London approached, rehearsals were ramped up… and I started to plan the really important stuff:

> I sat for a long time and decided on a dress for the future days. I had some tea and Ian and Alex came and we had a quartet practice which was not too hot but by the end we were all laughing. Ian's and Mike's strings have met disaster!

> We went to Ian's house and we were playing beautifully. We taped Beethoven - fab! We are so much looking forward to going to London on Thursday.

But there was one small annoyance to our sense of growing up and heading into the wider world: my parents still wanted to join us. You can hardly blame them, so into music as they were and this ambitious young group being fifty percent made up of their own offspring. But it became a bone of contention as we got older, and the seeds of discontent are already sprouting here:

> Mam and Dad are coming to Croydon. Damn! We must be independent.

So the day of departure arrived and the four of us boarded the train to King's Cross. All instrument cases and bags, we felt like a proper touring string quartet. Playing cards and chatting about the future, we may have unknowingly become the catalyst for the introduction of quiet coaches on trains, so irritating must our pseudo-intellectual specialist banter have been to other passengers. On arrival we made a beeline for Foyles Bookshop on Charing Cross Road. It had the best collection of classical sheet music nationwide and became a place of pilgrimage for every subsequent trip to the capital.

> We went by tube to the West End and walked right up Oxford Street. We went to Foyles for ages and bought Smetana Quartet, Shostakovich 3, Beethoven A Minor! Good eh?

It's quite telling that this was our priority activity having just arrived in London from two hundred and fifty miles away... no sightseeing or window shopping. Although later, after a feverish rehearsal in the hotel, we ventured back out for a walk around the seedy budget-hotel district that was Lancaster Gate. My diary is full of amazement to find shops still open at nine or ten o'clock! And a stark warning to the adjudicators in tomorrow's big event: If we don't win...

At the very tip of London's southern perimeter lies Croydon, home of the Fairfield Halls. The grand 1960s structure, housing concert hall and theatres, was reminiscent of the Royal Festival Hall in its architecture and, though in such a remote part of the capital – some would say it wasn't even London – it had a good reputation and was an important venue in Classical Music. We trekked down there on tube and train, full of our anticipated triumph but rightly nervous that we would again be disappointed. Here is my disgusted reportage of the debacle:

> We watched the first three, got ready and played, to my opinion and knowledge, beautifully. We really moved. We sat down and watched the rest - it was so boring. He (Morris [sic.] bloody Jacobson) gave his adjudication and we weren't even mentioned! It was trash... again.

In a depressingly predictable way, trying to impress with Beethoven seems to have been our downfall. And this adjudicator was the very man who'd singled me out for special mention the year before. Now he didn't even remember us! (Many years later, we were to become friends and collaborators with his son, the brilliant pianist Julian Jacobson. I told him of our shocking treatment at the hands of his old man and we shared a laugh over our thwarted great expectations.)

But my anger seems short-lived. We picked ourselves up and made our way to that other iconic post-war concert hall, where we lay on the grass and gazed at the Thames eating ice creams, then went in to hear the LSO in a performance of great Romantics. How we afforded the tickets I'm not sure, but I suppose we would have been on a Child Concessionary rate. My disgust at the tepid audience response – Bad London clapping! – was worthy of mention in the diary later that night. This place, too, became a destination of pilgrimage for every London trip; walking over Charing Cross Bridge would always bring a thrill to my being. Often we just sat there, soaking in the atmosphere, but it was a must for each visit. Its stage too became a well-trodden part of our future lives; here we were to perform our first high-profile Shostakovich Cycle in 1989, and again a breastfeeding session comes to mind, this time in the wings as the legendary Jeff Buckley sang *Dido's Lament* at Elvis Costello's 1995 Meltdown Festival.

In the pre-sale clear-out of my mum's house, I was delighted to find an old letter from my paternal granny describing the South Bank's launch in 1951 during the Festival of Britain, where she had a 'gay old time!'

So even though we'd bombed again in the Chamber Music Class, we still managed to rejoin our colleagues as some kind of returning heroes.

Got back to the hotel and the orchestra had arrived.

> They were all worried about us. It was a great feeling being important.

I didn't seem to be terribly embarrassed about our scandalous defeat in the competition and next day we swept the board in the Youth Orchestra section.

> Anthony Freeze-Green [sic] told us that we had the 'outstanding' award! We won! Hurray!

This triumph would mean an appearance at the first ever Schools Prom at the Royal Albert Hall in the autumn. Travelling back up the M1 with our friends in the orchestra, I was glad we hadn't had to take the train again. The excitement on the bus as the dark night closed in on us and all the camaraderie of belonging, especially to the Winning Ensemble – even though it wasn't the Quartet – made for a happy return North.

I haven't been back to the Fairfield Halls since and I certainly never breastfed there.

12

Pomp and Circumstance

In the autumn of '75 I was offered my first paid gig. The local amdram society was to stage an Offenbach Operetta, *La Perichole*, and needed a reduced chamber orchestra in the pit, for which I was to be the one and only cellist. The pay was fabulous – £3.50 per performance – and I jumped at it. But being sensible and conscientious, I saw that a ten-night run of evening shows might interfere with homework and make getting up for school tricky, so I asked my friend and TYO desk partner Alison Waines to do a job-share.

Middlesbrough Little Theatre was an iconic building in our enclave of Linthorpe. Built in 1957, one of the country's first post-war venues and opened by Sir John Gielgud, it was the only theatre in town. Here we had witnessed a plethora of hugely varied acts, from top international string quartets to, very much the other end of the scale, the Gang Show, that quaint variety of bygone times where boy scouts and girl guides – amongst them I do believe a certain Ian Belton – rode along 'on the crest of a wave' (or the Christopher Wave, as I understood it; having a brother of that name, it made perfect sense to me). It was home to an excellent youth theatre (of which said brother was a star member) with an eclectic repertoire of modern plays and standard musicals, and it hosted an annual pantomime, boasting B-list celebrities stuffed into bras and prised into heels, playing to a full house every night at Christmas. But the main attraction of this cultural hub was a ready supply of operettas by Gilbert & Sullivan and their ilk, performed by the Teesside Amateur Dramatics Society.

From the first rehearsal it was a hoot. I loved sitting in the pit and gazing up to see the action on stage when there was a long enough break in the music. Ali-bogs and I worked out an alternating rota for our job-share, but come closing night we found neither of us wanted to miss out. So we both sat in and played alternate acts, splitting the fee for that night between us. Partying with the cast afterwards, their exotic costumes and refined diction replaced by casual seventies' attire and local accents, there was camaraderie and a real sense of regional pride. But I knew the thrill of it was simply because it was short-lived. Regular pit-work wasn't an ambition for the future, accustomed as I had become to a much higher plane of existence. I was a member of a string quartet aiming for world dominance and, furthermore, I had spent this year as a member of the illustrious National Youth Orchestra of Great Britain.

NYO had come into my life with a bang. As the name suggests, members were drawn from all over the British Isles and therefore the standard of playing was pretty high for kids of eighteen and under. But the repertoire and succession of top conductors and soloists was truly inspirational, not to mention the thrill of belonging to an iconic clique. Mike had joined the year before and loved it, so the rest of the Quartet auditioned and the four of us went together for a ten-day course every school holiday. In that first year I got to play in Coventry and Norwich Cathedrals, Snape Maltings, the Royal Festival Hall and the Royal Albert

Hall. Charles Dutoit and Rudolph Schwarz were two of the luminaries invited to take us through our paces, Kyung Wha-Chung and Clifford Curzon amongst our soloists. It was a heady experience to be part of this huge gathering – over one hundred strong with desk after desk of strings, long rows of wind and brass, a heaven's gate of harpists and an armoury of percussion.

Rehearsals were regimented and serious. Most of the day was devoted to sectionals – to get each part just right under the direction of expert professionals – then the forces joined together at 5pm for a whole-orchestra rehearsal, known as 'Full'. To ensure the conductor arrived to a ready and waiting throng, we had to be in our seats thirty minutes early and remain in complete silence while the tuning process got underway, each section and solo part taking all the time they needed to be spot on to the oboist's A. When tuning was over, the silence continued right up to the grand entrance of our maestro. His laughing voice might be heard before he came into view, such was the stillness of these hundred-plus kids, thus creating a frisson of excitement and an aura around him. The whole orchestra would stand as one to greet him with fitting respect, and the rehearsal would commence.

But with the music came no relaxation of mandatory conduct. Pencils were firmly tied with string to every music stand to avoid the annoying – and embarrassing – interruption of a dropped one. We all had to wear regulation black plimsolls, to ensure total quiet, and no one was EVER allowed to speak – unless spoken to, and with an answer required. This honour was reserved for section leaders, whose voices would sound strange and out of place in this controlled atmosphere. The standing ovation was repeated at the end of the rehearsal as the conductor took his leave, and we would file out in silence, only speaking again once we had vacated the hall.

This military routine carried on into other parts of daily life, with concert-uniform inspection, strict lights-out and wake-up times, 'Coach Order' for journeys so you would travel with your section, not your friends (unless the two coincided), afternoon rest on concert days and so on. It was like belonging to an exclusive kind of private school and I quite relished the strictness. Somehow, having to sneak around the rules made life more fun, chatting after lights-out as quietly as possible so that one of the dragons posing as house mistresses didn't hear us. I made new and very close friends from all over the country and we would write long letters between the courses, missing our special times together and counting the days till we'd meet again. It became a huge part of my life for four years.

This being our first real involvement with players from outside our corner of north-east England, my Quartet and I experienced a bit of a culture shock. None of us had broad Middlesbrough accents, far from it, but amongst our new colleagues I was painfully aware of sounding unrefined, especially as there was a significant public school – or at least, southern grammar school – representation, as well as a particularly refined set who'd already 'gone up' to Oxbridge. I found myself living a double life, attempting a switch to received pronunciation every time I went away to one of these courses and having to lose the plummy tones on my return to school, where they already thought me hopelessly posh. It's odd I felt this way as there were plenty of regional accents within the orchestra, but somehow they were all more palatable and cheery compared to our downbeat tones.

Largely in those days (except on Teesside of course), kids who'd been offered the chance to learn an instrument and take it to a high standard were from privileged backgrounds and could afford the costs involved, so the demographic was decidedly upper-middle class and proud of it. Our Grande Dame Musical Director, Ivey Dickson, was of Scottish origin, but had a regal upper-class demeanour, and her soft Scots was more than a bit Queen's English. She always wore flamboyant flowing dresses that suited her big personality – and helped mask a generous bulk – and flirted shamelessly with the conductors she'd put on the podium for our inspiration and adoration. I felt grubby in her presence, especially at the annual auditions in Newcastle, (where she once told me to my face that I smelt and needed to buy some deodorant. My train had been late, I was hot and pubescent; of course I smelt. I was devastated.) Unjustly I'm sure, I sensed she was there through duty and would have been happier drawing the orchestra's membership from further south. I was fiercely proud of what had been achieved in the North-East, and of the freely available music education, and I didn't want anyone thinking we were a lesser breed.

The whole regional accent thing has thankfully lost its stigma in recent years, with the help of musicians like Lesley Garrett and Jess Gillam taking to our screens, but back then it was all BBC diction and Old Boys Network. Music, in the UK, being a profession wherein regional accent meant lesser pedigree, by the same token any foreign accent implied greater brilliance. We British nationals have long been the victims of that favourite Brexiteer slogan, bemoaning the trait of foreigners 'taking our jobs'; it has been a given in our profession forever, and no one ever complained. We love the chance to hear performers from all over the world filling our concert halls and welcome the diversity with open arms.

Yet there was, and still is, this preconceived idea amongst some promoters that foreign is best. When the Wigmore Hall celebrated its hundredth anniversary, not a single string quartet from these shores was invited to perform, so much did they favour the more exotic imports. This isn't to undermine the brilliance or legitimacy of others' celebrity, but I can't imagine a French or German concert hall meting out the same treatment to their own musicians.

On top of this, we regional types faced the indignity of being an underclass within our own country, sounding all wrong for radio appearances, struggling to be perceived to have an intellectual voice. Even as late as the 1990s, my niece went to the Guildhall School of Music & Drama and was told by her singing teacher to lose her Middlesbrough accent if she wanted to be taken seriously in the profession. Such snobbery is shameful and yet there it was, and there I was fitting into it and trying to temper my Northern soul.

This chameleonic way of life was quite confusing and I found myself even more schizophrenic: the school versus music double-life was one thing, but this added a third element into the mix. Now even at TYO, as we big fish returned to our little pond, the others must have found us unbearably affected. We adopted rehearsal techniques and jargon we'd learnt at NYO and tried to instigate their use on local turf.

Not all of it was a waste of time, but we undoubtedly seemed seriously pretentious to our friends, who had already had to put up with us being full of our own importance as the Fab Four, even before we went away. However, we also inspired some of them; the following year the NYO membership boasted seven players from Middlesbrough, five of us from tiny Linthorpe! Amongst us was Angie Daly, as expert on the viola as she was at singing 'in the Club Style'. This distinctive Northern technique made famous by Vic Reeves and Bob Mortimer (fellow Boro-ites) was delivered to perfection in the girls' dorms at NYO after lights-out, *She Wears Red Feathers and a Hula-hula Skirt* unashamedly celebrating her roots and rendering her genteel audience helpless with laughter.

That summer, my first year's membership of NYO culminated in my much-anticipated Royal Albert Hall debut – not only appearing in the iconic hall but as part of the Proms Festival, where a select few youth orchestras each year are invited to contribute to the two-month-long classical extravaganza. From its inception in 1895, the Proms has been an inclusive affair, offering cheap standing tickets to the lower orders, who cheer and call out exuberant slogans in a total departure from accepted concert etiquette. My diary entry was suitably full of awe at being a part of it.

> We arrived at the Royal Albert Hall. It was a great atmosphere. We unpacked our cellos and talked and went on and my God, what a fright. The Promenaders shout such funny but frightening things. We played the Kodaly very well and the Beethoven was superb. I had such a fantastic feeling in me. This was the best experience in my life. In the interval we walked around and around and tuned and went on again. Oh, the feeling. The Tchaikovsky... Well I can't describe how beautiful and amazing it was. I was in tears at the end - last time - and the cheering was tremendous. At last we came off and that was it, all over.

Later that same Proms season and to my utter delight, a group of us won arena tickets to the famous 'Last Night', experiencing at first hand the madness of the heaving throng in full voice as the orchestra took them through all the perennial hits: *Jerusalem, Rule Britannia!* and my early childhood ballad, *Land of Hope and Glory*. I'd come a long way since that infant school railings debacle. This promptly became the new Best Day of My Life.

So, that autumn, the time had come for the Teesside Youth Orchestra to take to this famous podium in the first ever Schools Prom. Children from across the country would congregate – choirs, jazz and wind bands, string ensembles and full-scale orchestras, an impressive roll call, all prizewinners in that National Festival back in May. The grand finale was to be a combined-forces performance of the very same anthem we'd sung along to at the Last Night, with us as overall winners taking centre-stage nearest the conductor, Anthony Hopkins (the musicologist, not the actor).

Preparation back home was at fever-pitch; earnest rehearsals aplenty of our orchestral solo item, Wagner's *Meistersingers* Overture, radio interviews and press conferences, and a rather unhelpful dry-run performance at a local secondary school, where the bemused pupils reluctantly sang along to Elgar's heart-wrenching tune with characteristic teen lacklustre. Finally we were on the bus, London-bound. I felt like a veteran returning to the glorious scene of my recent summer's outings here, all insider knowledge and fake nonchalance.

Our placement in the programme being last before the finale, we were to remain in place while the other musicians assembled around us for the all-in-together-sing-along. But the afternoon rehearsal didn't follow concert format and we were shocked to find that another orchestra, the Brighton Schools, was still in position after their rehearsal and were somewhat reluctant to make way for us. We couldn't get to our pre-assigned spot at the core of the combined orchestras. A shout went out within our ranks – "Brighton won't move!" – and there was almost a bunfight. We sucked it up and maintained our dignity. Our moment was to come.

As the audience filed in and backstage became awash with anticipation, it was time to show the world what had been developing up there in that scary corner of the North-East.

> I am writing this while I have just finished the best and NO EGSADURATION [sic.] day of my whole life!!! [AGAIN?!]
>
> We queued up to walk onto the stage. It was great and really scary. We went on after being introduced by Anthony and the uproar was great. Mr Raymond came on and it was back at the Proms again! We played the Wagner really well and got applauded greatly. Then Anthony came on and announced us all and we played 'Pomp' and they all sang and it was beautiful and I was so happy. We all went off stage after thunderous applause and packed away.
>
> We got Kentucky Fried Chicken and it was absolutely beautiful.

On the bus journey north we were serenaded by members of the orchestra who also sang in the Billingham Friday Choir, another of Teesside's famous and excellent ensembles. They were sublime, till we all joined in, having changed the words of one of their lovely songs to 'Brighton Won't Move!' It kept us going all the way home.

Shortly after the Schools Prom appearance, the Quartet was asked to provide the live demonstration for a lecture on Bartók's 3rd by a well-known musicologist, for post-graduate students at Durham University. When the lecturer spotted us entering the room his face dropped; perhaps he had envisaged an older, more experienced group who he could rely on to follow his complex and fast-moving observations, cut from one section to another at speed and to actually be able to play the notes. But there was no time for prevarication – the students were ready and waiting and he simply had to launch in.

As the talk progressed he relaxed visibly and it became increasingly obvious that he was delighted with our efforts; the thing went swimmingly. Afterwards we graciously received his compliments, tinged though they were with relief, and ventured to suggest that he might recognise us from a previous meeting. His blank expression showed not – but then that was understandable. The last time he'd seen us we were leading the sections of the TYO and massed orchestras in the Schools Prom, under his baton. Only a few weeks later, Anthony Hopkins couldn't reconcile the image of a bunch of excitable kids with this still young yet assured and mature string quartet. We were thrilled.

*

1975 came to an end. As we moved towards Christmas, I honoured the school concert with my presence, offering *The Swan*, accompanied on the piano by the pleasantly surprised class music teacher, who had just found out about my other life. I felt it was time to own up to being a musician; I'd reached an age at school, in the third year, when individual characters and interests could be safely revealed without risk of a ribbing, and I was proud to be congratulated by my friends as well as the teachers.

There is an inexorable sadness in my diary pages here. The year's close, cheap seventies' fashion, films and presents (I got two from my mum and dad – a game and a tiny perfume). Cosy home life battled with the pending NYO course and, after months of looking forward to going, I didn't want to. Carol-singing was our family tradition on Christmas Eve, raising money for Oxfam, with many hangers-on from amongst our friends… singing and playing instruments, with oil lanterns and woolly hats, tramping through the snow door-to-door. Mam's special chicken and tomato soup was always ready to warm us when we got back, then music and chat and off to bed, ready for a big family Christmas the next day.

The Quartet took one day off, reconvening for a practice on Boxing Day, followed by sledging and watching Disney Time on the telly. But work was always there in mind:

> Later I talked to Mam and Dad and Mike about dedication and wrote out a practice timetable. I will work. It is my career and life at stake. I hope it works, and so do you, for if it shirks, I wouldn't know what to do!
>
> Monday after tea I practised extremely thoroughly only one third of my repertoire which took 3 and a half hours! I will work through every day and through and through. I have good prospects for the future.
>
> I'm getting on very well with life and I am happy; good night Mam, good night Dad. Good night Jacksons, good night Jack!

It was hard to tear myself away from this scene to the cold dorms at the NYO course, but once there I had a good time. Straddling as it did New Year's Eve, it was even harder to be away from the Christmas family atmosphere. But despite the homesickness my determination remained firm.

> New Year's Resolution. I will always practise four hours if possible - it must be! I must make sure that I become worthy of a brilliant title and I would love a louder toned cello!!

During this course, I was to make a start with my new teacher, who would take me through to leaving school. It was at the famous sweaty audition that Ivey Dickson had suggested the NYO cello tutor would be ideal for my further studies. He was a professor at the Royal Academy but I would have private lessons at his home in Clapham, thereby avoiding the need to join the weekend schedule at Junior Academy. I'd bonded well with him in cello sectionals; apart from being a fabulous player with a warm and luscious tone, this jovial Irishman kept us all amused with long and funny stories for a bit of downtime in the hours of hard work perfecting those orchestral cello parts.

My parents made contact and were told I could stay the night with him and his family whenever the journey to London and back was too much for me, and he quoted some crazy reduction of his usual rate. Normally he charged the princely sum of £5 for an hour's lesson, but I could have two hours for £7. A most generous offer, especially as the lessons normally lasted closer to three.

> January 3rd
> I had my first lesson with DAVID STRANGE. Fantastic - he changed my Bach. Great. It was superb. Played the Shosta sonata really well. He said I had a brilliant bowing hand. The lesson was great!

13

Geeklemania

Amidst all this extracurricular activity, the Quartet continued central to my existence. All those trips to Foyles whenever we were in London, plus our local music shops in York and Newcastle, had built up quite a repertoire.

> *I practised my darling cello superbly again. I love it! Oh goodness. Then Ian and Alex came. We played Haydn – a couple of them – and then we sorted out our music. Oh, Ian, Alex, Mike – 60 quartets!*

I learnt a tough lesson the hard way when, at one of the NYO courses, we indulged in a bit of showing off. Not content with a full day's orchestral slog, members would gather in the evenings for chamber music, just for fun and with whoever was around. We, being this famously pre-existing String Quartet, felt we had more to offer – and might have been right if we'd chosen a piece we actually knew. On the way to the course, we'd made our usual detour to Charing Cross Road and come away with the iconic and notorious C sharp Minor of Beethoven, opus 131.

The excitement of having it in our possession led to a premature and disastrous busking through of the work:

> We had supper and went to the boys' place to play Beethoven Septet but ended up playing the C sharp minor quartet and we played really badly and I could've shot myself. There were loads of people outside listening! It was so bad I could've shot myself. I am disgusted with Jacky.

Why is there always someone listening when it goes badly?

Despite our growing collection of sheet music, there were some pieces we couldn't get hold of. We might have had a miniature score but been too impatient to wait for parts, so we'd write out our own parts from the score. Whilst performing this arduous task for Shostakovich No.1, my diary tells me I listened to records. A lot of records. (And the long list of those works bears witness to the time and dedication it took, though the job at hand might have been simpler without a Tchaikovsky Symphony blaring in the background.) Alex wrote out parts for Stravinsky's *Three Pieces* – I still have mine to this day and have used it when my printed part went missing in a hire-car smash-and-grab in Holland nearly forty years later.

In some cases we didn't even have a score, but were so eager to play a work we'd heard that we took it down in dictation from the radio. My parents having acquired one of those new-fangled machines that could record to cassette straight from broadcasts, we built up quite a collection of bootleg tapes, all catalogued and displayed neatly on the kitchen window ledge. When we heard that Shostakovich's latest quartet was to be broadcast, we recorded it and set to work making our own parts by listening back to the tapes, over and over till we had it all down. This was no mean feat for youngsters, and stood us all in good stead for the days ahead in further education, where a high level of accuracy in dictation exercises is expected. I can only hope we tried to order the parts – unsuccessfully – before setting out on this mammoth task.

Having also acknowledged the wisdom of choosing this kind of repertoire, namely Shostakovich, for our subsequent competitive outings, I had to make a score from our parts of the 3rd Quartet, as it was mandatory to present a score to the adjudicator and we didn't have one! (Again, I hope we tried...) A straw on the camel's back for a fourteen-year-old in the middle of school exams and Grade VIII preparation. This is actually the day of that milestone:

> Had a bath, went for a walk, helped Mam, had dinner, played the cello badly, did aural tests with Joy, relaxed then went to Richmond. I TOOK MY GRADE VIII CELLO EXAM!! Everything was just fine! My examiner said, "Are you going to take it up professionally?" "I would like to." "I hope you do!" We had tea at Dr Bull's and came home and I felt great and I was really glad. They got back from Brandenburg rehearsal. I wrote the score for Shostakovich 3 all evening.
>
> Got my school report as Mam had been to open evening. AAA,ABA,AAA,BAA,AAA,BAA,BBB
> I'm a backwards sheep!

Next day:
> More score writing. It's getting me down!

We felt a particular pull towards this incredible music of Shostakovich; its often sparse textures nevertheless felt rich and layered, always surprising, emotional depth juxtaposing sarcasm, irony or genuine humour. Perhaps it spoke to our Northern sensibilities, a kind of stoicism we identified with, especially as we were starting to come face to face with prejudice and snobbery. And somehow it suited our style of playing. It was often edgy and aggressive, so we could unleash all the gritty unrefined energy of our youthful approach. From the start, we had developed an unforgiving style that called for split-second accuracy in ensemble and attack, without recourse to the tricks of the trade we were able to pick up on as we matured. This style, when it works, can be hugely exciting and gratifying to the listener. But it carries with it a risk of sounding rough around the edges. It is at least totally honest.

We gave almost everything a short attack, whether or not the note had a dot. I was surprised years later at Gidon Kremer's Lockenhaus Festival, when we and several other groups shared a performance of the complete Shostakovich Cycle between us, that our friends in the Hagen were playing the *Scherzo* from No.11 with quavers on the string. We four exchanged bemused glances along our row in the audience. Surely they'd misunderstood? Later in the same movement, the quavers were delivered short like we played them. *Why the change?* we wondered. And yet on checking the score, we saw they were right and we were wrong. This composer asks for dots when he wants them and we had been making it up.

As in Beethoven, the directions in Shostakovich are absolutely specific and you misread them at your peril. How many times have we since revelled in the simple act of playing the dynamics or *crescendi, accelerandi* and accents exactly as written, only to find the music is infinitely more meaningful and rewarding for that attention to detail.

When teaching, I love surprising a group who've made some random half-attempt at following a direction, calling them out on it without recourse to a score (which added fact impresses the youngsters even more!). 'Where exactly does that hairpin begin and end? Look at it properly, now play it again.' So often just seeing a *crescendo* marking will make the less-experienced player increase the sound immediately – therein lies a favourite adage of mine: "*Crescendo* means play soft!"

So, we began to realise that any future outings on a competitive level should be with twentieth century music, specifically this giant of the repertoire who was at that time relatively neglected. Though he was celebrated the world over for his symphonic output, and the last trip he made to the UK in 1974 caused great excitement, not least in our corner of the country, there were groups who avoided all but a handful of the cycle of fifteen quartets, claiming they were too simplistic and even all too similar. As we got to know more and more of them, we found this claim utterly bewildering, but at this stage we also played just a few: numbers 1, 3, 7, 8, 11 and 13, the first and last from manuscript in our own hands. For a composer who was so often thought of as simplistic, the extent of his greatness is endlessly rewarding to those willing to plumb the depths. Back then, it was only just beginning to enter our psyche, but we somehow knew it was here to stay.

Decades later, performing in Latvia, a Q&A session in the bar after the concert revealed an interesting prejudice.

"How can you play Shostakovich when you didn't experience the System?" we were asked.

"Well, we identify strongly with the man and his music, have done since we were children. Does one have to live under a repressive regime to feel for its victims?" I replied.

"We also didn't live with incurable syphilis – does this mean we shouldn't play Schubert?" Ian chipped in, winning the argument.

As the audience tittered over their Prosecco, I realised there is a sad perception that certain composers are safer in the hands of their countrymen, whilst anyone is allowed to play Mozart, Beethoven et al. We are often asked to perform Elgar and Britten, being a British group, but I would love to hear more nationalities championing this great music. Elgar was a confirmed Europhile, and would have hated the jingoistic connotations his work often conjures up. Music is an international language; surely no composer would wish their works to be restricted by nationalistic tendencies, or played only by their own people?

No, Shostakovich was our friend for life. I vividly remember the news of his death breaking on the car radio whilst we were driving through the heat of the French Midi on a family holiday. On 10 August 1975, my diary announced sadly, and in a fourteen-year-old's touching attempt at dignified solemnity:

> Dmitri Shostakovich died last night but he still lives in my heart. I was nearly broken because of Shostakovich. The living soul composer of the Russian Republic, a fellow musician and human being – was denounced of his death the night before.

*

Rehearsals went on, dominating all evenings and weekends. We were working every day of a half-term holiday, even though my colleagues were in their O Level year. Despite this pressure, we would never tire of debating points of interpretation to the nth degree or consider any kind of shortcut. Back then we would learn everything together, rarely practising our quartet parts separately, so the music was absorbed gradually and organically. There was no sense that you were wasting your colleagues' time if you arrived unable yet to play your own part – that's how we functioned. It was years later that we understood work would be more productive if we'd learnt the notes in advance. But there is something to be said for the old approach – no one arrives with preconceived ideas; we learn together. It was endlessly fascinating to us and I seem to never have had enough of it:

> I did homework and had tea then Alex came and I did English till Ian came then we played the Schubert G major, Beethoven F major, Beethoven C sharp minor! From seven till 10. We played great and were exhausted. I am glad about our quartet and about the way life is treating me.

> We listen to Schubert G Major. Oh - it's ours! A recording, yes please!
>
> Played the record of Flight of the Bumblebee on 16 rpm instead of 33! It was hilarious!
>
> The saddest music is in the major key! People expect minor key music is sad, but I cry at the beauty of the slow major movements. Think of Beeth Raz 1 versus the Cavatina. I've been trying to decide which one makes me cry more, and I think it's the major one!

I record one occasion of a concert in a local church, where it seems the slightly inexperienced organisers hadn't realised how much space a string quartet needed to perform, something frequently bemoaned by many a professional group...

> They didn't know what they were doing in the church and there were piles of power cuts and it was lovely chaos and there wasn't much space on stage. And because we were cramped and silly we didn't play well and it was funny. Afterwards we all talked and we got on like cheese, bread, butter and tomato!

We would work on performance techniques, trying to be extrovert and flamboyant, but even at that age we knew that the music and the composer were more important than our egos. Nevertheless, we recognised from an early age the need to put the meaning of the music across to the listener; depict a scene, convey emotion. And to show where the theme is passed around, visually explain just what's going on. (Recently after a concert, a non-musician friend Poppy exclaimed, "If you'd been speaking to me in a language I didn't know, I'd have understood every word!" Mission accomplished. And such a brilliant and imaginative compliment!)

Our total single-mindedness of aim made for passionate exchanges and fierce arguments over interpretation, long before it became clear we could just as easily try it one way for now then change for another performance. I suppose when concerts are thin on the ground you have to get everything right there and then, and it matters oh-so-much to get it your way.

There are some lovely directions in our parts from back then that show the level of commitment and youthful enthusiasm... Ian once stood up and crossed the floor to come and write in my part 'Jacky' at a point in the work where he considered me important. It would have been more appropriate to write it in the other parts so that everyone piped down to hear me, but he was so pleased with his own observation that I guess he got mixed up. In Shostakovich 8 there's a bar where Viola and Cello have been playing a long line in octaves then randomly for one note move apart, then back again. At this point in the viola part Alex has written 'What is Jack doing here???', obviously believing me to be somehow at fault. I wonder if he ever asked me, even checked the score (if we had one) or just kept wondering... he never took the trouble to rub it out. Mind you, he almost always used a red pen to mark his parts, so that probably answers it. Also in red ink on the viola part of Ravel's glorious Slow Movement is scrawled 'Currn you are Cleo Laine!' as encouragement to himself to sing out the viola solo. (Must show that to my friend Jacqui Dankworth one day – Cleo's daughter and equally glorious songstress.)

Emil Currn (pronounced Curran) was one of Alex's nicknames, the others being Pob and Terry. I, having outgrown Jacksons, Monk & Rowe, was usually Jack, with Cindy Low Lin and Jaffa Cake-Tomás as alternatives, Ian was Kyp or Garridge McAnnick (being the only one of us able to mend a puncture) and Mike was Davey or Slide Horn Jim. In the very early days, we had even adopted nicknames derived from the infamous and short-lived Hungarian-inspired quartet name we'd wanted to adopt... so we became, respectively, Von, Nós, Nég and Yes.

Indeed.

Looking through my diary, I am struck by my idea of a great

night out at the weekend. Again and again, on Saturdays (and Fridays after orchestra) we and a whole bunch of others seem to derive pleasure from embarrassingly geeky activities. This first entry is following an immensely long drive home from London with my family, during which we ran out of petrol and were stranded on the A1 for two hours. Arriving home tired and hungry, what did we choose to do? Quartet!

> We had a good laugh then a good fair practice of the Brahms first, third and fourth movements. Then we played half of the Grosse Fugue!!!! (NB half!) then the Malcolm Arnold which was really great. Mike wanted to play the Shostakovich 13 but we didn't! We all mucked on and listened to records and absolutely freaked out to Janacek Sinfonietta. So great!

It gets worse…

> I was really worried that it was going to be another boring television Saturday night - but - when I was watching Mike Yarwood Ian phoned for a practice!!!! We finished watching Mike Yarwood when they arrived which was very soon after, then we had a great practice doing Haydn C major which was on the radio this morning. Then Brahms slow movement which is really romantic and beautiful because we played and made it so!
>
> After orchestra we danced in the garden to Mike and Alex playing Bartók duos!
>
> After TYO we had a party at Nigel's listening to Brahms 3 and Beethoven 6 as I had brought my record player. The music livened us all up and we were happy.
>
> Saturday night. Went for a long walk and met some kids who gradually believed we were Germans! It was

> superb fun - they were scary at first but so nice soon! Very clever. Came home and watched 'Face the Music'.
>
> After TYO - sang and worked on El Grillo (Josquin des Pres) and other madrigals and it was great fun. Then we sang it beautifully in the streets under the lamps and people admired us - also in the Chinese takeaway! An Apollo Male Voice Choir member was there - "keep it up" he said! We got chips and came back.
>
> Saturday night - had a hilarious laugh drinking soup and listening to Stravinsky Symphony of Psalms and watching Shostakovich 1 on telly.

I mean, really?

And we still frequented every available concert in the area, my diary providing a rigorous critique of each one. Disclaimer: I was very young.

> Utah Symph.orch. with Michael Tilson-Thomas (he's gorgeous!) Billy the Kid, it really suited them Barber Adagio - cor - Death and Transfig, the Beethoven 7th. We got Greensleeves for an encore. [sic] A brill orchestra.
> All the boys said my legs were great.
>
> Budapest 4tet played Mozart Hunt badly, Bartók 6 was absolutely incredible and I got so inspired and we had a great laugh in the interval. Went back for a really good Beethoven Raz and I thought a lot and felt great and inspired and we cheered (but I felt CSQ could've done better in Beethoven) all the same, I loved the first violin and cello and I threw him a flower! They did two encores for me!
>
> Went to the Town Hall and saw an excellent NSO - well on form. They played Suk Serenade and then Marius

May (18) played Tchaikovsky Rococo and it was superb! The odd notes didn't matter - he has such performing control and sheer enjoyment!

We were desperate because we missed the first half, but we went to MLT to see the second half of the Lindsay concert with Dougie Cummings doing Schubert quintet and my God it was amazing. Two cellos - togetherness!! The whole piece was just beautiful and they really seduced it and I cried in the second movement and the second violin saw me! Dougy was wonderful. The whole thing was sparkling - I have some of his bow hair! At the end we cheered and cheered and they thanked us. The others wanted to go straight home but I wanted to kiss the players so we did. They chatted with us like old friends!

Went to the Town Hall and saw a pathetic attempt, really amateurish, by Wolfgang Schneiderhan of Mozart G major and then he stood and got in the way of an otherwise beautiful performance by the excellent NSO of my Dvorak String Serenade - what memories flooded back. It really annoys me how a soloist - bad at that - sees himself as good enough to conduct - he had no idea - how far he was from Rattle and Boulez and how close to Raymond! The NSO would be far wiser to work alone - would make more fame and more money. They are excellent these days!

On TV the Aeolian 4tet was boring - op. 130. It was not at all good. Their cellist is too loud, their violist is bored stiff, their 2nd violinist is woody and Hurwitz was drowned.

Despite my unashamed pomposity and our collective terminal geekiness, we were also capable of behaving more like normal teenagers... almost. Sometimes there were disco nights at the Inn Cognito, Teesside's most exotic nightclub, or we could just as likely sit around after orchestra listening to *Sgt. Pepper* or Roxy Music, which even boasted one of TYO's alumni, Ed Jobson, as its fiddler. The Swingle Singers and Pointer Sisters on TV are worthy of a diary entry, and I even write about an argument with my parents about the validity of pop against classical, and how disgusted I was at their narrowness.

> Rick Wakeman is an excellent keyboarder. It is so nice to have such an open mind to all kinds of music. It is the universe! Oh l'amour de la vie!

Being open to all kinds of music helped a lot when Ian took a Saturday morning job as pianist répétiteur for a local ballet school. He would happily busk his way through their weekly repertoire of light classics, improving his piano skills whilst delighting in the vision of tutued loveliness flouncing around before him. 'Madame' was Anne Jeanes, a diminutive brunette with an immaculately sculpted face topped by a tight chignon, and a refined but distinct Geordie accent. Every year for their graduation concert at Billingham Forum Theatre, the Quartet would be invited as guest artists, usually in a solo spot but sometimes to accompany the dance routines they had painstakingly worked on throughout the year. The whole event was taken with the utmost seriousness and taught us a thing or two about presentation, poise and stage manner. And this was about to become useful…

14

Concerts Galore!

The quartet have been offered two or three recitals in Dunkirk at Whit holiday. Wouldn't that be fantastic!

Quartet practice - three hours doing possible pieces for Dunkirk.

Haydn G major, Prokofiev and Dvorak will be for Dunkirk. Really good practice.

Now I hear that Dunkirk is right off! Oh dear, this is too sad.

Concert invitations continued to trickle in, but still they were often shared with other performers. We were, tantalisingly, offered a short series of concerts in Dunkirk, the French town twinned with Middlesbrough (point of interest – many years later our local Redcar Beach was used as a film set for the Dunkirk evacuations in Joe Wright's film *Atonement*, with my nephew as one of the extras), and we set to work devising programmes and building up excitement, only to be told they weren't happening after all.

We still had our triumphant lunchtime recital to gloat over, but that wasn't going to keep us going for ever.

> We went to Ian's house and listened to a fantastically professional Cleveland String Quartet - us - at the Teesside Polytechnic concert. The Prokofiev was superb and the Dvorak was superb.

We had to settle for Dunkirk's alter-ego, Redcar, for yet another shared concert, which was almost derailed by a last-minute disaster. Luckily, my parents were able to jump to the rescue and Hamiltons, our local music shop, was still open.

> Mike's A string went! We stopped practising and Mam and Dad had to go and buy a new string. Meanwhile we all had a great laugh. Mike changed the string but it kept going out of tune! Then we got ready and I got changed into the most beautiful dress - Mam had finished it! Ian and Alex went home to get ready. I looked lovely. We had tea then Mr Belton came and took us to Redcar. We tried the acoustics and talked. We watched the first half - a really funny time. During the second half we got ready, steady, go! We were backstage and then on we went and played the Haydn absolutely superbly, only spoiled by the apprehension all-round of Mike's string and the bad acoustics. The last movement was fantastic. We got a really loud cheer and I thought it was great. In the dressing room we had queues outside! Admirers - great!

We shared a concert in Middlesbrough Little Theatre, scene of my operetta pit job and venerated venue for so many celebrity quartet performances we had witnessed. It was pretty exciting to be there as invited artists, but it was soured by a group tiff and a slight misunderstanding with the promoters.

> Called for Alex and met Ian outside MLT and went into our changing room. We talked and had quite a nasty vicious argument but when we played (after complications

> because they said we were playing first after the interval and then got annoyed when we didn't know as the programme said third) anyway, when we played it was all smiles - the Borodin was lovely and Dvorak great.
> Got home and watched telly.

I love the lack of ceremony that sometimes follows these esoteric events. Then on other occasions there can be a seriousness that belies our age and speaks volumes:

> Played Beethoven in front of a big audience at the DLI Museum in Durham. It was really marvellous but we decided that it certainly needed a discussion which would come tonight. Here again, was our understanding. Also Mozart will have to be approached well by us!

This latter observation proved to be something of an Achilles' heel – we remained afraid of Mozart for decades to come. It's a popular misconception that the endless complexities and depths of Mozart string quartets make for accessible music; it isn't easy, either for the player or the listener.

Eventually we were asked to play a short evening recital for an invited audience at a nearby stately home. I guess this was really our first experience of being the sole invited attraction and all the attention that goes with it. But the inevitable discomfort of playing in a carpeted room intended for parlour games, not energetic concert-giving, was a shock to the system.

> Ormesby Hall. It was such a beautiful manor house and we sat in our quartet room with a coal fire before playing in even hotter circumstances than the Prom and even deader than my bedroom! But it was a superb experience as we were frighteningly bare! But afterwards we were treated as great artists and everyone was very impressed and said so in 100 different ways. We felt

so good – we had to try to escape out in fear of being caught to talk, before we four had a lovely quartet walk. Oh how musical it all was.

It's true to say that, when the feeling is good between the players, after a nice concert we do sometimes just want to be alone. Even now we're often happier when we can just slip into some restaurant for dinner together rather than hobnob with sponsors or committee members – there's a kind of institutionalised sense of safety in each other's company.

Another lesson learnt: when buzzing from a previous triumph, the next get-together often feels flat. How young we were learning these things. Following the rarefied environs of aristocratic elegance, it seems our next appearance brought us crashing back down to earth, but we didn't seem to mind too much.

We had a disappointing practice – always is after a good concert like last week.

Went to Park Road Methodist and in a great mood gave a funny concert, but really good, to half-deaf OAPs, but some appreciative ones. We came back laughing and I revised.

But dedication and tenacity continued to prevail. My young self is seriously disappointed at any lack of commitment I perceive, both in myself and in the group.

Sunday. No Quartet – oh dear, dear, dear.

Only practised the cello for half an hour today. Oh I hate wasted days – why do I have such days? I always feel much better after hard work.

Next day:

> I got up nice and bright and fresh and played the cello and it went well at least but, you know, when I play great once - even playing the same later doesn't impress me! I practised the cello for a beautiful time and my muscles are becoming stupidly big! My arms and hands are like those of an old man - with my cello playing!
>
> Pizzed Bach is great! You really understand it!

Rehearsals could be fraught and argumentative. At one stage it seems we hit a real low point and nearly imploded. My reaction was such that I dedicated a whole page, at the back of my diary, to record the momentous Fall and subsequent – with huge relief – Rise of our little world.

> Here I must dedicate a passage to the Cleveland String Quartet.
>   This title was written in a feeling of great excitement at least 13 months ago (it's now December 13 '76.) You see, this ever-growing Quartet began as a great idea and modelled into the best thing since sliced bread! I think that I have had some of the most moving experiences as well as playing music with, and talking to, Ian and Alex and Mike - we understand each other fully and as a result of this, the togetherness as a group is perfect.
>   All at once I become first deep and involved with the pieces and playing, but sometimes this dies out and we are left in a rut, board [sic.] and completely lost for loss of our mutual and intimate friendship. Such has been the case these few '76 winter months - we have had a minimum of practices - a thought that would now make us cringe, for tonight we were back together again and planning on the great future waiting for us. In January '77 will be our debut full evening recital (alone) and in preparation an NYO recital at Christmas. We shall show everyone once again, what is here, in youth, in Middlesbrough. These days Mike and I are proving

so with our Concertante, and the Quartet, having begun that argument, will go on to strengthen it with a firm and immovable backbone.

Such is the greatness of the Cleveland Street Quartet (England!) I wonder how it will go on - already Alex is planning a new quartet (Cambridge) and we will all go our own ways, but I do not believe that this will hinder us - it will only make us realise that such a high standard cannot be achieved by any other combination of people except ourselves - that we were drawn together with one purpose - to make real friends' music - and we shall not deny the gift we have for this form of love...

Total immodesty aside, this youthful outpouring does show quite an audacious level of intent on longevity. Reading this forty-five years on brings hugely mixed emotions and regrets for sadnesses along the way. But more than anything, it reconfirms my assertion that we were always in this for the long term. When people ask how legitimate our claim to have been together since childhood really is, I can answer honestly that it was there from the very beginning. It is always nice to witness the disbelief on faces when I'm asked if I was a founder member. When I answer yes, as we approach our fiftieth anniversary, I still look young enough (just) for there to be a flicker of disbelief and even outright amazement. Ten is a very young age to set out on one's lifetime career... I sometimes used to wonder if it happened by chance rather than design. These kinds of declarations put paid to that.

So, with the advent of the New Year, 1977, I was intrigued to find out what this upcoming full recital will be. Reading on...

Hilariously, and not a little embarrassingly, when disaster befell us and Ian was struck down with a serious illness requiring hospitalisation and possibly surgery, the rest of us shamelessly declared the show must go on and called on an NYO colleague to take his place for this all-important CSQ debut recital, should the worst happen. (By which I mean Ian being too unwell to play, rather than dead.) So much for loyalty; all my grand assertions that there was no other four than us four, that we were irreplaceable and unique, conveniently forgotten in our eagerness to play this great gig.

But in the event, Ian pulled through – I think he even delayed the necessary surgery till after the concert had passed, such was his professionalism and dedication to the group. (I would repay this years later by taking little or no maternity leave and even performing whilst in labour.) So the concert went ahead. Luckily my diary comes up trumps with a full and glorious description, as I have scant recollection of the night.

Only one detail stays with me: we spent easily as much time perfecting the staging and lighting as we did rehearsing in the hall on the day of the concert. I remember a feeling of panic, as I knew this couldn't be right. The venue was the local further education college, a few hundred yards from my house, (scene of Wednesday nights' TSO and my Saint-Saëns Concerto outburst), a hall devoid of charm or atmosphere in its usual strip-lit state. We went to work. Alex, with his eye for visual aesthetics, made sure all the music stands were at the same height, equidistant from each other, with feet angled in perfect symmetry. Then the fluorescent lights were killed and the stage lighting was set so that interesting shadows were created around and about us, making us a little bit dazzled in the process, but we went with it in the name of dramatic effect. Given that most classical concerts in those days, and for many years after, were given in fully lit auditoriums, house lights up so that the audience could read their programme notes during the performance, our presentation that night was radical and new, which possibly added to our success. To this day we view atmosphere in the hall to be of paramount importance. People believe what they see and, with attention to this kind of detail, you are already a step ahead before you step onto the stage.

At 6 o'clock (1 1/2 hours to go) we went there and sorted out all the lighting and staging fantastically and most professionally and did last-minute practice etc and time was getting closer and closer and, tuning up backstage, one second to go, we went on stage and played the Mozart - it was excellent, the hall was packed, though the Shostakovich was wonderful. I had never played so well in my life - my solos - wow! And it was all so exciting, and then moving, and gee, they loved it. We were so happy and the interval was spent apprehensive but happy - but no need - our Brahms was so warm and so enchanting, and beautiful and well, just Brahms... Oh gorgeous - everything perfect and the tone just warmth personified... They cheared and cheared [sic.] - we had three calls and then, encore, we had wrong music etc and it was all so funny - Haydn "Joke" and they cheared even more! Oh, we were so happy - I was proud to have earned an encore and such an audience. So moving... We had finished, and I have never played/performed so well. Autographs, bookings, photos - my God - we are a Quartet - we are parting ways, but not for long. We all cleared up etc and came home, beautiful and ecstatic - all the time everyone was so pleased - they all loved and congratulated us and the enormous buffet/party was divine. We went for a walk and escaped - didn't like the outsiders - but returned. Went to bed at 3.30 so tired but ecstatically, wonderfully happy!

I am delighted to read that we made £100 on the box office, which we donated the following Friday night to the Youth Orchestra touring fund.

*

This was the spring term of my O Level year. I was fifteen, Mike seventeen, and Ian and Alex approaching eighteen, with university entrance and college auditions looming large on the horizon. Mike, who had dropped all A Level subjects but Music, decided he would leave at the same time as the other two if he could get into music college, for which only Music A Level was a requirement (and an ability to play an instrument of course!) Whilst Alex was all about arts subjects, Ian was doing Maths, Further Maths and Sciences, as well as Music – his dad still vaguely hoping he might wise up and get a good teaching job instead of this uncertain future of self-employed, pensionless insecurity. And so we entered this moment of flux, all of us under huge pressure of exams and decision-making.

In the event, Alex was admitted to Cambridge and Ian and Mike to Manchester – the Royal Northern College of Music – Ian opting for a joint course with the university so as to come out with a dad-appeasing 'proper' degree at the end of it all.

I, in the meantime, was cramming my headspace to the brim whilst keeping up all my usual hours of practice.

> Saturday - did quadrilateral equations all day! But I listened to music too and by the end I at least know how to factorise! Later... came to bed and felt a bit fed up. Why? Because I don't work hard enough...

(Really, girl, give yourself a break!)

On top of this I was asked to play continuo again for the *St Matthew Passion*, staying long into night to rehearse after everyone else had left. The cello continuo is a soloistic role within Baroque oratorio, seated with the harpsichordist, away from the other strings and alone in our bubble for long stretches of the work. The two players become as one, following every nuance of whichever singer is reciting the story; it is an exposed and tricky job requiring a high level of competence and concentration.

I was thrilled to have become Mr Raymond's go-to, but it did mean a lot of extra work in an already full schedule.

> It was like the Farewell Symphony - at 10 o'clock I was still playing with the singer Anne Lampard, oh it felt endless... it is disastrously long and I was almost crying with boredom and impatience.

I was regularly travelling to London for my cello lessons and fitting in Quartet rehearsals, preparing art pieces, projects for O Level. I cunningly managed to cross-reference my favourite subjects: for my Music project, I chose the NYO, an easy and delightful subject for me to spend time on and a joy to produce, whilst for my History project I focused on Coventry Cathedral, where I had played with NYO. (My History course was all about architecture through the ages and I adored it, leading to a fervent belief that I would have been an architect if not a musician, following in the footsteps of my Belgian grandfather.)

I also continued with dressmaking and a huge amount of helping around the house, tidying the kitchen from top to bottom just about every Saturday morning. I was eager to bring order to the chaos I'd grown up in.

All this to the constant soundtrack of symphonic or chamber music, including one day when I apparently wrote a Symphony 7 minutes long whilst listening to Symphony of Psalms, Lieutenant Kije, Schumann Cello Concerto,... (Huh???) I was leading the cellos at TYO, with all that that entailed – At orchestra I took the sectional then we did Tchaikovsky's Swan Lake. The cello solo was fun - I love cello solos! – and tripping off to NYO courses every school holiday.

Another Middlesbrough Festival came and went, but this time none of us entered, making way for our younger colleagues, we having outgrown it and moved on to more professional activities. We honoured them with our presence in the audience at the Prizewinners' Concert, having fun with orchestra friends in the Town Hall gallery, where we pretended we were Prommers at the RAH, all flags and cheering and silly chants.

Shortly after our Debut Recital (which was surprisingly late into our Quartet career, I now realise) we were offered a very different gig at the same venue: playing background music at a wine and cheese evening for the grand fee of £20.

> It was great fun and we enjoyed it and were enjoyed, and had gorgeous food and a hilarious time before playing again, having had a break, and finishing at midnight. We were knackered! But everyone liked us. We got £5 each and many thanks and came home.

We called it our 'Sleazy Palm Court Evening' and set about arranging all sorts of suitable short pieces, realising our usual repertoire wasn't going to work in this context. So, popular Debussy and Ravel Piano works, Scott Joplin Rags, as well as Beatles, James Taylor and Victorian parlour songs were all given the quartet-instrumental-arrangement treatment. This was enormous fun and helped us through the tedious weeks of revision for mock exams. The collection built quickly and came in handy for a similar night at Mansion House, London, with Charles and Di the guests of honour just a few years later. It also led to our trademark penchant for offering anything but regular repertoire as end-of-concert encores, eventually the recordings of these lollipops marking various anniversaries: *Brodsky Unlimited* (twentieth), *Petits Fours* (fortieth) and, coming up... As Yet Untitled, for the fiftieth.

15

La Fille Romantique et Révolutionnaire

Anyone growing up amidst the sort of musical environment I experienced will tell you that it's a great way to find love and romance. Peering across an orchestra in the throes of some gushing symphony, violins crying, cellos yearning, woodwind and brass thrilling, percussion crashing... it fills all the senses of teenage emotion to the brim and explodes into outpourings of affection and togetherness.

I would be in love with several different boys at once, or at least in very quick succession, eyes meeting across the heads of our massed throngs as the music filled the air around us, making the moment even more glorious. At that age, the thrill is always in the realisation, the first shy chats or even hugs, but rarely progresses beyond that. The occasional snog would be fun but wouldn't mean much or necessarily lead to anything more. Sitting on the floor in the semi-dark, listening to records and drinking cider, Friday nights were all about getting someone to be 'with', but it was an ever-changing set-up, understood by most to work that way.

Relationships that developed into full-blown exclusive Love might last a couple of months, more if they were long-distance, i.e. NYO-sourced and therefore mostly conducted through incredibly long and romantic letters. But once said correspondents were again face-to-face, the supposed romance might come to nothing, or merge into the common friendship and love that floated around the clique you happened to be in for that particular course. One might find oneself helping a friend hook up with the boy who was the object of one's own desire, wistfully hoping to curry favour by the service whilst secretly wishing it was you, such was the fluidity of our relationship merry-go-round. Given that I tended to set my sights on boys a year or so older, I could probably have been accused of being a bit of a tease, but I dare say none of them would have wanted to take it much further either, and were probably just as happy to be able to share their love around in that physical but totally chaste way we all had.

I never fell for boys at school – it was the wrong environment; there just wasn't the electric frisson of excitement I felt amongst my own type in that body of noise and sensory shared experience. (I would of course share the odd smooch at the infrequent parties held as we got a bit older, but it was with the same rotation of understanding as Friday night fumblings...) Only once, when I took part in the school play (not a small role, I might add – that of a master magician with many lines, crazy back-combed hair and ten-inch platform shoes to correct my height impairment), did I fall for a school colleague.

It's telling that this only happened because we were sharing an artistic experience, the energy and adrenalin, nerves and shared relief when it went well, heroism if we got through a tricky moment, bringing us together – akin to the orchestral environment. We had one date, at his house listening to Beatles records, but it was over before it began. As soon as he opened his mouth to sing along with the Fab Four, I realised he was tone-deaf. I got out as soon as politeness allowed and went back to my comfort zone of like-minded, high-minded musos.

*

> Went to the new CPO practice and we kicked up a fuss about equal pay etc and the way we, young and brilliant players, are being treated. The arguments carry on all the way home so - watch out, okay?!

Being trailblazers in our little world, with not only the Quartet but a weekly chamber orchestra, Cleveland Concertante, to run, pulling in membership from all our loyal friends in the vicinity, we were quite a busy bunch. On top of this, and of course Friday night TYO, there was the formation of the new semi-professional adult/youth orchestra, the Cleveland Philharmonic, whose management, in their wisdom, decided that only the grown-ups and not the youngsters were worthy of receiving the small appearance fee on offer.

Disgusted by this outrageous inequality, the youth membership formed a sub-committee and went on strike at one of the rehearsals, creating havoc in the ranks and causing the *Evening Gazette* to seek a statement. One unfortunate quote I recall from this notorious interview was that our Mr Raymond 'isn't exactly Herbert von Karajan', an assertion which, though undeniably true, demanded full and unequivocal apology from our spokesperson when the feature went to print. We fought our corner and licked our wounds and felt like suffererjets.

But with this gross injustice, the building sense that we were representing a town that didn't necessarily give much back (oh, sorry – free lessons and instruments for many years notwithstanding) and the pressure of pending exams and release into the world, it was only natural that we should call for a full-blown revolution.

I had completely forgotten about this short-lived episode till I spotted it in the diaries. It was vigorously passionate yet beautifully vague in its aims and doctrines, only serving to voice some sort of generic indignation and radical activist posturing.

> We talked about our Revolution. It is so difficult to explain because, if anyone asked me what it is for I couldn't give it a theme; it is just to go against bad things, and adults are the main offenders. We are so mature and know our own argument so thoroughly, and agree with each other so well, that their silly arguments cannot stand up. We must start straight away and make everybody know - it is just new and so true. It is our answer to Britain's state at the moment. The Peace Movement in Northern Ireland is having such trouble - it has support but it is not acknowledged. We will have support and we will help them and kill all overlordship ideas in county councils, committees, governments and the like, and it shall be fully accepted and understood. An understanding in a whole country is such a difficult thing to achieve but by the end we shall all think the same, because it isn't just one way of thinking, it is Truth, and no one can argue against the Truth! Our protests and appeals will be so peaceful that no one can be offended, so innocent that they have nothing to hold against us, and when they accuse us for something legal, innocent and different - revolutionary - the Revolution will laugh. It is an idea which has, you must understand, been with us for such a long time - it was on a small scale against the CPO people, etc, and against 'pro' musicians who aren't either (pro or musicians). It has grown and always shall, and any criticism shall be welcomed and crushed! Please help - all we need is support....

Eat your heart out, Adrian Mole – this is pure gold teen-diary material! A revolution on something-or-other and a manifesto that makes overuse of the word 'shall' for the purposes of gravitas. (Incidentally, I am gratified to read, on behalf of my future husband, that the war in Ireland was on our radar.) I even managed to sign my schoolfriends up to the cause. This was pivotal as we had recently become old enough and mature enough to accept our respective differing interests in life – I had lost my Pablo Casals stigma and was appreciated for my art, having by now given various school performances. Fake autograph-hunting was replaced by genuine appreciation as my journalism-aspiring colleagues sought to give me my own mini-documentary. (Some prime footage they took that I would love to get hold of now was of me helping a first year, by the name of Caroline Dale, struggling with an insubordinate cello peg on the school stage in the end-of-year concert, hailing me an overnight hero.)

These friends all had eclectic interests and we would congregate at lunchtime in our Little Room, a small classroom rarely used that we requisitioned for our own private purposes. Here we formed the pseudo-serious Casey Jones Appreciation Society, had singalongs of numbers from that and other cheesy TV shows of the era, swapped higher aesthetic beliefs and juicy gossip, and discussed boys and teachers we fancied.

Above all, there was finally an acceptance of the merits of articulate diction. One friend, Sara, had been subjected to lessons in elocution and had developed an unashamed command of Queen's English, which she refused to drop in the name of acceptance and playground cred. Her bravery in this was inspirational, and I stopped feeling like a misfit every time I returned from NYO courses with a bit more finesse to my guttural tones. She, along with lovely Nancy, Hilaz, Linda, Jill, Bridget and Alli, belatedly blossomed into the friendship group I had shirked in favour of my extra-curricular muso buddies, and we ended our comprehensive school years in style and great companionship.

During the course of our time there, a fully functioning theatre had been built, separate from the school, a place of oasis for us and our peers. Plays rehearsed and performed there, concerts and shows, brought us together in mutual artistic pursuit, again showing how powerful the arts are in forming characters and breaking down barriers. My lasting and fond recollection of the Art Suite – with The Eagles, Roxy Music and the *Sound of Bread* offering the soundtrack to our efforts – brings my secondary school experience to a gentle and happy conclusion. Although the Careers Officer never could reconcile himself with my conviction in my future as a musician, unable to envisage what that actually meant, until one day he finally hit on the inspired solution that I could apply to join the Sally Army Band.

The Revolution's short-lived trajectory provides an amusing interlude.

> Revolution - day one. It was incredible - I was amazed by the absolute understanding and support everybody gave. Mr Brett locked us out of our Little Room and ran away whilst we weren't there, so we couldn't challenge him - coward - this was what made us all agree wholeheartedly on the Revolution. Instead we looked after a gorgeous First Year in the Medical Room...
>
> At home Mike and I discussed the Revolution over Bartók and Stravinsky. I practised the cello for three hours with breaks for discussions with Mam and Dad about the use of the English language - I must use it carefully and perfectly, ok?!
>
> The Revolution has had a flying start - tomorrow I shall prove myself a true leader!

[Next day:]

> At school lunchtime we went to Acklam 6th Form for a Revolution but no one was there! We cut up rats in biology which was good.

> We were meant to have the meeting after school at home but no one came so it was a bit of a failure really. Later people came round but we just couldn't seem to talk about the bleeding Revolution! It is upsetting how we are continuously being boycotted... Anyway, we had a laugh.

So the great Revolution lasted precisely two days! (With the odd reference being made in later weeks, as a guilty afterthought.) But my radical spirit had taken root and soon found its voice through an art project I was struggling to devise:

> Then at 7.10 I had a brainwave. I decided on a chessboard which, having worked on it for three hours, turned out magnificently and is called "Check, mate!" - a dominating, large Queen and a small, recessive King! Women's Lib!

My diary had now become an outlet for my more mature outpourings, with less attention to irrelevant detail, childish observation and enthusiasm. As well as learning more about the world's problems and injustices, I was posing as a person of great mind and artistic temperament, which only succeeds in sounding unbearably pretentious and puffed-up.

> You may notice my incredible attention to depth - I find it important for everyone to bring out their most inner thoughts - I want everyone to share in mine and all the wonderful people I know, do... I love depth, love; it is all music, like words are all poetry, trees are all in the forest, everything is music... Food for thought, deep thought...

> In music there's so much I want to say and I get caught up without being able to say everything! Tonight I wanted to help Dad in lots of ways but had to think of how to say it all - I have not the patience

of a teacher. No one knows what sense David talks. I was so overwhelmed when I first saw what he could do - such an orderly mind and the problems set out in a red list with, which is more important, the answer to each problem. Almost a Hercule Poirot, yet such a musician, he is difficult to beat. David is not only music, but he can pass it on to me and he proves what selflessness is - if you can tell others what you feel then please do. Don't keep anything in; let it all flow out. As yet, I can't, because I have so much inside that can't come out, but soon it shall come to everyone and you too will understand...

Sunday. Had a great practice of Schubert Quartettsatz, Beethoven C sharp minor, and Bartók 5. The tempests changed while we rehearsed and inspired my new painting through the window called "When a confused March evening thought it was a winter's day". It's great!

Went to Kirby College and saw a film and talk on the very shocking state of black/white South Africa. Honestly, I had no idea - but I feel we are helpless and too weak - the WHOLE WORLD must unite against this terrible scheme.

Why do some works make me so nostalgic and tearful? There was an innocence that is gone now...Dvorak piano quintet, his symphonies, almost everything by Debussy. I connect it with trips to Richmond and the good old days before nuclear weapons and television.

I was fifteen and moody, though by all accounts not a terrible teenager to have around. I would listen tearfully to Fauré's Requiem or James Taylor songs. I had a new boyfriend from within our musical circle and this time it felt serious. But it wasn't an easy relationship; his being from a devout Catholic household made having a girlfriend fraught with guilt and conflicted emotions. I was faced with a new dilemma, that of being Eve to his Adam, temptress to his chastity.

Neither of us wanted to have sex, but even the preamble was against his moral beliefs. So I had to delve into my own conscience at a time when I should really have just been having a nice time with innocent snogs and the like. I hoped my adoration of Fauré Requiem and appreciation of ecclesiastical architecture would be enough to satisfy what I saw as his pious stance. I knew my dog-tooth mouldings from my zig-zag, Early English from Perpendicular, could identify flying buttresses or groin vaulting, apses and ogee arches.

But he told me churches were for the worship of God, not pretty buildings to admire. I agreed to try to understand his beliefs, read up and learn about it all, even try to join in. (I didn't like the sound of this 'Limbo' place where we unbaptised heathens were doomed to languish.) I would sit in my favourite cathedrals, blissfully enjoying the music whilst willing myself to have some kind of epiphany. But I wasn't convinced and would appear to be more than a little bit confused.

> Communism v Catholicism?
> On a walk in the woods, Mam and I discussed Communism - I don't know how to choose between that and Catholicism.

Finally, an outburst sums up the height of my conflicted state…

> Lots of Revolution action must be taken. I really resent everything!

16

End of childhood

Heading south for an NYO Easter course, the Middlesbrough contingent was forced to stand in the guard's van due to overcrowding. Here we made the most of it, took out our instruments and played through some of the repertoire we were about to perform. I imagine that was the one and only time the Intercity 125 service boasted a live on-board performance of the *Rite of Spring*. By now there were ten of us in the orchestra, which is an impressive ratio for one small town versus the whole of the UK – almost a tenth. We even had the principal bassoonist, John Whitfield, who was about to open this incredible work under the baton of the legendary Pierre Boulez.

The course began, before Boulez could make the time to join us, under the guidance of a very young Simon Rattle, with whom we also recorded the piece in a proper studio-style set-up. Looking back, I recall being thrilled by the process – the producer in some remote make-shift control box, twiddling the knobs and speaking to the room through a two-way voice mic, saying "Take 1, Take 2" etc. each time we were poised to play. It was high-octane stuff, with a lot of pressure on each of the young players to not be the one screwing up a take with an erroneous entry or a wrong note. We were thrilled with our professionalism as we came down the home straight after a day and a half of this intense process, and more than a little knackered. Decades on, with over seventy CDs to my name, I still find recording a challenge – having to be on top form for hours on end, three or four days at a stretch, performing with total conviction to an empty hall and a disembodied voice... not easy.

The opportunity this process afforded was invaluable. We got to a point where most of us could play chunks of this rhythmically complex work from memory, watching each other for key points in the music, noticing what the other players in the orchestra were up to. (Visiting conductors to the UK are blown away by players' abilities to execute anything thrown at them with ease, especially in the film session studio where the music is brand new so no one can prepare. This training at a young age must have gone a long way to creating that reputation.)

After the preparation and recording were over, Maestro Boulez arrived and his deputy joined the starstruck onlookers scattered around the hall. We had grown fond of Simon, who felt just like one of us, being a very recent ex-member. We loved his mannerisms, including an adorable chin-cupped-in-hand whilst addressing his players, which was mimicked to his and our amusement and remained a trademark look throughout his stellar career.

But now he stepped aside to make way for the commanding presence of this suave and mega-famous Frenchman with his impeccable technique and minimal, no-nonsense conducting style; it was awe-inspiring. I remember gazing up at him from my place in the cello section, struck by his Gallic grace and charisma. The rehearsals were efficient and methodical, but he remembered we were kids and managed to offer encouragement as well as direction, even declaring on the last day that, Bien! we had done enough, we were ready and we could finish early!

The other works for this course were Bartók's *Music for Strings Percussion & Celeste* and Berg's Violin Concerto with the wonderful Itzhak Perlman. Again, our guest star was not able to join us straight away, so in rehearsal we had a superb young stand-in from within our own ranks, Krysia Osostowicz, who nowadays just happens to be the Brodsky Quartet's 1st Violinist!

Following an electric performance at our beloved Royal Festival Hall, we headed straight to Dover and crossed the channel to France. It's hard to overstate the effect on this crowd of enthusiastic young musicians of what was to follow. Turning up at the Théâtre des Champs Elysées, venue of the Rite's disastrous premiere only sixty-four years earlier, to perform that very work... the Parisian audience lifting the roof with their appreciation, Boulez apparently delighted with our efforts... it has to live still in the memory of all those who were present.

> Back at Champs Elysées for the concert there were loads of people - all French too - it is so strange that they should come of their own accord to hear us! And then we gave the most fantastic performance in the whole world of the Rite of Spring. It was the most fantastic moment of my life to play that incredible piece and played so well, expertly and superbly. Boulez was thrilled!

> Perlman's Berg! It is incredible how we have such incredible artists flying from the other side of the world to play with us, and enjoying it. It was really brilliant - what a piece!

Sitting quietly on that stage amongst the orchestra while Perlman gave an encore – one night Bach Chaconne, peaceful and divine, the next Paganini – was truly inspirational, absolutely fantastic - literally. I had never imagined that I would witness such mastery.

After the last concert, in Le Havre, my cellist friend Clare Dolby and I were delighted to have managed a chat with Pierre, an autograph from Itzhak, and as we set sail for home we vowed to return together to these shores one day, to live in Paris and be thoroughly bohemian and French.

Back at Friday night orchestra, the returning NYO contingent were full of the experience, which injected TYO with a new energy to take us through the rest of the term. But O and A Levels were due to take precedence over all else, so Quartet rehearsals became very thin on the ground. I found the pressure exhausting and yearned for a return to normality. Any practices we did have were fraught and argumentative and I complained of being bullied or not listened to, and accused of dragging when others had dragged, then filling my diary with the injustice of it all.

As well as my own inner turbulence, there was a lot of emotional strain on all four of us at this time. Life was changing; plans by the three boys for leaving home to enter new unknown worlds created a sadness at the closing of our childhood years and a nostalgia for this amazing environment we'd grown up in.

I didn't even enjoy my trip to London that month. Though the lesson was, as always, a joy, my journey had been marred by the guard on the train spotting that I might not be the age my child ticket implied, and I was subjected to an embarrassing cross-examination followed by threats of prosecution. I had been travelling on the cheaper fare for every lesson since I was thirteen, with my parents' knowledge and blessing (they were coughing up for the fare, after all), but they never warned me of what to do if I got caught.

As soon as I arrived in King's Cross I rushed to find a payphone and dialled home in a panic, but no one answered, so I spent the day terrified that the police would be on to me or that I'd be caught again on my way home. That guard certainly put the fear of God in me and taught me a life lesson; I've never tried it again. (Though it has to be said, it was a ridiculous system that designated fourteen- to eighteen-year-olds as adults, till the student railcard could be obtained.) By contrast, my mother, who was never a vain woman, actually changed the birth date on her passport so that she would qualify a year early for her senior railcard.

I just wanted this dreadful period to be over – hormones all over the place, dealing with periods while the boys teased me about my changing shape, not enough music and too many exams.

> It's awful that my state of mind cannot remain the same – I am constantly at the mercy of changing moods – of not only me – and I don't know what to do. I am dying to live a totally musical life once more, after all this academic trite. I revise French and do the exam in the afternoon – see what I mean?

> I was getting ready to revise when Ian came and I learnt we had a quartet practice! Huh! So I gobbled down a sandwich and we started. Anyway I'm glad because it was excellent! Beethoven C# minor, Razumovsky 1 and Shostakovich 13.

> Played Dvorak quintet which was great and then the Beethoven quartet and I had a stomach ache. Mike was angry because I "held people up all the time" and Alex agreed.

A bit of light relief came in the shape of the Queen's Silver Jubilee. TYO (now renamed Cleveland Youth Orchestra) was to perform for the royal entourage as they toured the country. Feverish preparations – and the smell of fresh paint – were all around us. We played in a special jubilee service at Stockton Parish Church, which I declared depressing cos it wasn't Notre Dame, then performed for our monarch the next morning. I pontificate on the merits of having a Royal Family versus its drain on the public purse, how proud I was on Jubilee Day of all the TV coverage, the gorgeous choristers of St Paul's, the nationwide beacon-lighting and the oh-so-very Englishness of it all, whilst trying not to sound too patriotic and hypocritical.

> Today it rained so the Queen came! Prissick Base looked very smart and neat. The Queen arrived and we played well, she talked to us and the Duke of Edinburgh too. He was great fun in his mack - spoke and laughed for ages. She was small and quite pretty but had ageing skin. He had a large nose and was very tall and looked as little like the Duke/Prince/Queen's husband as does John Wayne! For want of a better comparison I thought I had better put in my views for pure posterity! Anyway it was all good fun and we left and came home.

But the respite was short-lived. We got back to work and all seemed to be suffering under the strain.

> Got up and had a big row with Mike and went to school and had a terrible biology exam.
> 8.30pm Ian and Alex came and we discussed London happily (upcoming NFMY Competition) - (we'd better win) and had a quartet practice which made me unhappier by degrees. I was so annoyed with Mike's objectionableness and my playing and totally weary of the whole thing.

I don't know if that means the Quartet, exams or life in general. Emotion was running high and I was at boiling point.

> I just have to last three more days - that's all, but I'm so tired I feel I just can't do it... help me please! I'm so so tired and fed up of the whole lot of them. I look back now and see I failed them all - the relaxation now will be no good unless I forget it all. I'm so tired that I shall find that quite easy, but just keep going for one more effort.

And then it was over.

> Wednesday, June 29th, 1977
> The day I've been waiting for - I left school!

My last exam coincided with those of my schoolmates so we met up for one last lunch ('The Last Supper', as we called it) and a final round of *Casey Jones* and other favourite songs in our Little Room, an emotional goodbye and vows to keep in touch.

A long hot summer stretched ahead of me, to be devoted purely to music and all the divine social activity attached. My schooldays over, I felt like a true professional with a world of experience behind me.

> Watched a programme called 'East plays West', with the Chungs and quite a lot of NYO footage. Do you know, there's a point where you're no longer excited at seeing yourself on telly - it seemed quite normal to me!

That elusive prize at the National Festival of Music for Youth was calling to us again. A nationwide competition with a Chamber Music category clearly had no business existing without acknowledging our formidable importance. We had to try again – could it be third time lucky? This time we had learnt the wisdom of presenting a modern, feisty piece suited to our youth and vigour, so Shostakovich No.3 was the obvious choice – the second and third movements were a tour de force we were sure would win them over. At this point we hadn't even learnt the final two movements but absolutely adored these two, one a foreboding precursor of coming trouble, the other all-out war. We boarded the train to London again, checked into another seedy hotel in Bayswater (where we all shared the same room apparently!) made our usual pilgrimage to Foyles and the next morning set off with trepidation to our Mecca, the South Bank.

> At the Purcell Room we felt ancious [sic.] about our opposition, until about 3/4 of an hour before we played, when we suddenly became really confident, in the Artists' room. What a performance we gave - it was stunning and perfect and what a cheer we got! It was incredible and we were so pleased! But the best was yet to come - Head of Jury: "Cleveland String Quartet... well what can we say... Professional... Perfect... Stunning". I collected our outstanding Award and they were all amazed by our brilliance! It was really wonderful! Our relatives were happy, we were happy, and the public, including many real musicians, were extremely impressed. And then we felt proud, and happy and light.
>
> We went to a concert at the RFH. It was lovely sitting there, feeling pure success, and love for the other three. Walking through London: Southbank, Westminster Bridge, Embankment, Trafalgar Square, The Mall, St James' Park, all gorgeous. We felt London, the World, was ours. Had an incredible laugh at Trafalgar Square and then sadly left London by tube to King's Cross and onwards north.

At last, proper recognition by the wider world. As well as a stylish etched-glass trophy and a bit of money, first prize earned us an appearance the following autumn at the next Schools Prom, scene of our triumph two years earlier with the TYO. Only this time we would have a solo spot.

*

It's been extraordinary for me to realise that during all this time since our intensive week in Devon, we never once received tuition as a group. I can't say it was arrogance, because we did try. The Dartington brochure would arrive every January and we would excitedly pore over its pages, only to find that the dates clashed with precious NYO or other courses. Or truthfully, we probably couldn't afford it: it has always been notoriously expensive and there were no grants available for our age group. Then we applied to study with the Allegri Quartet at their annual course in Birmingham, but it clashed with my Grade VIII so was aborted. Finally, I read in the diary that a planned trip to Aldeburgh for the Amadeus Quartet course, for which we'd won a scholarship, had to be dropped under our conductor's orders, as CYO were invited to Oberhausen, Middlesbrough's twin town in Germany. But then that too was postponed so we could have gone to Aldeburgh after all, and now it was too late. My frustration is eloquently expressed, though poor Edwin wasn't really to blame:

Stupid Crap Raymond!

With the arrival of summer came the last ever Cleveland Youth Orchestra concert for my colleagues and the realisation that I was to be last girl standing next year, as I stayed home and joined the sixth form college and they moved on to Manchester and Cambridge. It was a sad day all round – lots of other players would be leaving too and those Friday night parties would never be the same again.

Our more recent preferred listening at these get-togethers had been recordings of Monty Python sketches; we would laugh hysterically and sing along whilst sipping our cheap warm beer or cider, all seated as usual on the floor in the semi-dark.

We also enjoyed the collected works of a certain PDQ Bach, a fictional composer created by American musicologist Peter Schickele. His deadpan delivery, documentary-style, of the 'great man's' output, with its anachronistic misfit facts and geeky musical in-jokes (an Oratorio called *Iphigenia in Brooklyn* and his gloriously imbalanced *Concerto for Lute and Bagpipes* being firm favourites) had us rolling about in fits of laughter and ever-so-clued-in knowing smiles.

Leaving it all behind, we set off on a family holiday, camping in France and Switzerland, where I polished my newly qualified French, then Germany, where I gawped, stupefied, as the ghost of Beethoven emerged from the Bonn museum that was his home. Fumbling for my trusty Instamatic, I lifted it to my eye just in time for the great man to start singing some inane drinking song, a beer tankard in his hand; it turned out they were shooting a TV ad. My indignation at this effrontery towards the world's greatest genius was loudly expressed to all around me. (Strangely, the developed photo had no image of the composer – maybe it had been a ghost after all? Or I was just a hopeless aim.)

Returning to London in time to catch a Prom featuring the Rite of Spring, I bumped into many NYO friends and had a fine old time showing off our extensive insider knowledge of the work, putting the regular and musically ignorant Prommers in their places, we reckoned.

There followed the summer course of NYO, during which we finally performed as a Quartet, to the great acclaim of all those present. Though I adored orchestral playing, it was gratifying to be recognised for what I considered my main strength.

> We were rather nervous, but my first solo was great, so after halfway everything loosened up into an incredible flourish and climax and absolute roar! Everyone cheered like hell. It was fantastic! Three curtain calls – I

> was really happy! And afterwards we all were and it seemed I had played really well: "you stole the show - beautiful" etc. Well everyone is really amazed and happy! What absolute music!!

The course took us for the first time to play at Snape Maltings – to see many return visits professionally in later years – and ended with a Proms performance of Holst's *Planets*, tearful and emotional as so many of my friends, including Quartet colleagues, were playing their last concert.

Back home, we had a few intense rehearsals before I enrolled into my new sixth form college and the guys prepared to leave home and the life we had known so long. On their last night, we gave a concert at my sister's house for a small group of family and friends, to thank them all for the support they'd shown us through the first years of our group's development. Looking back over those years, it felt like a very long time. I was ten when we started; we had grown together, already become what we considered old hands at our art, yet with no depletion in our fervour and enthusiasm for it.

> At 7 Mike, Ian, Alex and I went to Joy and Pete's and had a good practice and sat in front of the fire and at 8 everyone arrived and we played the Shostakovich and Ravel most beautifully. And the looks we shared, and memories... made everyone nostalgic for the past... We were so friendly - especially in more Palm Court encore stuff which was superb fun. Everyone was pleased that we had thanked them for the past and we looked at ourselves, and we are sad, but not for long - we do not die.

The next day's diary begins with one simple sentence.

> None so sad as today.

17

Gap Year

With my Quartet colleagues gone I expected to feel bereft and lonely, but I actually have fond memories of this year home alone. My parents and I had an easy rapport in our quiet threesome and there was plenty going on in my life to keep me busy. I discovered an independence that had perhaps been elusive to me till now, being so much part of an entity – the family as well as the quartet – rather than my own person.

Turning up at Youth Orchestra that first Friday night was a sad moment, but those of us remaining soon made our own dynamic and settled down to the season's repertoire with a renewed vigour, which always followed the long summer break. We formed a chamber group and I devised a concert, involving mixed combinations of players, culminating in Mendelssohn's Octet. This string players' favourite, being such a joy to perform, was new to us all, so we had a lot of fun putting it together. My co-cellist Alison Waines comes to mind every time I play this work as her nickname, Bog (from Ali-bogs), is scrawled indelibly at the top of my music, she being the one who led us in for the exhilarating start of that first movement. Thankfully the word BOG! doesn't spoil the moment, though co-cellists in later years have often asked me why it's written there at the top of my part for this sublime piece.

I was a little miffed when I discovered Mike and Alex, who were home for the weekend, had only attended the second half of this concert. After all my hard work and planning, I expected them to congratulate me and take note that I wasn't simply pining for my Quartet colleagues. They had all moved on to lots of new activities in Manchester and Cambridge, and I was eager to show that we were just as busy back home.

We took on a couple of wine and cheese evenings à la CSQ; a nice little earner. I finally organised that sponsored play I'd wanted years before, though raising money for the Youth Orchestra Touring Fund, not the Quartet. We bashed our way through twelve hours' worth of continuous orchestral and chamber repertoire, taking only minimal breaks in relay. I even devised a prize for the player with the most staying-power – an LP of Andrew Lloyd Weber's *Variations*. (Well, it was very 'in' at the time, being the theme tune for Melvyn Bragg's *South Bank Show*, the electric cello sounding so cool.)

Edwin Raymond called on me again for continuo duty in oratorios, but by now I was able to appreciate the role and revel in its special place in the orchestra and the beauty of the music, however interminably long it might be!

> I was practising all day, more than anyone, for St John Passion and when the concert came I looked so pretty. I realised the bond between me, David harpsichord and the lovely Evangelist and Jesus and the other soloists and it was so superb. The Passion is gorgeous - I sat amongst the inner strings and the sound sent shivers up my spine. I was "an accurate, beautiful-toned, coherent, in-tune" continuo (apparently). My solos were so lovely! I was proud. There is something special now - never nervousness, always confident and accurate. Professional! That's me (us) (CSQ).

Edwin wrote me a lovely letter of appreciation, which I found amongst the house clear-out papers, very nice to read so many years later. He also invited me to play the Boccherini Concerto again and, later in the season, the Elgar for a planned tour of Germany and Poland. I was feeling valued and validated; more than just a quarter of a group, however much that was important to me.

In the meantime, the Quartet continued. We reunited every holiday when the others came home, and we even organised weekends in Manchester, working long into the night to make the most of the few days we had. But there was a serious fly in the ointment for us to deal with. As they moved from their cosy lessons in Newcastle to the heady heights of conservatoire-level tuition, first Ian and then Mike had to stomach the indignity of being told by their new teacher, Yossi Zivoni, that their learning so far had been incorrect and they must go back to basics.

This kind of radical and potentially debilitating gesture was quite common amongst a certain breed of teacher and turned many promising students into gibbering wrecks if they weren't strong enough to weather the total lack of self-worth it engendered. More seriously though, it would affect our plans for the group. The bad news came just minutes before my friend Carole and I had to play quartets with my dad and his friend, and my bad mood pervaded the moment...

> All my hard work has been ill rewarded - Ian has been told he must do NOTHING BUT SCALES for six months and no pieces AT ALL - I feel so sorry for him because he has a good technique and doesn't need to do that - it will do him more harm than good. And what's worse, our quartet recital (Darlington) has to be called off. Shit Zivoni, that Ravel and Shostakovich would have made us, but you don't care, you're already made. Shit Zivoni, thank you.
> And then me and Carole played quartets for two hours which was so mentally destroying - two old and

slow minds, Dad and Jack Robson - and I had to look after them and work so hard without taking any credit whatsoever.

I don't understand why anyone would want to undermine the confidence of young musicians in this way. Admission to music college ought to presuppose a level of excellence and ability that should then be nurtured and developed with sensitivity and care, enabling the student's progress. The RNCM String Department as a whole struck me later as being devoid of this kind of nurture, playing students off against each other in an unhealthy competitive culture. Mike and Ian had to turn up to masterclass every week to play their slow scales in front of their peers, after everyone else had performed real pieces. It must have been mortifying. (In hindsight, they feel Yossi had a point; their technique needed taking in hand, but the process could perhaps have been implemented less oppressively.)

As for the Quartet, besides derailing a recital that 'would have made us!', this new regime posed one particular and significant obstacle to our future happiness. By winning that nationwide Youth Music Competition in the spring we had earned a solo spot in the upcoming Schools Prom, and by now the letter of invitation, confirming the November date and our inclusion, had been joyfully received and accepted. To play two movements of Shostakovich No.3 with both violinists confined to slow scales was perhaps, even for our optimistic and imaginative minds, an insurmountable task.

The boys set to work trying to convince their notoriously dispassionate teacher that this was an opportunity he couldn't – and shouldn't – force them to miss out on. He reluctantly conceded that they could do it on condition that we promise not to rehearse! In the end it was a matter for insubordination – they ignored orders and headed for Piccadilly Station and the London-bound train.

I had travelled down the day before for a lesson and Alex was on the Cambridge Line, in time for us to reunite at our favourite hall in the world. Now all our orchestral training and experience in that iconic venue seemed to culminate in this moment – it was our turn.

> Tuesday, 29 November '77
> It was lovely to walk into the Albert Hall artists' entrance and be very much at home, settle into our dressing rooms, wander around and love!
>
> Then we went to a Wimpy and had a hilarious laugh till I remembered I'd left my music in the hotel! I ran there and back and nearly died! (It gave me licence to be bolshy and respected all round!) We rehearsed and weren't too pleased, then Mike and I had a great interview with the BBC overseas bloke and we all went back to our hotel. We changed at the hotel and had nerves and we all walked back in a great flourish! CSQ arrives! Apprehension, illness and noise filled the first half, with a broken C string from Alex and nerves, (slightly) which mounted in me as we stood ready but which had gone as we played - our best performance yet of this Shostakovich! We made it! RAH conquered! I received a lovely lovely bouquet of which we were all so proud and Land of Hope and Glory was played, with kisses and hugs ending the Prom and we were back in the silence of our hotel! Flowers and success!

The Royal Albert Hall is built up in layers like a great round birthday cake: a huge arena on the lower level – the Stalls – surrounded by the raised seating levels of the Upper Stalls, then the plush gilt-etched boxes in several tiers, and finally the Gallery. The whole set-up creates a sense of a Roman Circus, especially during the Proms Festival when all the seats are stripped out of the Arena, leaving it free for the audience to stand, sit or even (subtly) sway as they watch the concerts. The centre-piece of this Arena is a beautiful rockery complete with fountain (switched off during the music) around which you can stand or sit in comfort, leaning up against its wall if you're quick on the uptake.

Henry Wood, creator of the Proms, conceived this standing area as a way of offering cheap first-come, first-served tickets to 'those less fortunate'. These days it's a computerised system so you queue online then turn up in time for Doors. But the traditional way was far more fun: young people queueing all day, sitting on the ground with picnics, singing or sunbathing – or cowering under umbrellas and makeshift awnings – building up a wonderful party atmosphere as they snaked around the hall and down the steps towards the Royal College of Music and beyond.

When the doors opened, there would be a great surge by seasoned Promenaders, all vying for the best spots. If you were too slow to make it to the front few rows, the central fountain was the next best option, giving a good sightline to the stage, good for sound being halfway back, and somewhere to lean if you started to flag.

Then out come the banners, flags and silly hats – if it's the Last Night – or, on regular nights, chants and banter are passed from Arena to Gallery and back again, the youthful, cheerful Prommers putting on a pre-concert show for the more staid regular concert-goers. My favourite back in the day, being such a fan of that new-fangled London-exclusive delight now known as KFC – when a certain lookalike conductor took to the platform, they enthusiastically chanted, "Sir Charles Groves is finger-lickin' good!"

Overseeing this fiesta from his perch in the organ loft is the bust of Sir Henry Wood, dusted off and given pride of place for the eight-week duration of the festival. But once a year for the Schools Prom, this bust is replaced by one of Beethoven wearing a striped school tie and cap at a jaunty angle, and the

Promenaders are a much younger demographic, though no less vocal and certainly no less excitable. Their higher pitched chants and cheers could be heard from off-stage, where we stood waiting to make our entrance.

We already had some experience of playing to school kids and knew it wasn't a given they'd be kind and listen attentively or appreciate us, even though we and all the other performers that night were pretty much their age. But the organisers had dreamt up a whole new challenge to make our experience even more intense: we were to play on a stage erected over the iconic fountain, bang in the centre of the Arena and this heaving throng of young faces. And we were to follow a hugely upbeat performance by the Doncaster Youth Jazz Orchestra. Gladiators and lions could well describe the feeling as we launched into a not tremendously accessible movement (the second) of Shostakovich's 3rd String Quartet.

Though it begins stridently, there are moments of delicacy that demand pin-drop silence for full impact. Our young audience didn't let us down. And once we launched into the second of our two movements – the Quartet's third, entitled 'War' – they were with us all the way, almost jumping to the marching rhythms, like head-bangers at a heavy metal gig. (This was good practice for twenty years later when we opened for Björk's UK stadium tour playing Stravinsky, to the delight of her open-minded fans.)

On this occasion back in '77, the 'chearing' had all the more meaning and poignancy as we felt we'd truly conquered a potential monster, finally making this hall our own, not with youth orchestras and conductors, just Us Four. A national newspaper reviewing the concert commented that we had perhaps been set an impossible task by the organisers, then wrote: 'Not a bit of it! The Cleveland Quartet demanded – and got – our attention with a concentrated interpretation of great musicality. This is not simply youth bravely having a go; rather it is maturing musicianship demonstrating that the heart of youth can shed light on music too often thought to be the preserve of older performers.'

One bitter lesson was to be learned during this episode. The concert had been televised but, true to form, the producers in their wisdom chose not to include our slot in either of the two relays. Chamber music is so often treated as the poor relation of our profession, perceived as less glamorous and more insular or even exclusive. And yet how much more exciting it might have been for young viewers, seeing a dynamic foursome like ours instead of the usual bland expressionless orchestral fare of youngsters under the baton of some unknown oldie. By now, my indignation had reached full maturity of expression:

> On Tuesday the Schools Prom on telly didn't show us - again - the fucking bastards.

*

During this year of separation, as well as meeting back home or in Manchester, we convened on one occasion in Cambridge, where I got my first taste of the cloistered life amongst those mediaeval cathedrals of learning. Darkening autumn days, with bicycle headlamps reflecting off damp roads, high walls echoing as gowned students chatted or sang, running to lectures or lounging on street corners, appealed to my fondness for *Brideshead Revisited* and the public school types I'd met at NYO. Here was an intellectual version of what we had grown up with – an enthusiasm for music just as fervent but seemingly even more entitled. Feeling slightly outside the clique but wanting to fit in, groups of us sat around on candle-lit floors sharing cheap red wine and listening to the latest hip sounds of our specialist genre: the neo-classical delights of Stravinsky's *Pulcinella* and the unashamed romanticism of Schönberg's *Verklärte Nacht*. Somehow these composers had proven themselves cool already with their more complex works that we had known as kids, so these 'new' discoveries were allowed to be enjoyed, despite their upbeat accessibility. Milhaud joined this gang with *Le Boeuf sur le Toit*, along with Maxwell-Davies' *Foxtrot*, their jazzy, easy-listening timbres exciting our heightened senses, Ravel's *Tombeau de Couperin* a brilliant throwback to the Baroque.

Hearing Stravinsky mimic the chord-structures and textures of ancient eras of music and even popular idioms, as in *The Soldier's Tale*, we were taken off-guard, shocked and delighted all at once. It was like when The Beatles came out with their Sgt. Pepper album, fans bemused and distraught at the departure from their characteristic three-minute pop songs, shocked by these experimental sounds and weird ideas. We too felt like the first to discover these works by our old favourite who'd penned the *Rite of Spring* and *Petrushka*, insider appreciation making the rounds throughout the seats of learning in the world of the undergraduate. I was tickled to read in Stephen Fry's autobiography that he and his Footlight friends had been soaking up these 'hip' pieces in his digs at Queen's at that exact time!

Just a few years later we were to return to these hallowed grounds as the University's first ever Quartet in Residence, barely older than our student groups and still with an uncomfortable feeling of not quite belonging.

The Quartet managed a few further reunions in London and elsewhere, including the Royal Overseas League Competition where we won first prize and a healthy bursary. Turning up separately from our different lives, me still travelling regularly to the capital by train, gave me a sense of being truly cosmopolitan and grown-up and, crucially, fully independent.

Monday was fun! We all met - only the quartet - in Overseas House and left, having played the Haydn

> to our "absolute perfection" (Ian Jewel). We had a hilarious time walking around the posh London shops and we all parted in a tube - "See you in Venice", "Have a nice time in Copenhagen", "Come to my Festival Hall concert" very loudly on the train. People gawped!

Contrary to this make-believe cosmopolitanism, none of us had yet left the country for anything other than family holidays. But this was about to change. A most inconvenient new kid on the block was making its bid for supremacy over my beloved NYO. The European Community Youth Orchestra was calling for young players from all over the nine member states to come and audition, and there was a buzz of excitement amongst my peer group.

But I had already decided to give NYO one more year and was quite excited at the prospect of being there without the rest of my Quartet. Some of the other Middlesbrough contingent were also intending to go, but we were all being tempted by this new upstart. I hoped that maybe I could make it work to belong to both bands...

The north of England auditions were held in Manchester, so a bunch of us trouped over to the BBC on Oxford Road, had our photos taken like celebrities, and played our audition pieces and sight-reading in the main hall of Broadcasting House to a panel of Europe's musical elite.

In the meantime, I made my annual pilgrimage to Newcastle for the rather more understated audition one-on-one with NYO boss Ivey Dickson, in the usual drab little room at the top of some ancient municipal office block. This time, being an old pro, I was treated to a chummy reception and she tempted me with offers of solo spots during courses and similar boosts to the ego. I felt I'd been admitted to the top rank, being spoken to as an equal and respected as a cellist. (It helped that I'd also remembered to use my roll-on.)

The letters of acceptance all arrived at roughly the same time, with players from Middlesbrough yet again disproportionately represented in both cases. Ten of us were offered places in an orchestra drawing membership from nine European countries – quite a feat for a small town like ours. Then the pressure began.

We who had auditioned for both received phone calls from Ivey warning us that we could under no circumstances belong to her orchestra if we accepted the other offer. This was a strange and ungenerous stance to take; only a date-clash should have decided the case. Most of my TYO friends chose the new and exciting and, judging by the audition day, more hip and modern band. I was conflicted; I still had many close friends at NYO and hadn't properly closed that chapter. The friendliness of my audition suddenly started to look suspicious.

Ivey Dixon is a stinking blackmailing old sow.

But I folded to the pressure and dutifully turned up for the three NYO courses that year, mostly wishing I was elsewhere but still managing to enjoy being in the top-dog clique of veteran members. Reports from ECYO painted a picture of glamorous foreign tours, made-to-measure designer suits and gowns for the players, not the school uniform-style concert dress we had to don. The young and free-thinking directors treated members as adults. They could drink, venture off campus and openly date each other! They had Claudio Abbado, Pollini, Beethoven *Emperor* and Mahler 6; but we had Charles Dutoit and Kyung Wha Chung, Beethoven Violin Concerto and the *Firebird*. Things weren't so bad…

The whole thing came to a head when both bands coincided at the World Festival of Youth Orchestras in Aberdeen. My last course after four years of membership in this venerable old institution ended and the next day I was in the audience for the ECYO's concert, already being introduced to my fellow northeasterners' new-found foreign friends in time to join up next year.

*

Whilst sorting through my heaps of 1970s' memorabilia in my mum's basement, I found the programme for this World Festival. It was a stark reminder of how things were and how, in some shameful cases, they remain. Out of a two-week festival featuring orchestras and soloists from many countries worldwide, the list of artists' and conductors' profiles showed not one single woman. Page after page of posed photographs and biographies of men holding batons, violins, cellos, or seated at keyboards, looking pompous and entitled.

Actually, I lie; there were a couple of women featured on these pages of blurb. Praise and thanks were offered to Lady Someoneorother, who had kindly hosted fundraising dinners at her stately home, and Mrs Husband's-Name, who skilfully coordinated the team of volunteer helpers.

18

Gap Year Continued

Ian couldn't come so we asked Dad to play with us for fun. He was chuffed! We played Shostakovich 11, Haydn and Prokofiev - nostalgic memories. We played really well - even Dad!

By now we had been together so long that old repertoire could cause a stir of nostalgia. The Prokofiev was a particular favourite from the early days, and it perfectly encapsulated our childhood sound and delivery, so much so that when we revisited it decades later we had to remind ourselves not to fall into old habits of juvenile unrefined playing. The four-square, solid metre of the first movement, with heavy accents and chordal motion, didn't encourage elegant phrasing and it took a disconcertingly long time for us to think of injecting some of our own! For me, that piece is forever associated with fresh faces and uncompromising enthusiasm.

As with many childhood experiences, the emotions connected to certain pieces are deeply embedded and can spring up and take me by surprise even now. There are moments in some works where the cello has a cadenza or big solo, and my young self would build up quite a head of steam as we approached the point in question. Then I would take a deep breath and launch in, my brain full of doubt and bravado all at once, the music happening to me almost as much as I made it happen.

The passages leading up to those big moments are still capable of causing a quiver of nervous excitement, my subconscious memory sparked, even if I'm not playing. I was teaching the Prokofiev at a course we held at Chetham's School of Music some years ago and found myself holding back tears as the children in front of me so closely resembled our young selves in their spirit and manner.

Many of the quotes from my diary have displayed a shocking degree of immodesty – I can't imagine ever feeling that sure of myself these days – but I'm glad to read that it was often backed up with genuine praise and validation from respected people in the profession. Gratifyingly, I notice that some of my performance descriptions now begin to include thoughtful observation of the process and show that even then I was endlessly fascinated with the machinations of my chosen art. The experience of sitting by the harpsichord amongst the inner strings for the St John Passion was lovely for me to read, as I had remembered it was a special moment but not quite recalled the details. And later for my Boccherini appearance with the adults' Symphony Orchestra, the observation is interestingly detached and astute.

> Practised non-stop during the day - Mam was with me, bringing tea and snacks and stuff! Anyway, instead of playing till the last minute I was sort of so casual and hanging around and I just didn't feel scared once! Not even as I went on and tuned and things! I was so calm I couldn't believe it! And I concentrated - every tricky bit I thought, and knew what I was doing. It came off - it was superb! Well, I had a lovely time. Afterwards everyone said wow and were thoroughly impressed.

> The orchestra was bad but that made it even better for me!

This last point is an interesting phenomenon known to many musicians. If those around you aren't up to scratch it can unfortunately lower your expectations of yourself and depress the spirit, but it can also inject you with a confidence that you sound so much better by comparison and can use it to your advantage! This certainly works in a concerto situation, where sticking out and shining is admissible – nay, expected.

But in chamber music, the levels must match and all should feel equal to their colleagues in ability and importance. Any suggestion that this is not the case can totally undermine the integrity of a group or an individual performance. Even as I play an apparently simple bass line in an Early Classical work, I know that I am influencing the other lines and informing their interpretation and understanding.

When I have a leading role to play, I have learnt over the years to have autonomy, not to be straitjacketed by the accompanying parts, but at the same time I never stop hearing them and allowing the harmonies or textures to influence my phrasing or choice of sound. Playing inner parts within the texture calls for another discipline again, whereby choice of vibrato and bow pressure can enhance or detract from the main theme one should be hearing. This calls for endless sensitivity and awareness, which becomes a fine art in itself. The bottom line is, in a string quartet one never stops listening.

The other observation in that diary entry was that concentrating and thinking whilst performing really works! It is a revelation to a young player that mindfulness can get you through a difficult moment, whereas up until then you may be forgiven for letting muscle memory and adrenalin take over – that deep-breath launching-in I mentioned. The older player starts to have moments of clarity in performance, out-of-body observation of that process at play; and if they're lucky, the true out-of-body experience that can lead to transcendental moments of absolute immersion and loss of self in the performance.

So as this year of independence continued, I was developing into my adult self and enjoying all the kudos my big fish/small pond afforded me. But the Quartet was where my heart lay and I couldn't imagine another year of being at home, completing A Levels and going to orchestra every Friday night after even more of my friends would have left.

I started to think of Manchester for myself; the call of a new level of learning and exclusive engagement with music was strong. Alex had intimated that he would be happy to leave Cambridge and transfer to Manchester so we could all be together. This was a huge sacrifice as he had loved his first year of university and was passing with flying colours. In the course of another reunion during my mid-term break, these seeds of change took root.

> In Manchester the quartet was playing 12 hours every day and playing beautifully! We had a break at midnight and carried on till 2.30am!
>
> I began seriously talking of going next year. I love the thought of having your own room and things. I could do my A Levels at the same time! It would be so good - I couldn't come here with nothing to do but what Mike does (i.e. only lessons). I would love it and it would be such hard work and a challenge. Ha ha - how happy I was at the thought of it! And miserable at the thought of being totally alone in Middlesbrough next year. I know I should go. And Mam said, "Well, do an audition. There is no need to get worried about all this - you're a lucky girl and in a good position and whatever you choose to do won't matter either way." What a fantastic thing for a mother to say when her daughter is making a drastic move in life!

And more to the point, when her daughter is the last to leave home and the nest will be empty. Although I take exception to her 'lucky' (as Gary Player quipped, 'I find the harder I practise, the luckier I get!'), I did feel guilty at choosing to leave a year early and leaving my parents alone prematurely. We'd had fun together this last year, making the now calm house more proper, me encouraging certain improvements and designing on graph paper great schemes of change, some of which were implemented. I was helpful and useful to have around, doing many washing-ups per day, keeping order and offering companionship, maybe even keeping Mam feeling young, sharing babysitting duties for her new grandchildren living nearby.

Nevertheless, even though lucky isn't the word I'd use if my daughter had been so diligent and hard-working all her childhood, her encouragement was unequivocal and helped me to make the move. Maybe she was seeing the light at the end of the thirty-one year tunnel she'd been in since having her first baby and would be glad to precipitate my departure!

At this pivotal moment, Conkey, the wonderful black and white Border Collie who had been a constant in the house for as long as I could remember, had become ill with cancer and was nearing his end. A short stay of execution gave him one more month to slowly and gingerly enjoy a few more walks in the Yorkshire countryside he adored so much, me nursing and stroking him in those precious last days alone together. But the time came for us to help him on his way and it resonated in a bittersweet way with my own sense of moving on.

> It's Monday and sad and our Conkey is dead. It was becoming impossible for him towards the end so I was glad he had an escape - he was so unhappy. Just before he left he knocked my cello over and it broke (shifted at the neck, so I couldn't play all evening and it must be mended but at the same time Dad has enquired and I can go and see some cellos in London on Saturday.)

> They took Conkey without telling me and I couldn't say goodbye - but I would have cried. I really loved him. I worked hard all evening and we put a picture up for Conkey in his box.

The end of an era.

It's interesting that I still had half an eye on the future even at this sad time. I had been aware that my 'lady's cello' was a bit of an oddball, with its long scroll and slim body – it just didn't look like all the others. A year previously I had commented:

> I'm sorry to say that I am not satisfied with my cello - it is not Celloish - I need a Celloish Cellistic Cello! Well, 20th of January Philips sale?

But I didn't get to visit that sale and now this incident led to a half-hearted search whilst the repair was carried out by a luthier in London recommended by my teacher. He gave my poor old cello a thorough overhaul; gluing ancient cracks and replacing the sound post, and fitting a new Belgian bridge (which thrilled my sense of heritage though I'd never heard of such a thing), and the sound was improved enough for me to stay with it another year or so.

In the meantime, I still adored those lessons in London with David Strange and would have happily continued.

> Bloody superb lesson. He was so pleased with my Lalo especially. We are now doing the second and third movements - it was really fantastic. He has again proved his ability to recognise faults and have an answer for them - my vibrato shall now be beautiful!

But Manchester had become my magnetic pole. I knew there were great teachers there – Ralph Kirshbaum was on my radar – though in reality it always felt as though the Quartet would be my 'first-study' instrument. The boys had let it be known during their first year that they had this quartet back home and just how much it meant to them. They had even enticed one of their new friends, Chris Craker (now award-winning producer and studio owner) back to Middlesbrough to join us in a clarinet quintet concert, playing Mozart and Brahms. He had reported back to his teachers that this was a pretty serious bunch of kids, and how excited he'd been to find such devotion in our group. Though there was no precedent for a foursome to arrive at college ready-formed, we were determined to break the mould and prioritise our joint vocation.

To complete this picture of flux and change, my diary, which had been a loyal and constant daily companion since I was twelve years old, was starting to bore me and become a burden. Doodles of musical quotes litter the pages, scrawled onto freehand staves. I was writing more and more philosophical stuff, reams and reams of pontificating nonsense that is amusing for me to read now, but I'll spare you the details…Then the increasingly distilled and sporadic entries start to be peppered with the futility of it all.

> Oh, I had a bath at 8 o'clock… So what? This diary is containing irrelevant detail and has no room for thought and I'm sick of it. Good night!

> Now this has gone too far. These nonentical [sic.] days are not worth recording - the idiotic and boring things are useless - this diary should be a taste of the wonder and beauty which I experience and it is only really good for lovely times.

> This is desperate - I don't know why I carry on with this diary, but of course I do.

Finally, two very short entries three days apart bring the whole thing to an abrupt and unceremonious end.

> Sunday 16 April
> It was pretty depressing and so sad to leave Clare at Euston. Manchester was good fun but I was so tired. My college audition went OK-ly and Ian looked after me. I came home exhausted.
>
> Wednesday, 19 April 1978
> I got a letter of acceptance at RNCM! It was a lovely hot summery day and we all sat in Joy and Pete's garden in the sun and in the evening we had waffles there! What a larf. Janet was there with her new baby. But, my God, the description of having a baby - good grief! Women are women!

I had travelled to Manchester directly from the end of the Easter NYO course to sit my RNCM audition. There was no particular ceremony in the event. A swarthy-looking dapper gentleman sitting in on the audition, who I vaguely recognised as Raphael Sommer, was somehow chosen as my new teacher. Right there in front of him I was asked who I'd like to study with – it seemed only polite to glance his way and mumble, "Erm..him!" It wasn't a decision I regretted, but I did feel a little forced into a corner; for Kirshbaum I would have to wait.

So my remaining summer term at sixth form college was spent persuading teachers to have faith in me that I would carry on my studies alone and return a year later to sit the exams. Then an event occurred in Middlesbrough that I had to Google just now, to make sure I wasn't dreaming.

Sure enough, the Newport Jazz Festival came to us; Ayresome Park Stadium, home of the Boro, hosted the dizzying spectacle of Ella Fitzgerald and Dizzy Gillespie, Buddy Rich, Oscar Peterson and many other big names. I had enough nouse to realise this was a one-off moment that would become legendary in local history, so along I went, all alone, to be a part of it. Upgrading from the standing terraces of 'the Boys' End' we used to frequent, I bought myself a prime-view seat. It really seemed like a sending off just for me.

Then my final summer course at NYO, segueing into the ECYO preview at the World Festival of Youth Orchestras in Aberdeen, felt truly like the closing of a chapter.

Fittingly, my last musical activity that summer was back with the old colleagues at TYO under the baton of our faithful and devoted Edwin Raymond. As shadows began to lengthen, we bussed and ferried over the Channel to Germany for a performance in the Rhein-Mosel Halle, Oberhausen. I was soloist in the Elgar Cello Concerto and truly felt like a star in this huge, modern and very proper auditorium.

On the long overnight journey home we sang, drank Apfelkorn and slept, reaching Hull harbour as the sun rose. Tumbling off that orchestra bus for the last time we said our tearful goodbyes, to each other and to childhood, in the cold air of a late summer dawn.

Two weeks later I was headed for Manchester.

19

Student Life

Leaving home for university or college is a frightening time for most young people; waving goodbye to the comforting cocoon of family life and childhood companions, facing an unknown future in a strange town with a completely new set of faces and names, tentatively seeking friends amongst that unfamiliar throng. I had none of this uncertainty: I was going where my Quartet was to be based and two of them had been bedding in for a year already.

As well as joining my colleagues, I had already met many of the friends they made in their first year and I'd even played in chamber groups with some of them. Several of my TYO friends also made the transfer to the RNCM and some NYO mates, including my best friend and fellow cellist Clare. So arriving at Hartley Hall, the halls of residence for music students, one rainy September afternoon, I only felt a sense of reunion and anticipation.

Naturally, a little homesickness tempered the novelty of that first night in my new bed, fond memories of family life bringing a nostalgic tear to my eye, but it was short-lived. As I launched into the excitement of a timetable of exclusively musical activity, and a lot of free time to devote to Quartet rehearsals, the novelty of being a Mancunian city-dweller, taking the orange bus to college and entering through those huge glass doors to a foyer full of instrument-carrying students and famous faces from the world of music, my childhood was unceremoniously left behind.

It is a well-known and oft-bemoaned fact that students can be wasteful of the exciting educational opportunity they're suddenly presented with; in charge for the first time of their own time-management they can easily fall into bad ways. Even music students, who have had years of training in the self-discipline essential for daily practice, can find that the switch to unfettered freedom and lack of scrutiny by parents or teachers leaves them floundering. The layout of college was no help in this dichotomy.

On entering the solid concrete, almost always rain-streaked building, you find yourself in the midst of a large refectory full of chatter and laughter, students congregating for banter, to pore over scores, compare notes on lessons or swap gossip and jokes. The sweeping staircase up from the grand foyer that leads to the practice rooms on the top floor is calling to you; you know you must venture up, but the fun is down here, where there's daylight, people, food and drink. Everybody keeps saying, "I must go and practise," but then stays another minute or ten, not wanting to miss the fun.

When eventually the guilt and panic that deferred practice instigates in all musicians gets too much, you make your way up the wide carpeted steps, daylight and noise still part of the scene, till the stairway narrows to a little concrete spiral into darkness, and when you emerge, you are in a new world. Seemingly endless corridors, narrow and badly-lit, form a huge square around the four corners of the building. Door after door you pass, hearing snippets of struggling student players and singers, little windows offering you a view in to check if the room is taken, but no view to the world beyond. Every practice room and teaching room is windowless – and airless, since no one thought of the importance of air-conditioning back in the seventies when the place was built.

It is possible to keep walking round and round this cube of endeavour for what seems like hours finding no vacancies, and the temptation to return to the everlasting party below is just beginning to win out when a student emerges hot and sweaty, having finished their several hours of slog, and you know that the room is going to stink, but you go in anyway – quick before someone else gets it.

This search for vacancies is extra tricky when a whole quartet wishes to rehearse. The regular rooms are too small for four people to work constructively and there are only a handful of larger rooms, almost always booked well in advance and available for just two hours at a time. On the lucky chance of procuring one of these studios, the hunt for music stands could delay the rehearsal even further, and your session is diminished to almost being not worth the bother. We liked to get stuck in to rehearsals and had been used to having limitless time in whichever home we chose to meet, not being curtailed by the needs of others around us. Still, when time is short it's amazing how much more productive a practice session can be.

My cello lessons with the dapper Raphael Sommer began. He was immaculately turned out; I'd never till now met a man who carried a clutch bag, let alone sported crocodile skin shoes. His smile was wide and generous; like his shoes, I never quite knew if it was genuine, but he seemed intent on helping me to progress.

The lesson followed a pattern that never changed. First, scales and arpeggios; four octaves starting very slowly, one note per bow, then two, increasing gradually to eventually attaining the not-inconsiderable feat of four octaves up in one bow, four down in the next. (This is very fast for the left hand!) And, a revelation to me, every scale used the same fingering, whatever key, major or minor, all the same. As long as you put a first finger on the third note ascending, and NEVER use an open string, this fingering is a universal catch-all and quite brilliant for it! Sommer was an ex-pupil of Paul Tortellier, whose book *How I Play, How I Teach* I had bought for myself with the earnings from one of my first playing jobs and devoured throughout my teens. This was his method. I'd wanted to apply for his school in Paris a few years back, had sent away for the entry forms, but somehow the idea was dropped. It was good to know that I was getting, if only second-hand, the teaching of the great man I'd admired for so long. If nothing else, my new teacher's exotic accent made it all feel very proper.

The analysis of bow technique, shifting and string crossing could all be executed during this rather musically ungratifying part of the lesson. Then it was time for studies. Piatti, Popper. Grützmacher... some were purely finger exercises, warm-ups for the digits and routes to greater agility and strength, but others were great works of immense structure, with long build-ups to crashing climaxes, all involving the repetition of one particular technical trick, be it playing in thirds, playing in octaves, bouncing the bow, fast passagework, trills or some other fiendish devilry of the cello. Students had to perform these monumental oeuvres in open classes, their peers listening and watching intently and just feeling glad it wasn't their turn yet. It was a good few months before we even discussed my repertoire of real music, and a great milestone when the time came.

I can count myself lucky that I hadn't been forced back to basics in the same debilitating way Mike and Ian had when they joined the first year, but it did seem odd that my whole existence was geared away from the driving force that had hitherto propelled me; that of the music itself. I had ended my summer in performances of extraordinary symphonic works – Britten *Young Persons' Guide*, Tchaikovsky 5th Symphony, Walton Cello Concerto – my own performance as soloist in the Elgar Concerto, and of course a huge chunk of the string quartet repertoire in which I considered myself thoroughly immersed and something of an expert, even at seventeen. And suddenly all that musical joy was gone as we sat around in little groups, scrutinising the studious efforts of our co-cellists under the watchful and somehow condescending gaze of our celebrity maestro.

There was one person on the staff for whom music could never lose its true purpose and who believed the Holy Grail was chamber music, especially the string quartet. Terence Weil had once been a wonderful cellist with a tender, human approach far from the pyrotechnics associated with many big names. His recordings of the Schumann and Brahms Piano Quartets with the Pro Arte and Melos Ensemble are legendary. He was first choice for many emerging ensembles after the war, the Amadeus Quartet amongst them – his being away on tour in South America lost him that ticket as they searched elsewhere. He was cellist of the Hurwitz Quartet and a founder member of the English Chamber Orchestra.

But drink was his enemy. At a time when it was quite normal to take some Dutch courage before walking on stage, and musicians were often to be found propping up the bar well after the audience left, Terry was one of the lads. Respect, and soon bookings, dropped and he had to rely on teaching to sustain him. But being a man of few words, and not terribly eloquent when he did speak, it was a special kind of student who could benefit from his tutelage.

Perhaps because we already had so much experience as a group and were able to bypass the preliminary stages of chamber music coaching, we found his lessons enlightening and enthralling. He shared our pure love for the music and belief in its importance. When we arrived at college, he was the only teacher exclusively dedicated to group playing. He was delighted to find us, already formed and well on the road to an aspirational career, and immediately took us under his wing.

'The kids', as he called us, became Terry's pet project. We would talk for hours about our favourite works and performers, he introducing us to players and groups from the old days, the Busch and Hollywood Quartets, which had so far been unknown to us, Szigetti, Hassid, Neveu. Vintage recordings of the great masterworks would be aired and discussed, he sitting in awe, head to one side, a smile of incredulity as a particularly ravishing violin shift or moment of expressive beauty filled our ears.

One exception to his total bias towards the classics was Alan Busch, a rarely performed contemporary British composer whose Communist persuasion led to ostracism in most countries west of the iron curtain. His Soviet-inspired style should have been right up our street, but we never did have a go at his *Dialectic for String Quartet* – maybe we should. (I've just listened to it on YouTube… maybe not.)

Terry's lessons were never boring. We would play through whichever work was on the table, then invariably, without making any comment on the performance, these words were delivered in his Cockney twang: "Play it again and I'll stop you this time." Being more instinctive than intellectual, he used actions rather than words to put his point across. Sometimes we would be mid-phrase only to be surprised by an abrupt movement from behind his desk. From a position of composure, head buried in his score, there would suddenly be a look of horror, a jolt or even a theatrical pushing back of his wheeled office chair, with him in it, till he hit the wall with a thud, like a cartoon character in shock. This meant that we had played an unexpected note or chord, or made a phrasing he didn't agree with. The first time it happened, we thought he'd let his cigarette burn to his fingers in absent-minded ecstasy at our playing, or maybe had been stung by a wasp… but we soon learnt that his OTT reaction was purely on musical grounds.

He always favoured expressive fingerings over 'safe' ones – a doctrine that stayed with us (sometimes to our detriment in competitive arenas). He quite often took my cello and my part, playing to show what he meant instead of relying on the inadequacy of words. I always felt a touch of jealousy as the other three seemed mesmerised by his artistry, and I was eager to get my cello back to show I could do it just as well. He had in fact lost his touch to a large extent– he had never been a technical whizz and confessed to being incapable of playing a scale in a rare lesson with Rostropovich some years before – but glimpses of his craft came through in odd moments of utter magic. Later we would progress to performing alongside him, in quintet or sextet works, and he never failed to inspire, even though his playing was sometimes shaky and uncertain.

Terry, like so many of his generation, had been addicted to cigarettes and drink his entire working life. Photos from studio sessions of old show all the players balancing fags on music stands between takes, or even holding them in the bow hand whilst playing. All the teaching rooms in college had at least a smell of stale smoke, and more usually were actually billowing with the stuff as you entered, the teacher a distant figure in the fog. Added to this in Terry's case was a bottle of kaolin and morphine mixture, which he kept handy on his desk for the occasional swig – essential to keep his stomach ulcer quiet. In a touching admission to his own self-destructive lifestyle choices, he used to say he was living on bonus time, having expected to die before he reached sixty. His wicked sense of humour and self-deprecation was a breath of fresh air, and he helped coin several phrases for the collection. His idea of heaven? Hearing yourself on a repeat broadcast on Radio 3. "You can sit in the pub and earn money at the same time!"

As well as lessons and practice, the top floor was home to tutorials and theory lessons, Solfège and Dictation. (With the terrifyingly brilliant Michel Brandt, who could sing at top speed using the Do-Re-Mi names for the notes without ever tripping up, and would set us fiendish tasks to write down by ear. Imposter Syndrome and little-girl inadequacy haunted my sleeping hours.) Additionally, I had my A Level work to fit in, with a little help from my tutor David Ledbetter if he had the time. There was the adorable George Hadjinikos with whom one could pass a pleasant hour being regaled with the joys of his beloved Skalkottas, a fellow Greek composer sadly neglected by all but this loyal champion. Here was a musician with an all-embracing generous spirit, going out into the community to conduct local amateur orchestras before 'outreach' was even a thing, bringing them impossibly ambitious repertoire to tackle and smiling blissfully throughout, hearing only the music he knew so well in his head, not the woeful performance. A *Rite of Spring* will stay with me forever, in which George gleefully filled in all the obscure instruments missing from the Bury Symphony's limited line-up – alto flutes, contrabassoon, Wagner tubas – by singing or running to the piano!

And so the day in college drew to a close. Whatever had kept you up there, the moment of packing up came as a relief. Descending back down from the airless top-floor corridors after a long lesson or practice session, returning to the bright welcoming refectory and whichever group of friends were still there lingering for a chat, one could spend another hour or so eating from the canteen as autumn darkness descended on wet Mancunian streets outside.

In the corner was the bar. Eleanor Warren would loudly call orders or offer rounds – only ever triples for herself and Terry – and hold court for whoever was available for pedagogic scrutiny. She was our Head of Strings and an ex-cellist, with a matriarchal demeanour that belied a somewhat misogynistic character. Again, women were women's worst enemy – she gave me the uncomfortable feeling that I somehow had to work harder to earn my place in the Quartet or to make it in music, being female. And our wish to focus on the group also seemed to slightly undermine our worth as individual players. Our teachers were wary of letting us go out and about performing – Mike and Ian had just about got away with that jail-break to the Schools Prom – as though playing in the group would somehow damage our development or interrupt our musical journey. (Oh, but all students had to report for orchestra twice a week without fail...)

But on the whole we were welcomed and celebrated for our dedication and the longevity we had already achieved at such a young age. Patrick Ireland and Eli Goren were added to our roster of coaching staff, and we were allowed to sign up for out-of-town dates, should any come our way. During this autumn term we had our first proper paid booking, at Rothbury Music Society in Northumberland. This charming little town held memories for me from a holiday in early childhood when I had fallen off a speeding bike down a perilously steep hill, resulting in stitches to the head and gravel-removal treatment by the dashing Dr Armstrong at the local cottage hospital. How long ago that seemed as we travelled together in Ian's Hillman Hunter, being welcomed and hosted like a real touring quartet. Receiving our joint fee of £80 plus expenses, we felt we were starting to be taken seriously. As time went on, we would be sent out as ambassadors for the College, on exchange visits to other institutions in Europe and on study courses in the UK.

Some weeks into my first term, a notice in *The Guardian* newspaper caught our attention: there was to be an International String Quartet Competition held in Portsmouth the following spring. A celebrity jury would be assembled, headed by Yehudi Menuhin no less, and prizewinners would be offered concert tours and recording opportunities, as well as money. There was even a Menuhin Prize for the 'most promising young group'. Given that we were well below the upper age limit, we already felt this prize was ours for the taking.

We would hear no opposition to our determination to enter this contest; our teachers simply had to go along with it. There was a big repertoire to choose from and some set works that we would have to learn from scratch, including the fiendishly difficult K590 of Mozart, his last and most complex quartet. Preparation fever gained pace and we continued the fight for rehearsal space as practice sessions became more urgent than ever.

If you couldn't find a practice room at college, individual work could always be done in your bedroom at the halls of residence (though strictly this wasn't allowed), but both types of room were much too small for groups. We were occasionally allowed to use the larger teaching rooms, and we had the Chapel at Hartley Hall to fall back on, but this was in high demand and we'd sometimes find ourselves scheduling midnight sessions... luckily it was out of earshot of the sleeping students. The luxury we had grown up with – that of permanent and exclusive rehearsal space 24/7 – was starting to be sorely missed and we yearned for a return to those days.

Accommodation in the halls of residence was offered to first year students only, but Mike and Ian had begged another year there so that we could all be together, once Alex and I had joined them. Less than a term in, we began to realise that there was no benefit to this if we couldn't actually work. As comforting as those canteen breakfasts and dinners had been, and all the camaraderie of snooker and table tennis in the common room with the other students, we decided that for maximum dedication to the cause we had to give it all up and look for a house together, just the four of us.

In the meantime, on completing the competition entry forms we became aware of one glaring problem. We had reached a stage where any kind of success might lead to a fair amount of international recognition; having the same name as a currently famous group from the USA suddenly seemed wrong. Waiting till after the event would be too late – if we were ever going to change our name, now was the time.

20

Life on the Edge

I realised early on in life that there lurked in me something of a property developer. Back when my O Level History course was focused on the history of architecture, I developed a passion for the subject. My Belgian grandfather's creation of an entire seaside resort was a story which fascinated and inspired me, and I dabbled before I left for college in home improvements that my parents reluctantly implemented, to my immense satisfaction when they proved successful.

Resisting change, Mam and Dad couldn't understand why a door should be moved to improve access to my newly designed kitchen, but their annoyingly precocious teen daughter had the answers and the tenacity to see it through, and be credited with justified appreciation. A grandiose library worthy of any stately home, complete with floor-to-ceiling dark-stained hardwood shelving, was created in the old 'Girls' Room' once all but I had flown the nest, and I commissioned (courtesy of the parental purse) my sister's hobby-carpenter husband to do the honours. It became the best room in the house and just the kind of man cave my dad didn't know he wanted, being a literary type and with his retirement-project Open University degree still a twinkle in his sixty-something eye.

And so, when the Quartet decided we needed our own house, where we could work uninterrupted at any hour of the day or night, I led the hunt. Being mid-academic year, it soon became clear that no student-style rental accommodation was available, so I suggested to my parents that investment in a house purchase in the great City of Manchester could be a good use of their hard-earned life savings. They didn't immediately refuse, so I set to work trawling the estate agents in the vicinity of our present lodgings in halls, so as to quickly offer a concrete option to their 'in principle'. In no time I had narrowed it down to a few candidates, with one particular favourite, and invited them along for a viewing one afternoon in December. With the rest of the Quartet in tow, we approached the door to No.5 Edge Lane, Chorlton-cum-Hardy, where the agent was waiting to show us around.

It was a substantial house, from the 1930s and with the generous proportions that era offered. It came well – if scruffily – furnished, the central heating worked, the wiring was intact and there were five good-sized bedrooms. This was great – we'd be able to have one each and also dedicate a room entirely to practising, with music stands and chairs permanently erected, never needing to be cleared away or tidied up. There was even off-street parking for Ian's Hillman Hunter, so loading up instruments would be easy. The clincher was on entering the kitchen-diner; there in the centre of the room was a square dining table and four chairs, as if we were expected. We laughed and beamed at the prospect of making this our workplace and home, a Quartet House to match our seriousness and single-minded devotion.

Luckily, this was the 1970s and, though it probably seemed a lot at the time, the price tag of £15,999 was easily procured by mortgage from one of Dad's business contacts; in the event, he got it for £15K on the nose. He named a ridiculously generous nominal rent of £8 per week each, and we returned to Hartley Hall that night full of the news of our imminent escape. I was chuffed to bits as, at only seventeen years old, I had brokered my first of many property deals, standing myself in good stead for a life in classical music, where buying, renovating and selling the home you live in is pretty much the only route to a pension of any kind. (I just Googled Manchester house sales and saw that the next-door house sold in 2020 for over half a million. What a shame we didn't hold on to ours!)

In a bizarre twist to this tale of independent bravado, the warden of Hartley Hall, a rather insipid, annoying man of little imagination or character, took offence at the news of our departure. Hadn't he allowed Mike and Ian special dispensation to remain in halls despite their being in the second year? Hadn't he allowed us to rehearse late into the night in his Chapel? (No, he usually tried to throw us out.) Wasn't I too young to be living off campus? When none of his arguments worked, he pulled out what he considered to be his trump card. As warden, he had been appointed 'in loco parentis' to me, still ostensibly a minor. My dad's rejoinder (with the help of Mam's scholarly Latin training) put him in his place.

"We are ipsa parentes so I think that trumps your in loco, gratias tibi valde!"

So, as we approached the Christmas holidays with the exciting prospect of our house-move to start off the spring term, there was still the not-inconsiderable question of finding a new group name to concern us. Without it, we couldn't send off our Portsmouth entry form, and the deadline was imminent.

Frantic brainstorming and head-scratching took over our lives for a few weeks. Our North-East heritage suddenly seemed less important now that we were based in the North-West, but it felt disloyal to choose Manchester over Middlesbrough, so geographic considerations were ditched. Looking at composers' names, we considered Britten, Aram (after Katchaturian), Dmitri and Shostakovich, then realised the latter two were taken. And who were we to assume the name of some of the great composers with whom we'd had no links? We knew we wanted something exotic and looked at the usual Italianesque names, based on musical terminology – Allegro (too like Allegri), Presto (too fast), Bellissima (too cheesy), Stradivari (totally unrealistic). And anyway, we weren't Italian. We felt we needed something strong and earthy – like our Northern roots but more global.

We were all seated in Eleanor Warren's office, heads in hands as another series of names bit the dust and frustration threatened to bring yet another day to an inconclusive close. Suddenly, the head of the Head of Strings spun around to face a huge portrait that was hanging behind her chair. A kindly smiling figure was staring out at us, handsome and serious in his grand armchair and tailored tweed suit.

"What about him?!" exclaimed Eleanor, beaming with the thrill of her revelatory idea.

"Who is he?" we chorused in such perfect unison you'd swear we'd played together since childhood.

"Adolph Brodsky! One of the founding fathers of this very institution and a brilliant violinist and teacher. He was Russian but he settled in Manchester, to lead the Hallé; he pretty much assured its place as the musical capital of England at the time."

Further quizzing revealed that he had also been a friend of Tchaikovsky, had premiered and championed the violin concerto after its dedicatee Leopold Auer had declared it unplayable, and had formed his own quartet, to whom Elgar had dedicated his one and only work for the genre.

We all tried the name out, rolling it around on our tongues to see how it sounded. The Brodsky String Quartet. It was certainly strong, with an exotic flavour that nevertheless didn't sound too pretentious. And we could claim the right to use a Russian name, which by default paid tribute to our love of Shostakovich, as Mr Brodsky was so inextricably linked with our place of study and Manchester as a whole. We liked it.

With this momentous decision taken, the sense of relief was huge. We quickly completed the entry form with our chosen title and stuffed it in an envelope ready for early posting the next day. Christmas was coming and we could now relax for a week or two, then take up residence in our quartet home to begin work in earnest with the start of the new term. As we descended the grand staircase to the college refectory below, there was a lovely festive atmosphere and we made a beeline for the bar. I wasn't old enough to drink yet, but they made an exception this night and a bottle of bubbly was cracked open to welcome in the group's new era.

Soon afterwards we were *Driving Home For Christmas*, probably sitting in the same traffic jam Chris Rea was stuck in as he penned this evocative perennial hit. Yet another Middlesbrough musician, he was the son of a locally famous Italian/Irish ice cream-making family whose café had been a frequent haunt of ours as we trekked up Linthorpe Road to orchestra. Though the song wasn't released till a decade later, this was the year he wrote it, as the snow fell onto excited and weary travellers, my first Christmas home after flying the nest.

It was good to be back, reunited with family as well as old friends and traditions. Carol singing on Christmas Eve brought many TYO chums back together from our various new lives, so that departing once more for college in the cold January rain brought a fresh sense of homesickness and nostalgia. No.5 Edge Lane looked drab and unwelcoming, arriving straight from the festive comforts of parental home life, and it had a musty smell about it. The cold and damp seemed to have pervaded the walls, and the old heating system took a few days to make a difference. We set to work in a nesting frenzy, each taking their own room and filling it with personal touches, the communal areas becoming warm and inviting with every added lamp or picture, particularly the front room, which was designated the practice room. All our music, accumulated over seven years of togetherness, finally found a home in a set of carefully catalogued shelves, all neatly labelled. A state-of-the-art four-way music stand was erected – custom-built in brushed steel by Ian's dad – partnered by four chairs, and we ceremoniously held the first rehearsal in our exclusive new studio.

What a feeling, knowing there'd be no interruptions, no curfew and no limit to the noise we could make. (We'd already spoken to the neighbours – a house of dubious-looking bedsits where no one seemed particularly bothered what we got up to next-door. We had thoughtfully chosen the room that had no communal wall with theirs, to ensure limited sound leakage.) Even though we were now all four students with individual timetables and demands from college, there was an understanding that rehearsals took priority and, if we all found ourselves at home at the same time, we were expected to report for duty in the now newly Marine Blue-painted Practice Room.

Eventually there was an acceptance that start-times should be planned, so as not to waste each other's time waiting around, but no rehearsal was ever given an end-time, such was the expectation to be totally devoted to the cause and willing to continue till it felt right to stop. This later led to impassioned debates as one or other of us wished to go to the pub with non-Quartet friends, practise our instrument, work on essays or assignments, go to the cinema, or any other normal activity young people get up to. But in the beginning we pretty much did everything together anyway, so it wasn't really an issue.

Further exploration of the area around the house revealed some excellent shops, including a supermarket just ten minutes' walk away. There was a quaint little enclave around the corner, with an ancient half-timbered pub and a real feel of country village about it; this was Chorlton Green. At only four minutes' walk, the Horse and Jockey became our local. Just behind the house, a couple of blocks away, was the start of a huge heathland, Ivy Green, excellent for walks and fresh air. Best of all, right there on our road, adjoining the next-door house, was a tarmac play area perfect for footie. Chorlton-cum-Hardy was turning out to be a real find.

In the name of domestic harmony, there was a rota for shopping and cooking, a kitty for shared expenses and a vague, informal cleaning schedule, with the ineffectual use of an ancient old Hoover found in the basement next to an even older washing machine, which mangled one's clothes to a twisted oblivion. (I immediately set to planning a self-contained basement flat conversion for possible future income, then noticed some rather impressive fungi growing from the concrete floor and realised it was too big a job, even given my considerable interior design experience.)

For a short time, we stuck to a regime wherein we ate together every evening, each one with their speciality meal. Whilst home that Christmas, I had asked Mam for her basic recipes, the ones she had seemed to do so effortlessly on a daily basis for as long as I could remember. So I came armed with a little notebook with my scrawled instructions for tomato sauce, cauliflower cheese, chicken and rice, pastry, some of which I managed to produce with moderate success. With the exception of one particular night.

Ian had invited special guests over for dinner – Anne, the ballet Madame from his répétiteur days, and her husband Tim. We wanted to impress them so I was designated chef and chose to make a chicken casserole. For ease I bought a pre-cooked chicken from the local supermarket and tore it to shreds, poured in a tin of Homepride Cook-in-Sauce and threw it in the oven. I reckon I must have got confused and thought I was making a chicken pie, which Mam used to do by this method, except she'd have used her own sauce and fresh mushrooms to bulk it out. This paltry, decimated 'pulled' poultry was totally inadequate for a casserole-style dish for six. Everyone was eating politely till Tim could help himself no longer and, holding up a sliver of meat, declared, "Well, I think I've found a bit of chicken. Anyone else?" My embarrassment was dissipated by our laughs and I never allowed myself to be volunteered as head chef again.

As for my colleagues, Ian's speciality was a risotto with Campbell's Tomato Soup as its base, followed by a comfortingly childish blancmange of tinned pineapple, jelly and Carnation Milk, which we all adored. Alex came armed with his standard mince and mash – in Cambridge this had been Wonder Mash granules made up with boiled water, but here he progressed to real potatoes. Mike had varied success with a toad-in-the-hole, more often than not coming out as a glutinous stodge as he'd forgotten to preheat the oil. The scream of "Jack!!" from the kitchen usually accompanied one of his cooking sessions and elicited my ready help. I at least knew how to make Yorkshire puddings. In fact, I considered myself such an expert that I once, around that time, entered the kitchen of a pub serving Sunday roast with mediocre specimens of the fare, to offer my tips on the perfect technique. My mother always said to heat the oil thoroughly, I told them. I think they were gracious, but I cringe at the memory.

Before long our inward-looking exclusivity seemed a touch over the top. Which other string quartet would choose to live together, never mind spend all their leisure time in each other's company as well? Soon there was a healthy mix of other student friends in and out the door, and we avoided being too insular, though our mates probably thought the whole thing a bit precious and self-seeking. Middlesbrough friends weren't at all surprised – they'd grown up with us.

Alex, being the artist, got to work creating a huge mural on the upstairs sitting room wall, depicting a string quartet of course, in abstract shapes and sweeping strokes. It somehow resembled his scribblings on our big Dover Edition full scores of Beethoven, Schubert, Mozart and Brahms, great arrows arcing across the musical phrases, scrawled comments like 'Inversion of theme', 'Counterpoint' or 'Development', 'Neapolitan 6th!' plus an analysis of the entire key structure. All done in biro, this graphic calligraphy was intended to last, displaying a precocious and assured self-belief in his analytical skills.

His year in Cambridge had been responsible for this newfound aspect to life, belonging to every musical group going, all with their special acronyms, from CUMS (Cambridge University Music Society) to CUCO (the Chamber Orchestra), and CUSO (Symphony Orchestra). (One wonders what the Netball Team was dubbed). But he must have been missing this rarefied and intensive environment. There he discovered his academic fascination for the form and structure of the pieces we had hitherto been assimilating as naturally as food and drink.

Of course, we had all been expected to delve into this kind of specialised and detailed content when preparing for school exams, and certainly now in weekly lectures and theory tutorials. But no one relished it like he did, and it gave us all a greater sense of the why and wherefore of our decision-making in rehearsals, backup for arguments on interpretation, foundation for the things that came naturally. Debates became more passionate as the level of language increased, with a competitive element in the form of outdoing each others' use of long words and notational terms, as well as who could be proven to have the most acute ear.

Arguments over tuning became micro-managed, each offering advice to our colleagues on placing a note higher or lower in increments barely audible to the human ear but apparently screamingly out of tune to any one of us. Non-musicians may be hard-pressed to hear the difference between what we players can manage to find fault with. Many of the notes in my cello parts have directions over them to be higher or lower to fit in the general tuning of the chord around me.

"Jack, that B flat is too high."

"It's not a B flat, it's an A sharp! It needs to be high as it's the leading note to the B minor chord on the next bar!"

"But I can't place my E tritone – it's clashing!"

"Well, you're the seventh going down to resolve on the minor third, so you should be lower anyway!"

"Play it then, everyone, without vibrato."

"You're too high! Lower!" (Moves one billimeter.)

"Not that low – now you're exaggerating!"

"I haven't been able to play an open string for the last hour – is everyone hearing that? Should we tune?"

And on it goes: the need for impeccable spacing of perfect fourths and fifths for maximum purity of timbre; bow changes on long-held notes, for instance in Shostakovich – how to make them inaudible, changing in staggered sequence so as to ensure seamlessness; covering free open strings lightly with a spare finger so they don't interfere with the written chord, especially important for me as the cello resonates more than the smaller instruments.

We rehearse this stuff in microscopic detail – not just us, all musicians – but we were getting well stuck into it at this early age and managing to turn it into another source of rich competitiveness. Ian's keyboard skills and harmonic understanding quite often led him to the piano to illustrate his point and the other two were pretty proficient in that area too. And Mike and Ian would face each other, violins in hand, as if ready to duel, and play random chords that the other would have to repeat, note for note. It wasn't an easy game as they chose more and more obscure combinations of notes, laughing as they tried to outwit each other. But along with this highbrow repartee there was still plenty of idiotic banter – we hadn't lost our juvenile taste for farce and hilarity altogether.

As we settled into our new life in Chorlton-cum-Hardy and began to grow accustomed to the group's new name, a newspaper article appeared announcing the entries for the Portsmouth Competition and giving a preview to the repertoire, members of the jury, public access, tickets and so on. We being listed as one of the entries, under our new title, prompted a certain Edgar Fuchs to write to us, tentatively enquiring how we had come up with the name, and what connection we had with Mr Brodsky? Imagining we were about to be told we had no right to use it, we explained the connection with Manchester and our college, and prepared to defend ourselves. There was no need – the next letter revealed that this was the son of the founder cellist of the Brodsky Quartet, Carl Fuchs, and he was delighted that we had resurrected the name and would be paying homage to the legacy left by the original group. He promised to send us some memorabilia from the time and we awaited the promised package with great anticipation.

He didn't disappoint. There were some old programmes from Brodsky String Quartette concerts in and around the Manchester area, one in Bowdon Festival, where we were about to give our first local concert since arriving here. We were excited to find a score of the Elgar Quartet, with the composer's dedication to Brodsky and marked up with comments.

There was a book written by one Anna Brodsky, which turned out to be a memoir by Adolph's wife recounting their travels and adventures throughout Europe and America before they settled here. We were thrilled to read of his playing folk music with peasants in the fields of his homeland, and fighting for the rights of his fellow musicians as a formidable union trailblazer in New York; our namesake was turning out to be a true soulmate.

The memoir proved invaluable years later when I came to write the sleeve note for our Tchaikovsky Quartets recording, containing as it did detailed descriptions of the first private performances of the works, the composer reduced to tears of joy and gratitude, his closeness with Brodsky palpable.

And most endearingly, in the parcel was a set of photographs depicting our man, not in his formal attire or the pose that we had seen in the college portrait, but surrounded by family and friends. One such sepia image depicted a happy group, including Edvard Greig no less, eating and drinking in a countryside setting. The caption carefully inked at the bottom of the frame caught our eye and had us all gasping in coincidental wonder: 'Brodsky and friends picnicking on the Heath near his home in Chorlton-cum-Hardy.'

21

Portsmouth

I think I'm right in saying that the Portsmouth String Quartet Competition in 1979 was the first such international contest ever in the world, or at least one of the first. If this is the case, what an extraordinary fact it is. With so many long-established and celebrated competitions worldwide, inferring kudos and accolades, as well as leg-ups in the industry, on deserving young musicians – pianists, violinists, singers, conductors, composers and so on – yet for the string quartet, in some eyes the pinnacle of musical expression, nothing. This puts into context our sense of amazement when arriving at music college to find a pitiful amount of importance or time being devoted to the genre of chamber music, and just how much we felt like second-class citizens for wanting to concentrate our efforts and ambitions on this goal, which wasn't even deemed worthy of competitive status.

Surprising as it was, the Portsmouth Competition attracted a lot of attention and spawned many imitations, including Banff in Canada four years later, where we also joined the inaugural list of laureates. Portsmouth was the brainchild of local music and arts enthusiasts Richard Sotnick (Mayor of Portsmouth) and Peter Zander. After the first decade, with four triennial events under its belt, its success was proven and the competition was moved to London and renamed as such. But the small naval city of its humble beginnings put on quite a show and is rightly proud of the legacy created.

Groups from all over the world were enticed to take part and, being the Easter holidays, university halls of residence were available as comfortable accommodation perfectly suited to the job: four-bedroom apartments with kitchen, bathroom and, crucially, a large central quartet-sized living area ideal for rehearsal, complete with a set of music stands. We were one of twenty groups admitted to the finals and checked into our allocated flat with a healthy mix of excitement and trepidation. I think by now we had upgraded our expectations from winners of the Most Promising Young Group to Outright Winners. As we took our seats in the auditorium for the welcome speech by the competition president Yehudi Menuhin, I genuinely pitied all the other competitors around me who would inevitably go home disappointed.

Following this introduction, the business in hand was to draw lots to determine the playing order in Round 1, which was to be held over the following two days. Things got off to a bad start straight away as I climbed the stairs to the stage to draw our number, only to reveal we would be playing first on the second day; sessions started at 9am. For any musician early morning performances are not to be desired, but for us four hopelessly late-risers, this was seriously bad news.

Inevitably, we had travelled south with an entourage, my parents leading the way. Their advice following this disastrous start was to set an alarm for 6am then shower, breakfast and warm up for a couple of hours, so that by nine o'clock the day already felt well underway. It was good advice and we followed it to our advantage, playing well in the first round once we'd conquered our nerves. But having parents in tow is never a good feeling. Yes, I was still only seventeen and we were by far the youngest group there, but we soon got a reputation around the place for the over-zealous support of these hangers-on. They would accompany us to later competitions too; on one occasion I remember overhearing a music journalist describing us as 'the ones with the pushy parents', as if we were some kind of Jackson Five boy band. The insult was particularly stinging as it had been no one's idea but ours to form this group, stick to it and make it our lives' work. The idea that credit (or blame) could be imparted on my parents was anathema.

On top of this sense of being babysat or nurtured in some way, which was embarrassing enough beside all the other groups who'd arrived independently and stood on their own eight feet, was the added stress of their being always around at these tricky times. The pressure at competitions is huge – having to ready yourself for concert-standard performance at any time of day, in unnatural circumstances and in front of professionals who know all the works backwards. It wasn't easy feeling compelled to spend time with parents when I'd rather have gone off to do some practice. They would treat us to meals out, which was of course kind, but meant keeping up the conversation and being attentive to them, rather than relaxing alone or having banter and understanding between just the four of us or amongst our peers. (We also had to deal with their disappointment, as well as our own, if things went badly.)

Terry too had made the trip south to support his 'Kids', along with Eleanor Warren who, being best friends with some of the jury, considered herself an honorary member of their team, free to offer opinions and guidance. How this was allowed I'll never know: in recent years I have been invited to judge at several major competitions and there are always strict rules in place, keeping the jury separate from players and public alike until the competition is completely over. But in the old days I guess things were different, or maybe she just ignored the rules. She would seek out the judges at mealtimes and share a drink at the bar, gleaning updates and – frankly – interfering.

In the evenings we would be in the pub with Terry, he knocking back double shots and smoking himself to an early grave, when I for one thought we should have been peacefully in our own space and, crucially, not having to entertain these extras. But it did lead to a bit of light relief when things got heavy. Terry had made it his business early on to add some important non-musical aspects to our education by introducing us to the joys of backgammon and cribbage, both of which he excelled at. He took no prisoners and regularly won money off us poor students. But at times like these it was a welcome diversion from the stress.

During these evenings we also enjoyed some camaraderie with the other quartets, nervously bonding over the shared excruciating experience of competition. We likened the whole thing to a football league and made jokes about major signings and free transfers between groups, devising a whole load of imaginary new prizes, including the Tampax Award for the best all-female group. My feminist self hadn't developed sufficiently to see this as a slanderous piece of sexist nonsense, so I laughed along happily.

I wasn't too naive, though, to be shocked and offended that the jury was made up exclusively of men. Were there really no female experts in chamber music available to be chosen or deemed worthy of inclusion? In hindsight, I see it was the norm; probably no one even noticed the glaring omission at the time.

But, also in hindsight, I see we unintentionally made a big gaffe regarding this self-important line of men at the back of the hall, hunched over their softly glowing lamps and scores. As the seventies drew to a close, we had updated our black shirts and white ties to another staple of the era: brown and cream. I was in a dress – demure autumn shades in crimplene, another of

Mam's creations – but when the boys marched onto the stage in those brown shirts, Menuhin and his mostly Jewish team must have quaked in their boots at the sight. Why did no one warn us against this obvious faux-pas? Our two pedagogues of the same religious background who'd bothered to come all that way to support us would have been more help in that small tip than any amount of beer they ended up buying us.

We did well in the competition, playing to our own high expectations, and won a lot of praise from our peers as well as from the public. That set work for Round One, the terrifying K590 of Mozart, was clearly chosen with a view to sorting out the men from the boys (not to mention us girls). It starts with the whole group playing a unison passage involving running scales, fiendish for the intonation and ensemble. Each movement has its pitfalls, the last being a tongue-twister for the fingers, calling for dexterity and clarity, as well as beauty, at top speed. But for cellists the work holds another challenge altogether.

Long singing phrases high up the instrument give the cello a starring role unusual in the Classical Era, and all the more scary for it. Written for Friedrich Wilhelm II, King of Prussia, who was a keen amateur cellist, one can imagine Wolfie's delight as he stretched the poor man's abilities to the limits. "*You wanted an interesting cello part? There you go!*" Martin Lovett of the Amadeus Quartet actually refused to play this work later in their career, so much did he fear its exposed high-altitude moments. Stepping out at 9am to play that work, in a hall of punishingly dry acoustic, was an Everest in itself. But we scaled the heights and, with the Ravel, our work of choice to follow the Mozart, we proved ourselves equal to the challenge and earned a place in the second round.

Here we were in our comfort zone; a new work by Alun Hoddinott was handed out to be learnt on the spot by all the successful groups, along with another work of choice from a list of late Classical or Romantic quartets. We had chosen the Schubert

G Major, a monster of a piece at around forty-five minutes, but a great favourite of ours. We were well used to working on new pieces quickly – at College we'd already become guinea-pigs for friends in the composition department – so the Hoddinott didn't pose too many problems. After our performance of the Schubert, I remember one of the other British quartets coming to congratulate us, bemoaning the ease with which a bunch of kids had dispatched that giant of the repertoire. I was chuffed at the praise but also humbled by their self-deprecating honesty.

It's never an easy choice to make at a competition – whether to attend the other groups' performances or stay away in your own bubble. The former can offer either a boost to confidence or a debilitating sense of hopelessness, but staying away isn't much better, as you can only imagine the worst... Sitting in the audience to hear the opposition, I was inspired by many of the works I was hearing, some for the first time. Schumann A Major by the Takács-Nagy (now the Takács) Quartet blew me away, and I made sure to add it to our repertoire as soon as possible, where it remained for many years. Pete Hanson – who is now a close friend and neighbour – and his quartet played Debussy beautifully. That made its way into our playlist soon afterwards.

Also seated in the audience, I distinctly remember feeling sorry for the Endellion Quartet, who were giving such a neat and fresh performance of the Brahms B flat. "Isn't it a shame that players this good won't win anything!" I patronisingly and misguidedly whispered to one of my colleagues, sure in the knowledge by now that we would supersede all opposition. We had our opus 95 ready for the all-Beethoven Final, and we were raring to go. Gone were the days of coming a cropper when presenting Beethoven in competitions – here it was actually on the curriculum. And we'd grown up; our parts and scores were full of those intellectual observations and analysis – 'Truncated development!', 'False recap!'– arcing arrows as well as bows, depicting this magical music's trajectory in academic as well as practical terms.

How the smug smile was wiped from my face when we gathered in the hall for the announcement that evening, only to hear that we hadn't progressed to the final. Oh, and the Endellion had – where was my misplaced sympathy now! (We have laughed together about this since, as they have become friends and we've collaborated several times over recent years.) It emerged later that Ms Warren had decided we weren't ready for the kind of pressure and fame that would come from winning one of the main prizes, so had persuaded the jury not to admit us to the final. Instead she suggested they award the prize we'd set our sights on right at the beginning of this adventure, but which now felt like the booby – or at best, consolation – prize. We didn't want to be the Most Promising Young Quartet now – we felt we deserved more.

Undoubtedly, had we progressed to the Final, we wouldn't have won – the Takács-Nagy Quartet took First Prize, and deservedly. The Endellion were second, equally deserving, but none of the groups had been together as long as we had, even though their combined ages were well above ours, so we felt outdone by latecomers, however well they played. And Eleanor was right, they were of an age more ready to take advantage of the benefits of winning: an extensive concert tour, radio exposure and access to agents. Nevertheless, sitting in the audience listening to the final round, we felt cheated and frustrated, especially as the group from Czechoslovakia who'd chosen our opus 95 didn't do it justice and looked awful in their hastily purchased George of Asda gaudy shirts and ties.

Later that night, after drowning our sorrows in rather too much beer and cider, we stumbled back to our digs, where we met the victorious Takács guys coming out of the lift. "Bravo!!" we drunkenly cheered them, eager to show we had no hard feelings and admiring as we truly were of their excellence and polish. Indulgently amused by our youthful outpouring of emotion, they put their fingers to their lips to shush us, out of consideration for the sleeping residents as much as for their own modesty.

The competition drew to a close with a Gala Prizewinners' Concert in the larger and more acoustically forgiving Guildhall, with first and second place groups performing a quartet each, followed by a joint-forces performance by all the prizewinners, including us, as backing band for the Bach Double Violin Concerto. Menuhin and his great friend Yfrah Neaman took the solo parts, and we felt proud to have been included in this select group. We returned to Manchester with heads held high, glad for something solid to add to our biography.

- A December 16 diary page (Week 51), Thursday.
- "QUARTET" and "1975" visible vertically.
- "CLEVELAND" vertically along one strip.
- "Friday, July 29th, 1977" — fragment about walking to the Chateau, a coach to Montreux, rain, a concert.
- "It is my birthday!! I got 3 cards (Joy & Pete...), a letter off Ivan, got up, had a shower, a necklace, a writing pad..." — dated Monday, 24th May, 1976.
- "Tuesday 10th August 1976" fragment mentioning Shostakovich — "the Russian composer... a fellow musician and human being... was denounced..."
- A letter dated "12.4.76" beginning "Dear Jacky, This came this morning. I am very pleased. Thank you ... Many congratulations. He would be... Lots of love — the Palm-gar! / Have a good time with NYO. / Best wishes from us / A.J.R."
- A letter dated "June 7" beginning "Dear Jacqueline, It was on ... that I first came across ... the opportunity ... I was very much hoping ... Once more I thank you ... a splendid performer ... I could hear again ... With all good wishes for you and your family. Very thankfully, ..." signed "Lutoslawski".
- "Dear Jacky, I don't feel I suppose to you my..." — a longer letter signed "Julian Raymond".
- A Wednesday, 19th April, 1978 entry: "I got a letter of acceptance at BNCM! It was a lovely hot summery day — we all sat in Joy & Pete's garden in the sunshine... waffles there... What a lot Katie Emily Tom... all wonderful. But my God, the description of Shapely — a baby — good grief! Women are..."
- A page fragment mentioning: "Went back to the Purcell Room and felt anti-climactic... suddenly became really confident in our artists' room. What a performance we gave! It was incredible and we were so relaxed. But the best was yet to come — Cleveland String Quartet — well, what can I say — professional — perfect — stunning! I collected our autographs afterward... it was really wonderful. Our teachers were happy, we were happy, and the public, including many real musicians, were extremely impressed. Together we felt proud and happy and light. Everyone felt what we had — a great heart — and then a concert in the CFH of Okanagan YO (really good) and Kontor — always offers..."
- "C.S.I.G. — Playing pieces every time / The journal gets together / the bits of fun and there is a real cake in every... / Brahms, Beethoven, Shostakovich, Shield / Never da Capo / Will like / So come / We grand"
- Various other fragments: "INTERLUDE", "WHOLE BOOK", "by Mike C..."
- Vertical text at right: "on this that I am a ..."

Taking the applause for the Elgar Cello Concerto in Rhein-Mosel-Halle, summer 1978.

8 EVENING GAZETTE, Thurs., September 14, 1978

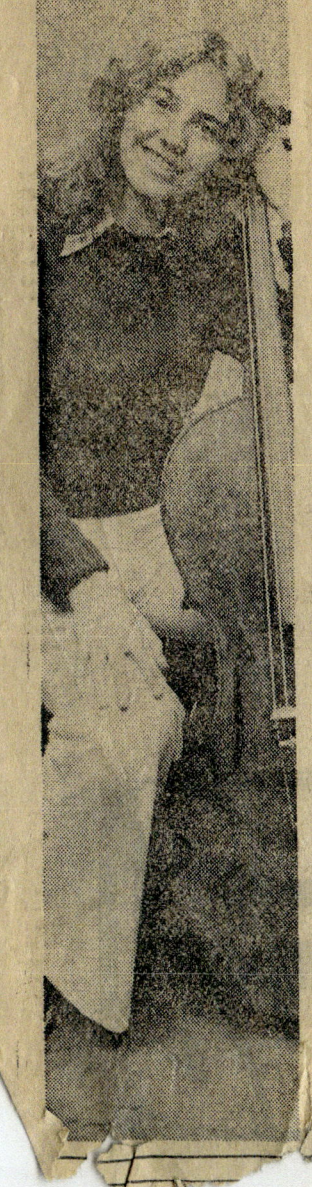

Cellist packs her bags for college

PACKING her suitcase is becoming a way of life for cello player Jacqueline Thomas, left, who was with the Cleveland Youth Orchestra on their recent visit to Oberhausen, West Germany.

Jacqueline, who is 17, arrived back in England, only to dash off to Canterbury to see three of her sisters who live there. Then she made the journey home to Cleveland to prepare for taking off again, this time to start a four-year course at Manchester's Royal Northern College of Music.

"I have been very busy, but I have enjoyed myself," said Jacqueline, the daughter of Francine and Alfred Thomas, whose eight children are all musical.

The youngest of the family, who live at The Crescent, Linthorpe, Middlesbrough, Jacqueline played the Elgar cello concerto before an audience of 600 at Oberhausen city hall. And she wasn't nervous.

She's a member of the Cleveland String Quartet, and has fingers crossed that she and the other musicians will turn professional when they have finished their studies.

I made the papers on my own!

Pre-concert rehearsal, guesting for Madame Anne's Ballet School, Billingham 1978.

Mr Brodsky lends an air of serenity to our new rehearsal studio at Edge Lane.

Adolph Brodsky and friends in the fields near Chorlton-cum-Hardy.

The newly renamed Brodsky Quartet in the fields near Chorlton-cum-Hardy.

Cellist's-eye view of Claudio Abbado, ECYO '79.

Luxuriating in Hotel Danieli, Venice.

Busking on the steps of La Fenice.

The infamous brown shirts.

The Brodsky Quartet, whose members are RNCM students, has already achieved considerable success at international competitions

From a newspaper clipping for the Manchester Evening News – resplendent in tails and dickie bows (and white socks?!). The magnificent floral car crash of a frock must have been one of Mam's creations.

A concert in Bowden, 1979.

Receiving the Menuhin Prize at Portsmouth, April 1979 with Yehudi Menuhin, Richard Sotnick and Yfrah Neaman.

The Menuhin Prize Certificate.

On the steps of the Czech Filharmonie, Prague, Autumn 1979.

The Janecek Medal.

Film still at Evian Competition, 1980.

With the Kodaly Quartet, touring Mendelssohn Octet, 1980.

Another dubious publicity shot... wonky ties and collars... squinting and sandals. But I get to be one of the lads in my men's suit from Oxfam!

'Entertaining' the Ballet School in a bit of Scott Joplin.

In rehearsal for Brahms Double Concerto in the Maltings, summer 1981.

First publicity shot with Paul, 1982. At last, a professional photographer, although... shadows, crumpled shirts and dickie bows, trouser legs of varying length... and I'm out of focus!

That's more like it – back in the Oxfam suit and ever so hip!

With Terry shortly before his retirement concert.

Back at the Town Hall with Mam for the Teesside University Honorary MA Award Ceremony.

22

Post-Portsmatic Stress

On the long journey north, we were newly inspired to pursue our goal of worldwide renown and make the most of all the opportunities available to us. In college, Nobuko Imai had joined the teaching staff straight from her recently quit post in the Vermeer Quartet, and she was an absolute joy to study under. Her viola playing was exquisite, her energy intoxicating. I remember bringing her the Mozart, that epic we'd had to play in Portsmouth, and how she reduced the fiddly passagework of the last movement to its bare bones, singing in her high-pitched sweet voice what sounded for all the world like a Japanese folk song. Suddenly the line was clear and the music spoke through any annoying technical difficulties; it made perfect sense.

Happily, her exit from the Vermeer had been amicable and her ex-colleagues soon followed her, with their new violist Jerry Horner, to perform and give masterclasses in college. We immediately liked them, as people and as players, their concerts having a contagious sense of spontaneity as well as masterful polish. They also seemed to like us, and taught with respect and consideration to our longevity, adding finesse to our still-unrefined edges without taking away the honesty of our approach. Their cellist readily offered me help with tricky parts like the Mozart, something I'd never had from Terry, whose cello playing was entirely instinctive. He tended to mostly rely on just two fingers on his left hand, leaving him terrified of anything above fourth position. All those soaring cello parts were out of his league, weirdly, even though he was our mentor. And I never felt I could take problematic quartet parts to my individual teachers, as they would consider them inappropriate for cello lessons. This may have been entirely in my head, but there it was. Someone like Marc Johnson, who lived and worked for his quartet, could offer the kind of help I needed.

Inspired by this experience, and by the encouragement we'd received from one of the jury members in particular, Sigmund Nissel of the Amadeus Quartet, we applied and won a second scholarship to join that group's masterclass course the following year at the newly created Britten-Pears School in Suffolk, offshoot of the Aldeburgh Festival. Following our success at Portsmouth, college was starting to take us more seriously and we were chosen to represent them on two exchange trips – in Frankfurt and Prague – also the following year, and more concerts were coming in for local music societies and festivals. So approaching the end of my first year, I had a lot to look forward to.

In the meantime, there was the small matter of sitting my A Levels. I'd been keeping up with revision and practice papers in my own time, such as it was with all the college classes, cello lessons, Portsmouth build-up and preparation concerts that had come before. Now I had to knuckle down and see this thing through. I'd promised my teachers, my parents and myself that I wouldn't chicken out – now the time had come to prove it.

Leaving for Middlesbrough with all my old school books in a suitcase felt like a journey back in time, especially turning up at my short-lived sixth form college to sit the first paper. So much had happened since I left in a flurry of excited decisiveness just a year before and I felt more grown-up and experienced than my neighbours in the examination hall. After the trials of an international competition in front of luminaries from classical music's higher echelons, walking into an A Level exam hall felt like a doddle. The Music and French papers seemed to go well and I headed into the weekend with only English to worry me the following week. I had all my revision notes to pore over – Austen, Milton, Heaney, and... wait! Where were my notes on Shakespeare? An entire exercise book containing all my meaningful scribblings and quotes designed to get me through the exam – nowhere to be found. Which could mean only one thing: they were back in Manchester.

I dialled the Edge Lane number. The wall phone on the landing rang for a long time... it was Saturday morning and there wasn't much sign of life. Then a sleepy Ian picked up, heard my desperation and did the honours, hunting out the precious notes from my desk. But now what? This was the seventies – there were no computers or mobiles, no email, text or even fax machines. It was by now Saturday lunchtime and the exam was on Monday morning; too late to use the post. Then I had a brainwave. What if Ian would read out all my notes over the phone? I could record him so I'd have it all to listen to at my leisure, not have to take it down in dictation. I could tell he was leafing through the pages and pages of scribble as we spoke, totting up just how long this was going to take. Alone in the house, he was my only hope.

Bless him, he agreed. I set up my old cassette recorder while he got dressed and made himself a coffee, then off he went. I'll never forget the pitiful sound of his voice each time I returned to the phone; still there, orating quotes and annotations from *King Lear* in a non-comprehending, Middlesbrough-inflected monotone.

"Pathetic fallacy here, foreshadowing Gloucester's demise. Alliteration brings military symbolism to the metaphorical device… Anaphora heightens Lear's desperation and descent into lunacy… Shake uses anthro... anthro… pom.... orphism to depict..." Blah,blah,blah...

Somehow Ian's frankly bored ramblings helped the information to stick better than if I was reading the notes myself. The whole exercise saved my exam and, though he has never considered himself a literary type, I can honestly say I owe my English Literature A grade to Ian Belton. (And Music too, to a certain extent, as he had helped me with the dreaded Bach Chorale form. The French was all my own doing!)

When I returned to Manchester shortly after the A Levels trip, I turned eighteen and the boys took me to Chorlton Green for my first legal drink at the Horse and Jockey. For a present, they clubbed together and bought me a leather music case and a shiny mock-gold alarm clock. As term came to an end, us four fully ensconced in our own house, even though I'd left home a year earlier this felt like a landmark moment. I was an adult.

That summer I joined the ECYO, touring Europe with Abbado, Perahia, Pollini and a hundred bright young people from the nine European member states. Bruckner No.7 in the Berlin Philharmonie; Prokofiev *Romeo and Juliet* in the Salzburg Felsenreitschule (that giant cave-like hall, scene of the Familie Von Trapp performance for the gathering Anschluss audience); Mozart Piano Concerto in La Fenice, Venice, followed by a gondola ride with Murray Perahia, staying in the grandeur of the Hotel Danieli. This was a step up from NYO and considerably more grown-up and free. I was on the second desk outside chair – no sexist power games going on here – and there was a strong sisterhood of hip young women from Holland, France and the Irish Republic, who knew their rights and weren't afraid to make some noise, both on and off stage.

Even here, though, I experienced a bit of the old dialect shame. One day I overheard a German violinist showing off his linguistic competence by pointing out disparagingly that I had a regional accent.

„*Sie spricht sehr schlecht Englisch*," he sneered knowingly to his colleague, sure I'd be too uneducated to understand him.

Quick as a flash, and with a pleasant smile, I rejoined, „*Aber kein schlechtes Deutsch!*"

Touché.

I was in good company too; the Middlesbrough contingent was no less formidable than at NYO, quite incredibly making up almost one tenth of this multi-national orchestra.

Before the course began with rehearsals in the French Alps, there was to be a preliminary concert in London, a sort of inauguration of the European Cultural partnership. Under Sir Edward Heath we played the recently adopted EU Anthem – Beethoven's *Ode to Joy* – and were joined by a selection of celebrity musicians, including once more Yehudi Menuhin. In the rehearsal James Judd, resident conductor and Artistic Director of ECYO, excitedly pointed out to our violin soloist that laureates of his recent Portsmouth Competition were in the orchestra behind him. Menuhin beamed and looked around the string section, trying to spot familiar faces.

"Oh, the Endellions?" he asked delightedly, as he scanned the assembled company.

"No, the Brodsky," answered James, somewhat crestfallen.

"Ah, the Brownshirts," mumbled Yehudi. "Well, yes, well done, jolly good," he continued hurriedly to mask his inadvertently rude utterance.

We all smiled wryly, trying to cover up our embarrassment as the rest of the orchestra looked quizzically on.

Later, we had a nice chat with Menuhin and laughed about the jury's nickname for us. There were no hard feelings and he went on to be extremely supportive of us in future years, even inviting us to perform at his seventy-fifth birthday concert near his home in Highgate, truly an honour given the number of string quartets he had come into contact with during the course of his illustrious career.

Back in Edge Lane for the start of the autumn term, we were itching to return to quartet life. To our delight we had been head-hunted by a concert agent. Dave Robson from Darlington, a burly man with a characterful Yorkshire accent, had watched our progress in the North-East with interest then read about our competition success and was eager to get us on his books. His style of management was a little akin to undercover detective work; he would talk of things 'on the grapevine', 'sniffing out' an opportunity or 'hearing a whisper'. It was all very cloak-and-dagger and all the more amusing as we joined in with the spy-novel jargon. His territory was exclusively North-East England, so when later we were approached by Ibbs & Tillett of London, the conflict of interest wasn't considered a problem and we were able to remain loyal to Dave and accept this new suitor with alacrity.

We attended every professional quartet concert on offer at college, taking notes and appraising others' efforts with detailed scrutiny. I found some of these notes amongst the old papers in my mum's house clear-out. Our devotion to duty is touching. Scrawled on the back of a piano volume for want of some note paper, a whole list of observations.

Me: 'Very smooth 'n' elegant. Clear tone. Take time on arpeggios. Nothing rushed. D'yer like the speed?'

Alex: 'We have to apply all their phrasing etc to the faster speed.'

Rehearsals continued to dominate all our spare time as we took on more and more complicated repertoire, including Lutoslawski, a work somewhat improvisatory in its execution, and a similarly experimental quartet by the French/Bulgarian composer André Boucourechliev, titled *Archipel II*. This comprised a huge score with what could only be described as islands of musical extracts, floating apart then being drawn together by linking material in a series of symbols and graphs. Players could choose what and when to play, taking different routes each time, like one of those kids' adventure picture books with a choice of direction at the end of each page to find the treasure.

It was literally like playing a drawing; Alex was in his element. Out came the red biro and in came the sweeping arrows and visual signals. Before long we had deciphered the code depicted in the map and devised a performance we were happy with. (This openness to experimentation later brought us to the attention of composers eager for commissions and we found ourselves inundated with requests to learn this and that new work, till it became too much and we put on the brakes for fear of being pigeonholed.)

As our scheduled trip to Frankfurt and Prague drew near, this was to be one of the pieces we would take, along with some core repertoire and specifically Janáček, which we were eager to play for the Smetana Quartet violist and Janáček expert, Milan Škampa. Excitement for the trip was building when disaster hit – again Ian was struck down by illness. Just as our debut recital back home had been threatened with cancellation, so now was our debut foreign tour. This time though there was no question of his being fit to continue regardless – he was hospitalised and operated on immediately and ordered to convalesce for at least two weeks.

I will never forget the German word for kidney stone – *Nierenstein* – as we had to recount the sad story so many times on arrival in Frankfurt-ohne-Ian. The Hochschule für Musik, with whom our exchange arrangement had been struck, had insisted that we come anyway, take advantage of the teaching on offer and do what we could to fill our scheduled concert as a trio instead of a quartet. We did manage, with a swiftly-learnt Mozart E flat Trio Divertimento (not something you want to learn in a hurry to play to discerning students and teachers at a major German Conservatoire), Beethoven G major Trio (ditto) and to fill the programme I ended up playing a Bach Cello

Suite (double ditto). The famous Gerhard Mantel was the cello professor and I enjoyed a Masterclass with him, but my main memory of this week was of incessant rehearsal and panic!

We did manage, though, to have a bit of fun, bonding with the Cello Quartet who were invited to Manchester for their part in the exchange. They took us out to Bierkellers and for walks in the nearby countryside, and we enjoyed returning their hospitality back home when the time came, a few months later.

The wonderful news had reached us that Ian was sufficiently recovered to fly in and join us for the Prague leg of the trip and we were over the moon to be reunited with him after our long train journey east. Back in our comfort zone of quartet repertoire, we had a quick rehearsal then ventured out to explore this majestic city. Having sampled our first hilariously disappointing taste of Communist-era Cuisine, and taken on the required amount of alcohol to make it palatable, we returned to our beds tired and giddy, ready for a good night's sleep.

The cold and austerity of Soviet-style student digs was a shock, especially compared to Hartley Hall back in Manchester, where the heating was always on full pelt despite the rainy Mancunian climate rarely dropping below 'mild'. Here, in freezing temperatures, we endured the student accommodation from hell. Each room doubled as a practice room and my neighbour would wake at 6am to start her slow practice of Chopin *Etudes*, the piano right next to my head on the other side of a paper-thin wall. I was too cold to get up and escape, so I lay there cursing and feeling homesick.

Meeting up with the others when the frugal breakfast was served, we would head out to the crisp but feeble sunshine to try to thaw out before classes began. At least Maestro Škampa's teaching studio was warm – in fact, too warm as the low winter sun poured through the high casement windows, mercilessly blinding the poor students within. We watched another group playing to him before it was our turn and I really felt for the cellist who was facing the full impact of the glaring sun, playing with one eye closed to try to escape its force. Many years later at a festival we took part in, I saw a shadow of this young man in a much older one and realised I'd been listening to an early incarnation of the Prazak Quartet!

Whilst in Prague we were taken on excursions to the majestic surrounding countryside – memories of TYO's performances of Smetana's *Vltava* came flooding back as I gazed down on the rushing waters of that mighty river – and within the city's noble buildings. We were awarded the Czechoslovak Contemporary Music Award and subsequently befriended by celebrated composer and national treasure, Petr Eben. He invited us into his home and opened our eyes to the suppression and deprivation of life under Communist rule, especially for those in creative industries. We were to come into contact with many such suffering artists in Eastern Bloc countries over the coming decade, but this first encounter was all the more shocking for our ignorance. We vowed to do all we could to help, performing Petr's quartets in the UK and in Europe whenever possible and perhaps in some small way helping with the pitiful situation.

But our main reason for being there was the daily classes under Maestro Škampa, and what an intense experience that was. Together we would pore over Janáček's original manuscripts, led by this scholarly professor through the meaning behind every ink splodge and chaotic notational doodle. The work on paper was very much a visual encapsulation of the tortured composer's musical outpourings. We learnt a lot about the man, his crazed infatuation with the much younger woman, Kamila Stösslová, his musical style and the Nationalist roots behind it. Škampa was preparing for publication his own edition of the Second Quartet and had made many changes from the version we had grown up with, interpreting some of the indecipherable squiggles differently to those early recordings we'd marvelled at as children, and at odds with our own attempts at this mad and passionate music.

Not all the changes met with our approval. Too many of our favourite chords and notes were changed, based on thin evidence as far as we could tell. The most shocking was the last movement that began, according to our expert, with a *pizzicato* accompaniment to that most wonderfully joyous dance theme, rendering it weak and unbalanced. Then later in the movement, inexplicably, it reverted to *arco*. We dutifully wrote every change in our old parts, Tipp-Exing over the printed notes, which felt like defacing an old friend. We'd lived with these sounds since childhood – this process was painful and confusing.

It's hard to overstate the sentimental connection we felt, and still feel, with this piece – from the very early days, as children gathered around the record player, to much more recently when we took part in Brian Friel's superb play *Performances* and actually shared the stage with the ghost of Janáček, played by Henry Goodman, with Rosamund Pike as his young student, the two passionately debating his music and his muse; it was a highly emotional experience. As students in Manchester, we witnessed a performance by a respected Hungarian quartet which had us loudly and openly booing, to the horror of the rest of the public. What they didn't know was that this group had changed the score, giving all the important 2nd Violin moments to the 1st Violinist. This inexplicable effrontery on the integrity of the composer, always democratic and equal in his part-writing, was so abhorrent to us that we couldn't hold back. (The insult was also on the audience, imagining that no one present would know the piece well enough to care.) How hideously arrogant we must have appeared to our fellow students and teachers present. I'm afraid this image of us probably lasts in the memories of some of our old friends, both in childhood and student days; we were full of our own importance and must have been insufferable at times. At least on this occasion we were arguably justified.

Through the long study sessions with Maestro Škampa, we would argue every point, but to no avail. After all, he had lived with the work his entire career, was a fellow countryman of the composer, and thirty years our senior. Out of politeness, we allowed him to think he'd won us over, but agreed to mostly stick to what we knew. Luckily, we'd learnt the piece from memory, so we could remember all the original notes now cruelly struck from the visual record.

It didn't stop Alex peppering the score in red ink though, just in case.

23

Britten and Britain

It was nearly ten years since my formative experience in Middlesbrough Town Hall, when *Noye's Fludde* swept me away on a wave of musical revelation. Britten's genius for drawing in young players and listeners alike had worked its magic on me, as wind and waves, raindrops and rainbows found ingenious depiction in the notes we played. The composer had been dead only three years when we made our first pilgrimage to his adoptive home of Aldeburgh and Snape, and his spirit was all around on the stoney beaches, in the huge old farm buildings and malt houses, and amidst the golden grasslands of the estuary. We very much regretted so narrowly missing the chance to meet him; close as he was to Shostakovich, the two friends had died within a year of each other. Just as my younger self had mourned the loss of one in my 1975 diary, a touching question was asked the following year after a visit to the opera to hear one of his many great works for the genre: Is this another poor heart failing?

Taking part in the Amadeus Quartet Course in the so-new-you-could-smell-the-paint Britten-Pears School was a joy.

Named after the composer and his close musical collaborator and life partner Sir Peter Pears, who had started the programme of masterclasses just a few years before, the school was a welcome addition to the cultural hub emerging in this quiet backwater. The peaceful surroundings with far-reaching views over the fens made for a sense of calm isolation where study was easy and unrushed. Each student group had its own room, well built with sound-proofing a priority so we really felt alone and undisturbed, and the members of the Amadeus Quartet tripped from one to the other to offer guidance, encouragement and fun.

We brought to the classes Schubert's G Major, one of their confirmed specialities, and some Mozart. Despite their celebrity – they were the absolute top of the tree worldwide and had the longest history of any living quartet so far – they were down to earth and kind to students, with none of the pretensions adopted for show by some pedagogues. It helped that the classes were closed, with no audience to show off to, and this made the whole experience all the more precious and genuine. Driving between the school in Snape and our accommodation, the famous Swiss Cottage Guest House on the seafront in Aldeburgh, one would often pass Peter Schidlof pedalling his pushbike. By far the fittest and most health-conscious member of the Amadeus, it was tragic and surprising that he was the first to die, ending the group's long history, just a few years later. We came across them several times in those final years, including in Paris at the Théâtre des Champs Elysées, scene of Stravinsky's disastrous *Rite* premiere and the NYO's triumphant one. It must have been one of the last concerts they performed together.

Somehow we seem to have made an impression that week in Snape, even though I don't recall there being any student concerts or showcases. Hugh Maguire was running the string courses and Sir Peter Pears was very much around the place, welcoming and gregarious to all, despite the recent loss of his partner and soulmate Britten. The upshot was that we were soon invited back to perform, in The Maltings no less, teaming up with the celebrated clarinettist Thea King in Mozart's famous Clarinet Quintet. I had grown up in the era of 'Watch with Mother' on the BBC and was well aware that the lovely clarinet solo, when it was 'Time to go Home' for Andy Pandy, was played by Thea King. At four or five, I could read well enough to think it a marvellously clever name, being so close to THE King. And now here we were, being paired as her equals on one of the most famous stages in the country, if not the world. She was a delight and treated us with a respect our thirty-five years' age difference didn't necessarily demand.

Further invitations followed; sharing the stage with Sir Peter Pears in Britten's *St Nicholas* in the lead-up to Christmas, where the Suffolk countryside took on a whole different character to its summer incarnation, felt like being admitted to an exclusive club. Then a starring role at the Lutoslawski Symposium where we would finally get to play his Quartet to the man himself. He very much liked our interpretation, which we had the pleasure of playing in his presence several times over the following years.

After one such outing, at Dartington, as he stood to take the audience applause he loudly declared, "It's theirs!" This was quite a coup, given the status he held as one of the world's most celebrated living composers. But it was difficult to take advantage of the accolade; wording it in our biography sounded awkward and self-congratulatory, so we left it out. We also tried to persuade him to write another quartet, for which we felt sure to be named dedicatees, but he claimed to have perfected the medium in his first attempt, so declined the request. (How happy I am that Beethoven, Shostakovich and so many others didn't feel the same satisfaction following their opening quartet opi!) Unbeknownst to me, the other students performing in this Snape Maltings concert counted amongst them a certain Paul Cassidy, our future violist – and my future husband!

The Brodskys' relationship with Aldeburgh brought us there regularly, and they asked us to play the solo quartet parts for the Britten opera *The Rape of Lucretia*, both in The Maltings and on a national tour. Britten operas held uncomfortable memories for our group teacher Terry, as he somewhat shamefacedly recounted the story of the World Premiere, in Venice, of *Death in Venice*. He and another member of the chamber group had spent the day in canal-side bars, becoming so hopelessly drunk that they turned up over an hour late for the show, incapable of playing a note. Being on solo parts with no other cellist around to take his place, it was a bad day to choose to fall short of accepted professional standards. That occasion probably marked the beginning of the end of Terry's performing career. But there was an upside to this for me; having no more use for it, he allowed me to play on his wonderful Tononi cello. A rich-toned, dark-varnished specimen once owned by my teen-idol Pablo Casals, no less. It certainly improved my quality of life for a while… till he had to sell it to fund his retirement to the festival town of Cadaqués, on the Costa Brava.

We had a great time with Lucretia. We hadn't yet got to know the three masterworks or any of the earlier pieces Britten had penned for String Quartet, but from within this small chamber group his magic caught hold and we were eager to start learning them. About twenty-five years later we would return to the Maltings to record these immense and wonderful pieces, which paint so evocatively the scenery surrounding us, memories of our early visits coming back as ghosts from the past.

Sir Peter Pears was to feature further in our Quartet's journey. He was so moved by Paul's performance of *Lachrymae* during one of the student courses held at the Britten-Pears School, that he donated Britten's viola to him. So the first notes I ever heard him play were on this very instrument. Soon afterwards, we were invited by Sir Peter to perform for his seventieth birthday celebrations and, five years later, at the tenth anniversary concert of the great composer's death. But by the time the concert came around, sadly he too had passed away.

With the Quartet, I continued to return to Aldeburgh and Snape regularly, and on one occasion as soloist in the Brahms Double Concerto. Mike and I had won the Bass Concerto Competition in college (no, not an award for instruments of low frequency, but rather one donated by a local brewery, Bass Charrington) earning us the chance to perform our work of choice with the RNCM Symphony Orchestra. This performance took place on the day of Mike's twenty-first birthday, to be followed by a mighty party. Not long afterwards, Ian and Alex were to perform Mozart's *Sinfonia Concertante* with the RNCM Chamber Orchestra. Our comfort zone in each other's company clearly made joint concerto performances more palatable to us.

Somehow news of our success had reached Aldeburgh and they invited us to play the Brahms with the newly formed Britten-Pears Orchestra under Gennady Rozhdestvensky in The Maltings. This concert was broadcast by Radio 3 and felt seriously proper, and pressured. Playing the whole work from memory onto live radio was a challenge for us aged twenty and twenty-one, and performing under such an auspicious conductor was a real coup for the Quartet as well as for ourselves.

Again, our paths almost crossed with our future colleague, as Paul had been meant to join the orchestra for that course. In the event he couldn't make it but, so I'm told, his friends reported back to him about this audacious brother and sister team who they found so impressive and, in the case of the sister, pretty hot! It's nice to think his curiosity may have been piqued by me long before we met.

Back in Manchester, professional life was starting to find a place alongside student life. Bookings were coming in through the college outreach programme as well as through our man in Darlington, Dave Robson, but our professional awareness was still developing, landing us in a few awkward situations. Even just planning ahead sufficiently to arrive on time at whichever music club had booked us, reading a map and figuring out the projected journey time, seemed to be a learning curve which had to be… well, learnt.

On the day of a gig up near Huddersfield, Mike had been bed-ridden with a bad flu and was doubting his ability to join us that night. Instead of alerting our hosts to the potential problem ahead and allowing them a part in the decision of what action to take, we chose to wait and wait, in case he recovered. He didn't. Far too late, Ian, Alex and I climbed into the car armed with a selection of trios, duos and solo works, and hit the late-autumn rush-hour traffic of the M62 in a frenzy of discussion and virtual rehearsal as we crawled through dark rain-lashed country roads to our destination.

Long before the days of mobile phones, the promoter was in a panic when we pulled into the car park, but apoplectic when he counted only three musicians emerging from the battered old car. There was about an hour to go till concert time and we hurriedly rehearsed our hastily thrown together replacement programme. The committee was not amused, there was no sense of the Blitz Spirit or appreciation of our resourcefulness; we were lucky to get out of there with a modicum of goodwill once our depleted and distinctly sub-standard concert was over. Lesson learnt.

Travels through the red- and white-rose counties of Lancashire and Yorkshire, our early stomping ground, put Ian's hand-me-down Hillman Hunter well and truly through its paces. More often than not, he was forced to coax it into submission as we snaked up Snake Pass or scaled the heights of the Pennine-traversing M62, the poor old car groaning under its load of us four plus instruments. More scary was the return journey in the small hours, when a breakdown might leave us stranded for hours while someone walked to find a phone or Ian tinkered with the mechanics of the thing.

Our soundtrack for these journeys was a mixtape compiled over successive weeks from Radio 1's Sunday Evening Hit Parade. Far from esoteric, the playlist had us gaily singing along to a selection of cheesy oldies and current hits. Abba, one of Ian's preferred bands, gave us *Thank You For the Music*; we had *Summer Nights* from *Grease*; *Video Killed the Radio Star*, *Hit Me With Your Rhythm Stick*, *I Don't Like Mondays* and *Bohemian Rhapsody* being the more hip numbers. One favourite was the newly released *Message in a Bottle*, that brilliantly rhythmically quirky Police tune, penned by our fellow north-easterner. We used to marvel at the fact that, in the chorus, the vocal never once sang on the beat, only on every off-beat, and strictly at that, and we'd clap along filling the gaps. Over twenty years later, whilst rehearsing together on his magnificent Tuscan estate, Sting revealed to us that he likes to play his metronome off the beat, to avoid being too four-square; so, I realised, remembering those car journeys long ago, in this case he'd have been singing *with* the metronome, against his own wishes! (Coincidentally, unaware of our connection, Sting donated some priceless memorabilia to be auctioned in aid of the TYO 50th anniversary touring fund, for their trip to New York.)

Though our playlist grew, it never renewed, so the original tracks were always there for our enjoyment; those road trips remain in my consciousness now whenever I hear the songs played. I am transported back to long journeys on the back seat, my cello wedged beside me, singing away en route to pre-gig rehearsal, tea, quiche and egg sandwiches, changing in the toilets, concert with raffle in the interval, then pile into the car back to Edge Lane, crawling into bed in the early hours.

Eventually, Mike passed his test and another hand-me-down car was available when needed, courtesy of Dad's upgrade to a new one of his own. Now for the occasional Quartet-plus date, we could take two cars and spare Hilly the burden. We proudly offered transportation to our Hungarian colleagues of the Kodály

Quartet, with whom we'd been invited to tour the Mendelssohn Octet throughout Northumberland and the Scottish Borders. Biggar, Peebles and Moffat became regular haunts in those early touring days around remote parts of Britain. We even crossed the water to the Isle of Arran.

Mike's zippy Toyota – and his somewhat more adventurous approach to driving – invariably got him there first, his passengers white-faced and shaken by the speed-crazed journey. One such concert, Dave had booked us to play the Shostakovich Piano Quintet for Newton Aycliffe Music Society, with Mike's then-girlfriend Dina Bennett on the piano. Arriving well in advance of the rest of us, they entered the venue – a rather drab assembly hall – to find one of those curtain-clad pine-framed upright pianos so beloved of primary schools back in the day. Dina's face dropped as she envisaged performing that giant of the repertoire on what may as well have been a toy keyboard – it didn't even have enough octaves for the top notes in the *Scherzo*. On closer examination, she found that even the notes it did have in the higher registers were woefully weak and tinkly, while the bass notes had no depth whatsoever.

By the time the rest of us pulled into the carpark, all efforts to find a replacement piano had been exhausted and we were left with no alternative. Hasty rewrites of the violin parts to incorporate some of the missing notes at the top of the piano led to a unique performance of the work which, I can only imagine, would have met wholeheartedly with the composer's approval, used as he was to the total disrespect of the powers-that-be and the endless flexibility and swallowing of pride demanded of great artists like himself. We had a hoot, giggles only narrowly avoided mid-performance whenever the top or bottom registers came into play.

Hopefully Newton Aycliffe also learnt a lesson that day – stick to booking musicians who come ready kitted out with their own instruments.

24

Concours Français

We had our sights firmly set on the next triennial Portsmouth Competition, to be held in April 1982, having made our mark so indelibly on the first one. Surely, we surmised, if we were the Most Promising Young Quartet last time, we would be winners when we returned; stands to reason.

In the meantime, we were on the lookout for similar opportunities and came across two such, recently started up in France. Evian, on the banks of Lake Geneva, looked promising, with another impressive roll-call of celebrities on the jury and the improbable setting of the Hôtel Royal Evian-les-Bains, a stunning Belle Époque hotel, spa and Michelin star restaurant.

On arrival at the gates to this veritable palace, we were wide-eyed at the spectacle of French opulence before us, hardly daring to believe that we were to stay here, certain there had been some kind of mistake. Or that we were simply here to enrol in the competition, after which we would be shown to our humble quarters somewhere in the town. But no, check-in was completed and we were shown up the elegant sweeping staircase by an army of uniformed bellboys. Portsmouth's student flats, functional and fit for purpose though they undoubtedly were, came a very poor second to the sumptuous accommodation offered here. Each musician was given a luxurious double room, high-ceilinged and spacious, some with lake view. The aroma of French polish and ancient thick-pile carpets, fresh bed-linen and flowers, lace curtains gently rippling at tall open windows giving on to the balcony and view of the lapping lake water across an impossibly green lawn… This was a new experience for us and would be the start of a life-long flirtation with similar places way out of our league, which every touring musician experiences.

We frequently find ourselves, in the course of our work, surrounded by the stunning interiors of grand palaces, castles, stately homes and even private houses, whose high-end fixtures and fittings, decorative features and furniture we cannot and will never afford. We may simply be offered access in the form of makeshift changing rooms, a high tea or sometimes a post-concert banquet, but occasionally one might be accommodated overnight in these palatial settings, treated to the privileges of life within their cosseted confines. It's a bitter-sweet part of touring life – pleasant in the moment but often quite tough to later return home to a small apartment or cramped family house.

Here at Evian, as we emerged refreshed from our stately boudoirs to make our way down for dinner, we were brought down to earth with a bump. Passing the doors to the magnificent dining room, we glimpsed the rosy-cheeked faces of some well-known figures in classical music deep in the throes of demolishing a sumptuous buffet of gourmandising extravagance.

"Non, messieurs-dames, ze dining room is for ze jury and organiseurs. Les musiciens eat elsewhere. Please follow me," whispered a small lackey who had suddenly appeared at our side.

Sure enough, as we tripped behind him, through a green baize door into a decidedly more sparse corridor and down a metal spiral staircase, we found ourselves in a hot, steamy, windowless space: the servants' canteen. Now we lowly musicians were put in our places alright. Here, we were to take all our meals, while the VIPs were wined and dined in splendour upstairs. It became clear during the course of the following days' events that the afternoon sessions were distinctly accompanied by the gentle sound of snoring and the faint odour of garlic and Bordeaux; no-one questioned the right or the advisability of drinking with the five-course lunch on offer to the Chosen Ones. A debate started up amongst participating groups as to the pros and cons of playing before or after lunch...

The other disappointment, given the beauty of our environment, was that the competition performances were held in a modern, windowless lecture theatre; just like at Portsmouth, good for the listener, nightmarish for the player. All blemishes were made painfully obvious, any scratchiness to the sound amplified, receiving no help as it might in a warm acoustic. But we did well, all things considered. Again we were by far the youngest participants and we came away with top prize for the twentieth-century section of the event, winning the Janáček Medal, in honour of a performance of our old favourite, his 2nd Quartet. We also made an impression on several impresarios and promoters present, including a Belgian composer by the wonderfully sing-song name of Wilfried Westerlinck, and invitations to perform at their various festivals, broadcasts and series soon followed including, to my delight, our debut tour of Belgium.

My recent triumph in the language department rendered me team spokesperson when French was required. Flushed with the success of a few simple conversations, I allowed myself to be volunteered for a live interview on Radio France 3. Face-to-face talk is one thing, but attempting to be fluent in front of a microphone with an intense-looking young interviewer was a step too far for my A Level French. I was tongue-tied and blank under pressure and politely shown the door, while the producer feigned a technical fault. With my mother standing by (yes of course, they had made the trip with us and were as ever a hindrance and a pleasure to have around), I could have easily asked her to help, but it was too late. I slunk off, embarrassed. Again my frustration at my parents' missed opportunity to have eight bilingual children came to mind. I put matters right some years later by going to live in rural France, where doing up an old ruin and getting married improved my language skills no end. Now whenever an interview in French is called for, I'm confident of passing myself off with a modicum of dignity and being understood on the receiving end of the airwaves.

On the whole, the experience in the rarefied air of the French Alps had been a good one. Satisfied but eager to try again the following year, we returned home with our medals and a presentation carafe of the famous Eau Mineral, bottled in person at the actual spring.

During my second year at college, we had all returned to Middlesbrough for the Easter break and the joys of two weeks' pampering with proper food and home comforts. Until Mike passed his test we tended to see Ian's car as the group transport, so it was a given that he would have passengers every time he made this trip. I'm embarrassed to recall that I would try to influence his leaving time, or even date, to suit my own needs – why I felt I had the right to do so is beyond me. It was his car, not ours. Somehow we had become an entity and were losing sight of our individual autonomy.

One day during this holiday we got together with some of our old friends from TYO for a friendly kick about in the garden next door to my home. This was the grandest of the four big-houses-on-the-corner connected by secret passages and strange layouts, the one lived in by the patriarch who had built the other three for his sons, if legend was correct. Many of the football matches and other fun and games we'd enjoyed over the years had happened here, especially just before we left home as the neighbours were living in America for a few years and we were given free reign to spend time there, helpfully making it look inhabited (and sneaking indoors to watch their colour television). With its extensive gardens, huge greenhouse and kitchen garden, massive lawn (football pitch) and summer house (grandstand), this was an invitation that didn't need repeating. The three kids of this family had been friends with my older siblings, being closer in age. Back then, my brother Pete and his gang had converted the sizable stable block into a music venue, complete with half-barrel bar, pull pumps and the authentic smell of stale beer. Genteel Mr and Mrs Hopkins were endlessly patient with the comings and goings of hordes of young people and the loud music emanating from the happening scene. In tandem with this, us Little Ones would often be found wandering the grounds unattended, stray waifs in pursuit of whichever game was ongoing around the exciting lanes and hidden corners of this wonderland.

So here we were, back on home turf for a Reunion Testimonial match with a bunch of old pals. Being somewhat untrained and less skilled than the boys, though equally enthusiastic, I tended to be unaware of what constituted a fair or even safe tackle. I would go in for the ball with no chance of getting it, the consequences being sometimes messy and unsavoury. On this fateful day, I lived up to my reputation and Ian was my hapless victim. I landed a booted heel to his left ankle and landed him in Casualty for the rest of the afternoon. He emerged with a huge cast and crutches and a generous sense of humour, much to my shame.

The timing of this unfortunate incident could hardly have been worse. After our scheduled return to Manchester for the start of the new term, we were booked on the boat train and the TGV to Colmar in the Alsace region of France, a country newly obsessed with this Concours de Quatuors-à-Cordes phenomenon, where the next one was due to start in a few days. Obviously Ian couldn't drive, so we had to hitch a lift to Edge Lane with his dad. A few quick rehearsals and packing up of all the required music and we were off, Ian with makeshift shoulder straps fitted to his violin case so he could use the crutches, the rest of us sharing in carrying his luggage. It was an arduous and undoubtedly painful journey, with the added bonus of being unseasonably warm, to his further discomfort.

My memory of the competition is sparse, but I have a clear picture of two things. First, every time we were to perform, the simple act of climbing up to the stage was an ordeal in itself, Mike carrying two violins and bows while Ian hobbled to his seat, lifting his leg onto a small footstool to prevent swelling. We must have looked a sorry sight, not at all prize-winning fodder.

The second memory was not injury-related but was the icing on the cake for this jinxed competition outing. Approaching the final straight in Bartók's 1st Quartet, Mike's instrument made that sickening explosive noise that every player knows means a broken string. And yes, it was the E; the top string and probably the most indispensable of the four if you're playing the top line. Being close to the finish, it seemed crazy to stop, so the boys gave each other a knowing look, found a pause in the music and made a swift swap so we could carry on relatively smoothly. Only there was one problem which they hadn't calculated on.

In those days, Ian didn't use a shoulder rest but instead stuffed some padding under his jacket to give his violin extra lift that way. Mike, on the other hand, did use a shoulder rest and had it on a pretty high setting. So when they swapped, Mike looked like a trad fiddler, the unsupported violin slipping further down his chest with each gesture, while Ian's chin, with its double elevation, was forced ridiculously high, giving him the appearance of a werewolf in full metamorphosis. Needless to say, the Bartók had sounded better. The unison passagework was excruciating and those exultant rising flourishes that end the piece had a somewhat scrambled desperation. Happy it was all over, we swiftly stood to take the generous/relieved applause. Well, three of us did. Ian reached for his crutches and fumbled with them whilst trying to return Mike's violin to its owner for the too-long journey off the stage.

The following year we made the return trip to Evian. Again we did well, receiving the Schönberg Medal as well as the Audience Prize, but that elusive Big Win remained out of reach. We had a feeling our performance style just wasn't competition material – the honesty of bow attack and adventurous devil-may-care shifting in the left hand (thanks Terry) making for an exciting overall effect, though perhaps falling short in the polish and finesse departments. But we stuck to our guns, determined not to compromise for the sake of accolades, whilst desperate to receive them.

This time, the College Chamber Orchestra was also present for some concerts in the Evian and Lucerne Festivals, including my then-boyfriend who played in the violin section. A few days after the Quartet arrived and had embarked on the competition rounds, the orchestra, having driven all the way from Manchester, were closing in on their accommodation somewhere in the main town. Passing the impressive gates to our hotel, Chris, recognising the name, asked the bus driver to stop so he could make his way straight to my room, where we had agreed he'd stay. But the gate to the grounds was some considerable distance from the Belle Époque palace of splendour. With his oversized battered suitcase and studiedly scruffy bohemian appearance – threadbare corduroy jeans tied at the waist with an old school tie – he cut quite a picture as he emerged from the rhododendrons lining the interminable drive into the light of the sweeping forecourt, sweating and puffing on a bent Benson & Hedges. That we had planned to sneak him in past the reception staff, not to mention my parents (yes, here they were AGAIN...), seemed to have slipped his mind. The competition continued for me in an uncomfortable conflict between doing the job I'd come to do and making sure all the entourage were happy, smuggling them into various parties and events, making sure not to neglect them. It just doesn't work.

The next attempt on our competition trail was to be the second Portsmouth, a year later. I was determined to enter this one with minimal distractions and maximum concentration, with no parental attendance and hopefully keeping Eleanor Warren's potential interference at bay, if she chose to make the journey again. But by the time that event came around, something seismic had changed in the Brodsky Quartet. We were facing our first defection.

Interlude II

Jacksons makes a comeback – a momentary leap forward to the nineties

When a big family gets together at Christmas, the idea of presents being exchanged in the usual way goes out the window. As our family grew, new nuclear units sprouting up, we nevertheless made every effort to congregate at the Big House on the Corner for the few days of the festive holiday. Luckily, some siblings lived nearby with their young families, so the strain was eased in the beds department. But on the big day, we would all gather around that sturdy oak table, extended to its full capacity, for the main meal, which was being prepared in the spaces left at the kitchen's periphery. The giving of gifts became problematic and awkward – too many to think about, too much unnecessary tat being exchanged for the sake of it, or not everyone reciprocating, leading to bad feeling. Then we devised a system: a kind of Secret Santa idea, where you only had to buy one thing for one other person, names drawn from a hat a few weeks in advance. But for this family of incorrigible performers and creators, there was an added twist. Each gift should be accompanied by an homage to the receiver, in the form of a poem, song, dance or whatever. It was a fun activity to pass the post-blowout twilight hours and we all took to the new system, some more readily than others.

Year after year the usual pressure of Christmas Day, which for some is huge – those in charge of the meal, those with young kids – was as nothing to the agony of meeting this deadline with your offering prepared and ready to perform. People would disappear to the attic for frantic scribbling sessions, or drag away unsuspecting partners for musical accompaniment duty. No one was meant to know who you had as your 'person', but slip-ups were frequent and by the time the event happened there were few surprises left. No matter – the surprise was in the performance. The present almost felt like an afterthought to the real business in hand, and a competitive spirit soon took hold.

There were some who always did poetry, from Dad's elegiac and serious iambic pentameter at one end of the scale, to comic rhyming couplets at the other. Mam always did a very last-minute prose, claiming she had no skills nor spare time to devise rhymes or meter. It was often hilarious without necessarily aiming to be. I usually offered a poem – my proudest being a sonnet on Walls and Divisions for Dad, quoting from The Style Council, with a lump of the Berlin Wall as his present – we had just been there to record, days after it came 'tumbling down'. Then there were the songs. It was quite a popular trick to take an existing song and put new lyrics to it pertaining to one's subject, a simple way to get started for the less creative. But occasionally we would get new compositions... and one such came to be sung to me in the Christmas of 1992.

The Quartet had spent the previous weeks in preliminary discussions and workshops with one Declan MacManus, aka Elvis Costello, brainstorming and swapping ideas for what we hoped might become an album but was as yet a few half-written songs and snippets of lyrics. We had met through a mutual appreciation of each others' performances and recordings, chatting like old friends from the very first meeting, but never imagining it might lead to the phenomenon our collaboration, The Juliet Letters, turned out to be.

Our starting point had been to play each other tracks we loved, from every genre of music, and also to collate words and phrases relating to letters or written communication. I was in the process of writing a song of desperate pleading, with the strapline 'Taking My Life in Your Hands'. Being slow to create, I was struggling a bit, but no problem; when we returned to work after the break, Declan had polished my bare bones into the skeleton of the song it later became, with further tweaking by us all of lyrics and of course orchestration.

That was the way we were working, in some cases starting from scratch with a word or phrase, or a musical motif, building a song together. By this point, *Why* had already emerged from Ian's hesitant child's questioning, with a series of disparate notes and words from a dream of Declan's. Some of the instrumentals were already completed – Declan's *Deliver Us*, Paul's *Dead Letter* and Mike's *Last Post*. The two parts of *Letter Home* were brought together – Ian's chorale-like melody for the address section and post-script, book-ending Declan's hurdy-gurdy tune for the letter... a bit like the creative process for *A Day in the Life*, if I may be so bold!

This was where we stood at the Christmas break. Later, and at breakneck speed, we would go on to develop together songs from fragments, like *This Offer is Unrepeatable*, written in one day, inspired by some junk mail and Béla Bartók, or the jaunty string backing-based *I Almost Had a Weakness*, another that began life with the string motif and developed its character from there. *Who Do You Think You Are?* similarly grew out of an accordion-style throbbing texture. *Romeo's Seance* again built on a Spanish-inspired riff by Mike, the song taking its identity from the musical basis, not the other way round. The music Paul wrote for *Sad Burlesque* and Declan's words to suit it perfectly, came spewing out like vomit the morning after the grim general election later in the spring. Within the two pivotal numbers, *Dear Sweet Filthy World* and *I Thought I'd Write to Juliet*, lurk an homage to Shostakovich – his 5th Quartet slow movement at the most poignant moment as Constance, the female soldier, introduces herself – and Wagner's *Longing and Desire*, the Tristan Chord for the suicidal words 'Don't try to find me'. This chord that had inspired so many composers through the ages, Shostakovich among them, found voice again in our modest offering.

These secret pearls that lie within those songs, the inspiration from some of classical music's greatest moments, are almost as much a source of pride to me as the original material that emerged. The real songsmith in our midst single-handedly produced some of the most beautiful tracks ever heard with only string-arrangement input from the rest of us – *First to Leave* and *Birds Will Still Be Singing* – but the joint effort behind all the material must not be underestimated. I recall sitting in Heathrow's departure lounge with a bunch of manuscript paper, dividing the glorious chords of *Birds* between the four strings, with the knowledge of our instruments only a player could have brought to the table, and which I believe helps make the song what it is. The open strings and harmonics infuse the words 'Banish all dismay, extinguish every sorrow; If I'm lost or I'm forgiven, the birds will still be singing' with infinite, delicate poignancy. Another configuration of the chords might have carried less beauty.

How often the textures of orchestration make the song; in our case, the Wurlitzer sound in *Swine*, created by alternating the same note on two different strings; the WW2 siren screeching from Mike's violin in *I Thought I'd Write to Juliet*; the overlapping entries in *Deliver Us* creating Bachian suspensions; *tremolo, sul ponticello, glissandi*, all bringing a third dimension to the textures. When it came to the live shows, audiences unfamiliar with our genre would marvel as they witnessed every sound being made right before their eyes by the four of us, nothing missing from the recording they'd been listening to.

When speaking with students who have played, studied and loved the songs since childhood, like that American Quartet in Banff who had so delighted me with their open-minded, unstuffy appreciation, claiming it was the soundtrack for their touring car drives (just like us with Abba and co), I am thrilled to share with them some of these insights. How much can be learned from the unprejudiced young. Contrary to the opinion of some detractors at the time, this was not a cheap selling-out crossover, and it was nothing new. Our own Adolph Brodsky had jammed with peasant musicians, Sir Yehudi duetted with Stepháne Grappelli, the Hollywood Quartet backed Sinatra, the Beatles wrote entire songs with strings alone – *Eleanor Rigby, She's Leaving Home* – and following our efforts with Declan, Top of the Pops hired a resident string quartet! It is a privilege to be able to claim at least a small part in introducing our genre to so many people who may otherwise never have heard it, new audiences who went on to discover more as their curiosity was piqued.

And many musicians around the world have opened their hearts to The Juliet Letters, with a wide variety of performances regularly emerging, by all sorts of combinations. Mountview Drama School in Peckham, London, recently devised a whole show of the songs, re-orchestrating every number and delivering them in a celebratory style, choruses and instrumental ensembles playing in the action, dance routines and comedy turns. It was an absolute joy to behold their joy in the work and to see how much it meant to them in their young lives, especially when we turned up to the show unannounced!

I just had a look on YouTube and found almost twenty versions of the cycle, in several different languages. It is so heartwarming... I cry at the endeavour and genuine love coming off the screen from all these artists.

Back to Christmas 1992. Mike had me as his 'person' and had written a song called 'Jacksons, Monk and Rowe', after my childhood nickname. Long since the days of my great prizewinning oeuvre, 'Sunday Morning', I was battling to complete my song idea for our return to work, having somewhat lost my muse. Meanwhile, he had a natural flair for composition, had been putting it into practice since before college and had an easy Gilbert O'Sullivan singing style. Seated at the piano in the grand bay window of the famous Music Room, he started with a short classical quotation intro, then launched into a raunchy funk-soul backing and sang of memories from childhood and my position in the family. There was a distinct undertone of menace – was I ready for the trouble ahead? Did I know my friends from my foe? But I, being one who notoriously doesn't listen to the lyrics of songs so much as the music itself, delighted in the clever upbeat funky chords and jumped up to congratulate him, calling to the gathered throng, "Remember where you heard that first!"

At this point, the family didn't know what we were up to with Declan, but I was pretty sure they would hear that ditty again one day, sung by a rather more celebrated voice. When we returned to work after the break, the song received a joint-effort makeover, adding another verse and a bridge and replacing the opening Prokofiev snippet with an original jingle by Elvis, as we weren't allowed direct quotes. The song became the poppiest number on the album, often got the loudest cheer, and was a hit all round.

Imagine the task, though, of explaining the provenance of its unlikely title; each night of the tour, Declan would chat easily with the audience, introducing the songs and giving some backstory to The Juliet Letters, and occasionally handing over to his co-performers for variety's sake. Leaning towards the mic, hearing my voice booming into the void of the Tivoli Gardens Concert Hall whilst I haltingly tried to explain my long-winded childhood nickname with its roots in a North-Eastern firm of solicitors, to a boisterous crowd of Danes more used to rock-and-roll banter, was a one-off moment for me; the next night I refused the proffered mic, leaving it in the hands of our infinitely more experienced frontman-cum-stand-up-comedian. It has to be said, that old law firm can't quite believe their sudden visibility on the world stage, more than 100 years after their fateful merger!

Whilst this song has an upbeat feel to it, the underlying menace is in the lyrics. Prophetic entirely sums it up, added to by my insertion of divorce proceedings in the third verse. Declan referenced the image in the Ealing Comedy *Passport to Pimlico*, when kids caught in a heatwave dare each other to touch the red-hot brass nameplate of a solicitor's office, hinting at getting one's fingers burnt when the shit hits the fan.

When Mike left the Quartet, six years later, the family did somewhat implode. My parents struggled with the change to what they'd known for so long and stopped coming to concerts, and – sadly for me – up to his death a couple of years later, Dad never again heard us play. Mam lived on for another twenty years and gradually got used to the new status quo, even regaining her love for the group. She would attend as many concerts as she could, including our first weekend Shostakovich cycle aged nearly 90. I was even able to persuade her, at 98 and post-stroke, to sing her favourite Tosca aria, which was put to film with us backing her. It was played at her funeral to a tearful congregation.

It's tough being the youngest in a big family; things happen before you're ready for them. You learn too early about the non-existence of Santa. You pick up on arguments and hatreds that teens develop for their poor unsuspecting parents – or, put another way, the sudden change in parents' attitude when a cute little kid starts to grow nubs, sprout hair and smell. I know that my younger self was infused with an anger that had nothing to do with my own image of them. But here there was the added complication of an underlying guilt that had tarnished their lives and probably marred their judgement. Yet they still felt qualified to judge.

Parental misogyny, favouritism, unequal opportunity, all these dichotomies and hypocrisies had peppered an otherwise happy family life with bitterness and torment, rivalry and resentment. So imagine how it went down when the true story of our parents' courtship and coming together – and our secret sibling – was finally out.

When my childhood nickname Jacksons, Monk and Rowe found voice once more in this new song, we had only recently found out about and met our new brother. Since then, Alan has become very much a part of the family. And after all he has to be angry about, he's not; what a generous, forgiving person he is.

For The Juliet Letters tour, one of the many encores we prepared was an original song by Mike. As we played it around the world – including in Hamburg, staying in the splendour of the Atlanta Hotel, where Tommy and Baby had eloped all those years before – I would try to get into the mind of that lonely boy who lost his dad. I also pondered the effect on families of all their closeted secrets.

The song was called *Skeleton*.

25

Dissonance

Inevitably, we had to accept that living together as a quartet wasn't necessarily the cleverest way to stay friends, considering the intensity that the group's working life was starting to develop. Ian was the first to go, moving in with his cellist girlfriend, leaving the rest of us somewhat crestfallen by his mature decision. Rehearsals continued to happen at Edge Lane in the Blue Music Room, now boasting another of Alex's wall murals – this time a blow-up detail of the old sepia photo, Brodsky in the nearby fields, which had so delighted us in our first days there. He in his casual reclined pose would watch over us and somehow lend a calm to our fervent and angst-ridden work sessions.

Though the Quartet still came first, we all had other things going on which took us, wisely, out of each other's orbit. Ian's joint course with the university brought him frequently to lectures and tutorials in that other institution on Oxford Road. With his friends there he had formed a Contemporary Music Ensemble and a Piano Trio, performing Fauré and Brahms at in-house lunchtimes and the like. Perhaps this was in an effort to regain his sense of self-esteem, which had recently taken a battering.

Following the Portsmouth Competition, it became a point of debate that Mr Menuhin had questioned the wisdom of alternating 1st and 2nd Violin roles, if we were to be taken seriously in the profession. Ms Warren, Terry and the other string department tutors all concurred and wouldn't listen to our arguments: that we had always prided ourselves on democracy and equality, even sharing the viola part in the early days. And if we were to choose one 'leader' – a title we have always eschewed, it being archaic and having nothing to do with the way our group functions – who should it be?

These two had grown up side by side, with the same teacher every step of the way. Both had loved their dual role within the group, revelled in the binary personality it afforded them. No one in a string quartet has the right to rely on others to take the pressure – there should be no role that allows you to take a back seat. We are all on high alert at all times, or should be, even in an accompanying role.

But Mike declared himself to be useless at playing the second fiddle part, it demanding so much more sensitivity and accommodation than he could manage. It is true that, wherever he sat, he had trouble melting into the background when it was someone's turn to shine, an attribute equally paramount to all four players, so he was essentially admitting to a failing on his part. In the end, this argument won and Ian took his place as permanent Second Fiddle.

I do wish there was a better, less hierarchical-sounding term for the two violinists in a group; instead of First and Second, why not Soprano and Alto, as in the origins of four-part writing, the voices being SATB – Soprano, Alto, Tenor, Bass. As Ian likes to observe, the old adage of 'playing second fiddle to...', a phrase used to describe a subordinate, lesser role, is all wrong. He calls it 'playing second fiddle with...', which is of course the correct interpretation when you know anything about music. (Not wishing to be a bore, but misappropriation of musical terms by writers is one of my pet gripes. I have no right to count myself amongst you, but can you professionals out there please invest in a bit of rudimentary theory? We don't BUILD to a crescendo; a crescendo IS a build!)

So while Ian was branching out in other musical groups, Mike was still composing for small chamber orchestras he would throw together; works with quirky titles like *Variations on King Derik the Not So Bad*, *Concerto Grobbo* or, in honour of our Icelandic contingent at College, *Io sóno Vikingo*, always with tongue in cheek to offset any sense of taking his magnum opi too seriously. Eventually he formed the Manchester String Orchestra as he was developing a love of conducting, but they would perform infrequently, its participants being somewhat tied up with their own studies, not to mention the demands of official college Symphony, Opera and Chamber Orchestra duty.

Alex had remained true to his Catholic roots and had formed friendships amongst the Christian community – the God Squad, as they were unkindly known. Not long after Ian left the Quartet house, Alex moved to digs with like-minded people and became thoroughly involved in church and musical community work. He became a bit of a misfit in college, wandering around in open sandals in winter, refusing to conform to rules – he offered a 'free improvisation' as his Final Recital exam modern work, putting a few backs up in the process. Saved having to practise, I suppose.

So Edge Lane became home to new students as bedrooms were vacated. My boyfriend had moved in with me, Mike's girlfriend with him, and we were joined by a succession of other students including David, a pianist (usefully with own piano and the house's first TV, complete with Teletext!); Angie, an ex-TYO violist; Cathy, a non-musician (uh???); and, briefly, Sylvain, a French violinist friend from ECYO days. We expanded our horizons; this was 1980s Manchester – The Hacienda, cocktail culture, Weather Report at the Apollo – and we embraced it all within our limited budget and tight working schedule.

The house was getting crowded but the Quartet maintained ownership of the Blue Room and I made a rather upmarket decorating job of the upstairs living room, the largest room in the house. Alex had taken his huge wall mural with him (luckily this didn't call for building contractors and RSJs – it had been done on lining paper loosely taped to the wall) so I moved in with delicate pinks and greens – wallpaper, matching frosted-glass light fittings and painted bookshelves propped up on bricks, a sofa bed and an actual new beige carpet. It became a grown-up haven from the squalor and noise elsewhere and a useful spare bedroom for when the parentals visited. Sometimes we'd hold chamber soirées in this more spacious room, inviting Terry to join us in a Quintet, Octet or whatever. If Dad was around, he would be included, to the amazement of our new housemates who had understandably presumed the father of this talented pair must surely be a reasonable player himself. The drink helped...

For my part, the intensity of A Level year whilst at college had left me content to concentrate on only cello studies and Quartet thereafter, though I did have a short flirtation with a cello ensemble and got roped into Mike's orchestra. I was due to rejoin the European Community Youth Orchestra in my second summer holiday, where I had been promised a front desk position, but somehow I decided to pull out. None of my colleagues was going, so I would have been alone there. I realise in retrospect this would only have been a good thing, but back then I had just got a new boyfriend and a couple of weeks' absence seemed all wrong. The following term I changed teachers and finally got to study with Ralph Kirshbaum, who had been on my radar for so long. His approach was gentle and nurturing, delving deep into the colours and meaning of notes and phrases, beyond technical considerations although not in place of them.

But the cello department as a whole was not a place of nurture. Was it my imagination that being focused on the Quartet somehow diminished my rights as a legitimate cello student? On top of this, our somewhat misogynistic Head of Strings Eleanor Warren, an ex-cellist herself, seemed to hold a grudge against our sex in the department. And elsewhere in college, I got the uncomfortable feeling girls had to outperform the boys to be accepted, especially in the traditionally male roles, like my friend Sian Edwards, now an acclaimed conductor. (This even though she was the only Conducting course student in college, male or female!) I was lucky to have escaped the insidious creep of institutionalised abuse rife at our college and at so many others, but there was a bullying and belittling ethos that could leave kids feeling confused, undermining their self-esteem.

Arriving at that bar, with all the tutors and their boss necking any number of triple tipples, you could always count on having to defend yourself against teasing or scrutiny, knowing smiles and winks. Lewd jokes concerning the students' merits – both musical and otherwise – would have to be endured. One of Terry's favourites was in reference to the generous décolletage of a certain female student, which he declared to be his main incentive for getting up in the morning. Only he didn't use such quaint language. It was brash and crude and totally unacceptable, yet Eleanor would laugh along with the boys and let it go. No doubt she had her own battles to fight in that patriarchal society, but to my knowledge, she did little to support girls who came to her with complaints of abuse or sexual harassment and simply facilitated its continuance by turning a blind eye, as did all the staff from the Principal down.

In the meantime, the Quartet was still our top priority and was taking on more and more work. The composers at college knew about us and would proffer their work for our perusal, sure of a swift and pretty accurate reading without much fuss. This led to us being offered up as guinea pigs to professional composers unable to get top groups to perform their works, or anyone visiting the college with egos to be massaged, our Principal co-opting us into service. We would be showcased in proper evening concerts, performing Schönberg and Beethoven to full houses of public, students and staff, and sent off again on exchange trips, to Yugoslavia amongst other places.

My first taste of hot chestnuts roasted over a glowing bed of charcoal in a wintry Belgrade at dusk comes back to me each time I smell them, now that all such foreign delicacies are ubiquitously available back home. This being only months after the death of Tito, his portrait still displayed in every building and school we visited, our travels through Split, Rovinj and the capital afforded us further insights into the challenging conditions of Eastern-Bloc life and paved the way for attempts at helping those people later in our career.

As well as trips like these, we had a growing itinerary of concerts both sides of the Pennines, into Scotland and, increasingly, further south. With Final Recital and exam pressure building, we were becoming increasingly tetchy in rehearsal. Even on the concert platform there were unseen arguments going on during the course of a performance.

I remember quaking with embarrassment as the turbulent opening theme of Brahms' C Minor Quartet was made all the more angst-ridden by the refusal of Mike and Alex to give in to each other, the theme wilfully oblivious to the accompanying quavers, which doggedly stuck to their own rhythm. Another pre-concert rehearsal had me in floods of tears as my lyrical subsidiary line in Schubert's Quartettsatz was deconstructed for intonation, when the real problem was in the tricky violin theme above. A case of insecurity leading to blame-shifting. We seemed to have lost the ability to bolster each other's sense of self-worth, so vital in a healthy string quartet environment. The carefree days of our early embodiment seemed far away at times like these.

Professional life was beckoning in a real and frightening way. Whilst Darlington Dave was still reading smoke signals and harvesting the grapevine, now Ibbs and Tillett, one of London's top agents, had taken us on and was busy promoting us for the following season, when the boys would have finished their studies and I would have only my final year Performance Diploma to deal with.

In this year, 1981, we gave just short of forty concerts with an extensive repertoire. Whereas many groups make a point of choosing just one or two programmes for the season, we seemed to admit all comers to the list (a trait we have yet to wise up on). So, whilst lessons and exams were still ongoing at college, we were travelling up and down the UK – from the Isle of Arran to the Isle of White – as well as over to Europe on exchanges and for competitions, performing a vast repertoire. According to the old contracts that Ian recently came across in his attic, this included Beethoven op. 59 nos.1 and 2, 131 and 135; Haydn Opi 20/4, 64/5, 74/3, 76/1; Dvorak op. 9; Janáček No.2; Shostakovich Nos.3, 7, 8, 11 and 13; Hoddinott *Scena*; Lutoslawski; Schubert's *Death and the Maiden*, *Rosamunde*, the G Major and *Quartettsatz*; Bartók Nos.1,3 and 6; Smetana No.1; Mozart K389, 475, 489 and 590; two Mendelssohn Octets – with the New Budapest and Kodály Quartets, also on the books of Darlington Dave; and Mozart and Brahms Clarinet Quintets. Any full-blown professional group would have trouble coping with this amount of work, and there we were fitting it into our college timetable.

Perhaps this increasing pressure led to what happened next, or maybe it was the natural line being drawn at the end of formal education. Or the challenges of being in this close-knit entity since early childhood – the passionate arguments, dangerously close-to-the-bone joshing, a sense that we were all fair game and belonged to each other, come what may. Whatever the reason, one day after a lunchtime concert in Bradford we were enjoying an Indian with a group of college friends who'd come along to support us. The banter got out of hand, rather more chicken Jalfrezi ended up on faces than in stomachs and Alex, getting up from the table, declared he would walk home (which he did – all thirty-five miles) and later announced his intention to leave the group.

It wasn't a surprise. He had been growing apart from the rest of us, becoming much closer to his church friends, and it made perfect sense for him to find a new life amongst them and closer to his God. He actually spoke of the possibility of giving up playing altogether, hinting that his religious conscience couldn't reconcile the earning of money with the making of music (though in a Quartet this was never going to be a real problem!).

So not a surprise, but the shock was huge. The next big thing on our agenda was the return to Portsmouth for what we considered our rightful prize. How could we do this with a new line-up? There were a few months to go till the event, so it might well have been doable, but we still held the belief that we had formed a special bond that was not going to be easily rekindled. And should we even try? It was a big leap to imagine the group without the original four.

Generously, Alex agreed to fulfil his part at the competition, hopefully thereafter leaving us in a better position to entice candidates and, with the pressure of college finals out of the way, a whole summer to introduce the new member. So we got down to work and put the search on the back-burner, maybe even hoping things would change to make that scary prospect go away.

If we really wanted to win that competition, we went a funny way about it. First, we elected to play Janáček 2. Being one of our favourite old friends of the repertoire, it is nevertheless fiendishly difficult, with each player forced into madnesses of constant double-stops, excruciatingly high chord clusters and crazily fast motifs; in truth, an inaccessible piece with its bitty stops and starts, fragmented motifs and mad outpourings.

None of this would have been an issue, but on the jury there lurked one Milan Škampa, he of the lessons in Prague with his proudly reconstructed new edition, shirked unceremoniously by us in favour of our own version. What suicidal madness then to include it in our repertoire for the competition, where he was unlikely to ponder, 'Hmmm, ze kids are playing well – if zey don't accept my years of research on ze piece and make ze changes I suggest, no matter; it's a free world!' More likely he would take exception to our arrogant dismissal of his greater wisdom and declare to the rest of the jury that we hadn't a clue.

To add insult to injury, we chose another work for which his Quartet were famous (indeed after whom they were named!) – Smetana's *From My Life*. Another tricky little number, it contains some of the most fiddly, gratuitous passagework you will ever come across – tongue-twisters for the coordination, endlessly passed around the group, looking for the next victim to fall foul of its traps. It is also a fantastic piece, with passion, romance and tragedy in its unfolding drama, but maybe not competition material; if you want to play it safe there are many better choices.

Finally, and out of character, Terry had got himself thoroughly involved in our choice for the Late Beethoven final round, should we progress that far. Whereas we had several options amongst the pieces we'd been playing since childhood – Opi 130, 131 and 135 – he insisted on the elusive and enigmatic opus 127. Not only had we never played it, none of us had even heard it, so this was a learning-from-scratch situation. And let me tell you, our cheeky chappy, smokin', drinkin', gamblin' Cockney was no help when it came to the home straight and that perilous cello stuff, all high scales and octaves, out of reach for his two-finger technique.

In the end it was irrelevant, as we didn't even progress to the Beethoven Final. We battled through the early stages with a nervous tension our younger selves three years earlier had not had to endure, and went crashing out after the second round. This time, Eleanor Warren, who'd made the journey south again, didn't have to interfere, and in fact decided to berate us afterwards for choosing Janáček as she'd had a tête-à-tête with Maestro Škampa and learnt of his dissatisfaction with us. Well, she could have advised us against it!

My parents also, of course, came along for the ride, contrary to my pleas that they stay home. Dealing with Dad's disappointment was almost worse than handling my own. Somehow sensing failure, we were too nervous to attend the gathering in the hall to announce successful finalists, so we sent them – at last they were useful for something – and waited in the student apartment to hear our fate. As I watched from the window overlooking the concourse below, Dad's body language told me all I needed to know… marching ahead of the emerging crowds, fumbling for a match to light his pipe, Mam trotting in his wake, no doubt mumbling platitudes.

Next to emerge from the building were the members of the young Hagen Quartet, punching the air and high-fiving each other, clearly exultant in their successful passage onwards to the final. They had been causing quite a stir amongst the public and were strongly tipped for the top prize.

"Surely they can't win it!" we exclaimed. "They're kids – and we were told we were too young last time!"

Lucas, their eldest, and I were the same age, meaning their group were exactly the age we had been when we won the Most Promising Young Quartet Award in 1979. Sure enough, and to our indignation, they won first prize. A fabulous group by any standards, we soon forgave them and became good friends when we next met in competition – Banff's inaugural one the following year – subsequently enjoying many fine evenings of food, drink and banter when we coincided at festivals in the course of our respective careers.

Emerging around this time, and doing very well for themselves with a long and illustrious career ahead, was an American group going by the name of Emerson. They were an unusual bunch – alternated 1st and 2nd Violin chairs... imagine that!

26

Harmony

Returning from Portsmouth, crestfallen and full of doubt, the reality of the situation could no longer be avoided. It was nearly May, Alex had given us till the summer holidays and we had done nothing to find a new violist. No glorious competition win behind us, not much work in the diary, but at least a growing reputation that we thought might help to entice someone like-minded to join our journey; we could delay no longer.

As with the name-search, we sat around batting ideas back and forth for long hours, trawling through candidates from amongst our acquaintance... college and university, NYO, ECYO, even TYO – how nice it would be to find another from back home – but no one seemed quite right, or they were already on their own journeys with chamber groups, or in salaried jobs with professional orchestras. We couldn't expect anyone to leave the security of a proper job to join us, with our uncertain diary and vague prospects, but neither could we work with someone who had any other pulls on their time. As it did for us, the Quartet must take priority. We needed to find a contender with the same passion for our art, who could deal with financial insecurity in the name of devotion to the cause.

Throwing the net wider, Terry spoke to Hugh Maguire. He was still an active performer and teacher but also ran the String Department of the Britten-Pears School, hotbed for talent from all over the world. Hugh immediately came up with a name – a young Irishman he'd met whilst tutoring the Irish Youth Orchestra who had gone on to study at the Royal College in London, from which he was about to graduate. He lived for chamber music playing, and especially quartet, had just the right sort of character if Hugh knew us lot, which he did. He spoke to his secretary and a number was procured.

Mike made the call from the wall phone on the landing at Edge Lane, Ian and I perched on the stairs, eagerly listening in. So many important calls had been made from this spot and this was to be one of the biggest. Paul Cassidy, in his soft-spoken Irish tones, declared himself very interested in auditioning; a convenient weekend was selected and entered into all our diaries.

Surprisingly, preparation for this meeting didn't entail any detective work on our part. As I recall, we trusted Hugh's recommendation and felt there was no need to check Paul's credentials with spies in the London colleges. My twenty-first birthday was approaching and preparations for my 'surprise' party took precedence. I should've received an Oscar for my feigned reaction that day; some of my family had come to Manchester for the occasion, all my friends were invited, and several hints were accidentally dropped, especially by Mam, who was hopeless at keeping secrets – well, all except one big one of course – and could always be counted on to spoil a guessing game when we were kids. I dutifully and subtly stepped in on each occasion, covering up her mistakes, sparing her blushes and pretending to be oblivious to the plans in hand.

So the family left, friends dispersed and the detritus of this great party was still being cleared away a few days later when Mike drove off to Piccadilly Station to meet Paul's train. After ten years of what we considered to be a Fab Four Set-in-Stone Ensemble, it was an odd feeling to be inviting in a stranger, almost like a betrayal, and all the more exciting for it. As I awaited their arrival I paced around, tidying the Practice Room, getting out the music I thought we might play, putting on the kettle, searching for clean mugs. I was in that kitchen/diner that had so enticed us with its expectant four chairs around the table when we first viewed the house.

The front door slammed, a fumbling of luggage could be heard, footsteps approached. I took a step forward and greeted our newcomer with some inane awkward welcome, which he met with an engaging smile and a warmly spoken nothing of his own. He seemed big in that doorway, sporting an impressively garish suit, tall, with a mop of wildly curly hair – *A perm?* I wondered, in horror – and could I sense an American accent? It certainly wasn't like any Irish I'd ever heard. But there was something immediately captivating about this person, honest and open, with not a jot of the defensive cool that is second nature to most Northerners. Clearly feeling massively overdressed, he asked to be shown his room so he could change into something closer to our quartet uniform: Oxfam Casual.

With Ian delayed by no one knew what, the situation threatened to become embarrassing, but cups of tea, a bit of warming up, stepping out for fresh air, got us through. The mug of tea handed to Ian on his arrival being immediately smeared with engine oil told us where he'd been, and his breakdown story managed to nicely break the ice. He washed his hands, brushed down his clothes, then we shyly made our way into the business centre and got to work.

How strange it was to have a new voice in our midst. Almost like his speaking voice, Paul's sound was warmer and less angular than Alex's, his approach more spacious and generous. Although we'd often played with other musicians, no outsider had ever taken a role in this repertoire that was so much a part of our lives. Like the foreignness of being in bed with a new lover when you know the ex's body so well, this was exciting and scary all at once. My overwhelming feeling was one of gratitude that anyone would want to join us, give up their old life for an unknown future, especially in this rainy drab city... Suddenly all my childhood certainty that we were the best thing since sliced bread, or whichever of the million overblown phrases I'd penned in my diary to big us up over the previous ten years, was in doubt. Did we really have anything to offer? What was so special about us anyway? I decided the only true answer to this was to delve into rehearsal with total conviction and let the result speak for itself.

The weekend flew by, with the intensity of new discovery, again like finding that the object of your interest/desire has just the same tastes as you, all the same opinions, likes and dislikes. The easy flow of conversation over an Indian, having ordered the same dishes; equal enjoyment of a kick-around, with just the right mix of seriousness and fun, skill and passion for the beautiful game; discussions on music, favourite performers and composers – these all added to the pleasant discovery that rehearsals can work just as well, ideas swapped as easily, with a newcomer. Oh, and the inconvenient discovery in myself that an attraction was forming even by Day 2, which was certainly not in my remit.

Paul laid his cards on the table and openly admitted to us three that this was what he was looking for in life; a group with the tenacity, devotion, passion, that our decade together stood testament to so eloquently. Instead of being reserved and cautious, he felt that there should be no game-playing in this most serious process. We three could easily have agreed between us there and then to ask him to come on board, so sure were we of the fit. But we knew good sense dictated a certain restraint, so we scheduled another meeting a couple of weeks later, in

London, giving everyone time to take stock (and for us to meet with some other violists we'd planned to trial, although that process now seemed irrelevant). For this part of the audition, we had agreed to prepare a work none of us yet knew, Janáček's 1st Quartet, learning it together over the weekend and performing it for teachers and friends. This was a useful exercise, placing us all on a level playing field and allowing us to discover the music together. Following this next meet-up, we all agreed things felt right and happily sealed our fate in this new incarnation of the Brodsky Quartet.

Just as in a marriage or relationship, once the decision is taken to move on, it's hard to spend any more time in the old order. We couldn't wait to introduce our new identity to those around us and the greater world. An end-of-year concert at college, playing Beethoven opus 127, was scheduled for June and we felt it would be wrong to go out there with the old line-up; much more exciting and positive to showcase the new group. We'd already worked on the piece with Paul, were delighted with the ease of our ensemble and understanding so soon into our collaboration, pleasantly surprised that it could be this simple after all the fear of change we'd been suffering. But the Powers-that-Be – namely the College Principal – vetoed the idea as impetuous and unwise, so we were forced to give this last concert with Alex, feeling awkward, sad and happy all at once. Our enthusiasm for the new order would have to wait.

We did manage one outing together before term ended – an audition for the post of Quartet in Residence at Lancaster University. This could be just what we needed, perhaps offering us the cushion of a bit of income, a safe working environment in which to build confidence and repertoire with our new friend. We didn't get the job, apparently because they didn't have faith that such a recent change of personnel would have longevity.

"Where do you see yourself in ten years' time, Paul?" they quizzed our newcomer at the interview.

"Right here in the Brodsky Quartet, of course!" rejoined the already devoted member.

The certainty of his belief, so early on, was touching and reassuring. We felt able to relax for the summer. Due to a previous commitment, he was going to be studying in the United States for the whole period, so we would be unable to get to work properly till September. We went our separate ways with optimism for the new start, a spring in our step and – in my case – a tightening in the chest, just where the heart sits.

One thing I'd promised myself in this whole process was that I would resist falling for the new guy; it was a scenario I was determined to avoid, not least because it was such a cliché. I hated the idea that the only female in the group should necessarily be 'with' one of the guys, as though that was her passport to belonging. 'Twas ever thus I suppose – being the sister of one of them might lead some people to doubt the legitimacy of my place… even within my own family, I later realised. (I thought of adopting my mother's maiden name, Philippart, to give myself more of an independent identity in the group. It would've had the added benefit of sounding a bit more exotic too!) In those days, bands of all genres were mostly men, women like Linda McCartney taking the flack – someone put a tambourine in her hand and she can join us on tour. Except no one thought of her dignity, in the light of media derision that she was there as wifey and for no other reason, regardless of her recognised creativity.

I knew that my situation was different; I had formed this band as truly as the other three, my place was legitimate and proven. But self-doubt is a terrible thing and I didn't want anyone to have reason to join in with my own self-destruction. Plus, everyone knows that mixing business with pleasure should be avoided, relationships within a group being the embodiment of exactly that. There was the added matter that I was already living with my boyfriend of two years.

All these considerations went straight out the window as I caught myself eagerly preparing for Paul's return to Manchester that late summer. I helped Ian to convert a downstairs room in his girlfriend's house, providing temporary digs so that the Quartet could get straight to work unconcerned by flat-hunting. I had a sense of anticipation for more than just the working life awaiting us. In the course of our early concerts together, the pull was strong and we had already acknowledged it by late October. But my earlier determination kicked back in and by Christmas, sense and duty put the whole thing off limits. We were to spend an agonising four years in close quarters, being 'sensible' against all instinct, before giving in to the love that was deniable no longer, hoping it wouldn't cause problems but determined to make it work or give up the group if necessary.

The Brodsky Quartet grew in those first months from eager students to young professionals. The restart after summer had been precipitated by an approach from a new agent, Ingpen and Williams' David Sigall who, with his dapper English gentleman demeanour and diction, was as far from Darlington Dave as it's possible to be. We had come to their notice at the recent Portsmouth Competition, so we couldn't have been all bad, and the opening gambit of the new management was to offer us our first proper London concert, at the Wigmore Hall, in October. Paul had dropped his studies in sunny California without a second thought, and joined the rest of us in a rather more wintry Manchester.

We set to work, quickly conjuring up a couple of preparation gigs in both our home towns, Middlesbrough and Derry, where we got to meet the new extended family in both places and discover the uncanny similarities of both home lives and their stunning countryside surroundings. Being on the same line of latitude, the two places felt like parallel universes. Both bore the trademarks of being underdogs to the bigger cities close by, with a fierce pride and grit that we felt had informed our character as a Quartet long ago. The fit seemed more and more right.

The Wigmore debut was a huge success, eliciting rave reviews in national papers; finally all our hard endeavour was rewarded with accolades and recognition. We returned to Manchester, where they offered us a rehearsal space in the beautiful and spacious Hermitage at Hartley Hall, and we set to work rebuilding our repertoire with the new line-up. As my final year studies continued at college, I was having to work around an increasingly busy performing schedule, as well as two more competition outings that spring, one of them – the EBU – extremely fruitful. As always one step behind my colleagues, I graduated on the hoof, rushing back from the St David's Festival in Wales just in time to play my Performance Diploma recital.

My college days ended with a Gala Concert to mark Terry's retirement; the Schubert Quintet, with him on Second Cello, and then Brahms' G Major Sextet with Nobuko Imai joining us. It was a moving performance for us all – the end of an era – and felt like a rite of passage into the greater world of music we were about to enter. The iconic Schubert was one of our earliest works, performed with William Bruce in the famous Music Room to a small audience of family and friends. Fifty years later, we have just recorded it, with the wonderful young Laura Van Der Heijden on Second Cello. I was touched to realise that the age gap between us is about the same as between Terry and me at his gala concert. Fittingly, and to our delight as we felt partially responsible for the inclusion of chamber music in the college curriculum, his parting gift to the RNCM was an annual prize for quartets, in his name.

Another Residency came our way, at Surrey University. This time the job was ours for the taking, but would mean the end of Manchester as the Quartet's base. Affiliated with the post were a concert series and free cottage accommodation on the grounds at Sutton Place, a magnificent Elizabethan stately home near Guildford, with the added support of South East Arts and all the incumbent concert opportunities in the region. Here we would soon make our first commercial recording – Elgar's Quartet, which he had dedicated to the original Brodsky Quartet. Somehow this brought us full circle and felt like a fitting tribute to the Northern roots we had transplanted to Chorlton-cum-Hardy.

Five years previously we had arrived here full of enthusiastic expectation and belief in our group. Now a huge change had taken place and we were a year in to proving ourselves with a new line-up, equally full of plans, eagerness and ambition. As we packed up the old house at Edge Lane for the move south, memories of our long childhood journey filled me with nostalgia and sadness... and an unknown future beckoned with all the excitement of imagined conquests.

Postlude

J, M & R signing off

After more revising I listened to Shostakovich 7 and got so carried away that I got up and danced.
 Then I did my English and Music, tried the dress on with Mam and came to bed. I wish you a very good night and cosy too and hope that your tooths don't irritate you! Gosh I didn't expect that to ryhme! Can't spell!
 Just now I'm thinking about music and how it is everything to me. I keep wanting to write down my feelings. I can't just go through life without keeping track and not letting myself forget the fantastic times I have had and will have.

Where is the girl who started this journey? Still here, believing. After half a century, I suppose I'm fast approaching a world record for membership of the same string quartet, along with Ian of course. It hasn't been easy to keep the faith in this notoriously difficult dynamic, with all the emotional and stressful challenges that come with the territory. Even though we've had relatively few personnel changes, each one has been difficult in its own way, testing my resolve to keep going.

Paul and I were married in 1990, in a fairytale French chateau as we had 'moved' to Normandy. Coinciding with a time when all four of us had reasons to either live or spend long periods in countries other than the UK, it seemed like a good idea, but became impractical and an expensive way to work as a full-time quartet. We were back in London and starting our little family a few years later. And suddenly everything is given a new perspective; nothing matters but these utterly wonderful beings you want to hold and protect and love with every minute of your day.

Having babies and young children within our lifestyle is hard, as it is for many self-employed parents. Work routine is ever-changing, income unpredictable. Maternity leave wasn't even considered, by me or my colleagues, so we had to fit my pregnancies and births into specific time periods, neither thing guaranteed to work to order. I would be performing up to the wire – on one occasion actually in labour on stage – and sometimes feeling decidedly unwell. Given the lack of routine, there was no fixed childcare that could fit with our needs, so the cost of the necessary full-time nanny wiped out one of our earnings. And alongside a schedule of up to one hundred concerts a year, it was exhausting.

On an emotional level, I was torn about separation and even when we travelled with the children, which was almost always, I hated leaving them for long hours while we rehearsed, performed, recorded, had meetings. When we left them at home it was worse. I found an extract of a short-lived diary begun at this time. My pain is palpable – after speaking on the phone to Celia who had been stung by a wasp, or Holly who'd felt unwell in the night... the separation was a constant visceral ache. Even though, it has to be said, going off to work sometimes felt like a holiday, as so many working parents of young children will testify, I experienced a powerful urge to give it all up and be at home with them; to give up the quartet and maybe playing altogether.

Paul was hugely supportive in these moments, reminding me what I'd built since I was ten years old, pointing out that the girls would never thank their mother for jacking it in for them, that rather I would be an inspiration to them if I continued. He was right – as they've grown up they have said so repeatedly. And they feel they've benefited hugely from the life experience; travelling, having adventures, meeting weird and wonderful people, hearing music... While we played our refined notes on stage, the girls sometimes listening attentively, sometimes sitting backstage with a DVD on the laptop, cosy on cushions on the dressing room floor, we would indulge their musical tastes on our travels – Australia filled with KT Tunstall, Switzerland with Green Day, America with Ed Sheeran. Or our choices for them to soak up, blissfully new to the joys of a host of iconic tracks – *Take it to the Limit* in Gran Canaria, *Bridge Over Troubled Water* in Canada, *My Baby Just Cares For Me* in Italy. We have built so many precious memories together. And despite any sense of success in music, I feel that these two wonderful girls have been my greatest achievement and joy.

Ah, music. The soundtrack to my life has made this writing project such a pleasure. Memories never fail to move when music is involved. What is a life without music? Looking back on the experiences I had as a child – and so many like me – how can governments so callously make cuts and undervalue this most important art form? Music is everywhere – every shop, restaurant, theatre, television, cinema, radio, social media platform. How would this world function if musicians were not formed, nurtured, cherished and rewarded? The insulting implication is that writers and performers will find their way, against the odds, because it is a vocation and they can't help themselves, doing it 'for the love of it', so there'll always be more coming through the ranks, providing the soundtrack to everything, creating as well as playing an everlasting stream of original music, all meaning something to someone.

Taking centuries of classical music out of the equation, just look at the legacy of Western popular culture in my own lifetime, all created by someone out of the same twelve notes. The tunes accompanying all those old TV programmes, real music with harmonies and touching chord sequences to catch your emotions and stay with you forever. The old fuzzy images of *Robinson Crusoe*, with the fabulous undulating theme tune and exciting polyrhythmic action music; *Belle and Sebastian*, with two alternative tunes sung by an adorable French boy treble, a countermelody for the discerning child to sing along to; *Magic Roundabout* also with its clever counterpoint; *The White Horses* and their sexy young women chanting '60s Peace; *Song of Norway*, featuring an entire playlist of Greig's greatest hits; Malcolm Arnold's heart-wrenching score for *Whistle Down the Wind* bringing at least as many tears as the storyline; *Everybody's Talkin'* at *Midnight Cowboy*; that bicycle scene in *Butch Cassidy*, with Burt Bacharach's *Raindrops*... Meanwhile the Beatles are gifting the world *Good Day Sunshine* and *Yesterday*; Bob Dylan, Carole King, Nina Simone and thousands more, filling our senses and enriching our lives with their generous offerings. On and on through the decades, from The Monkeys to 10cc, Arctic Monkeys to UB40, song upon song upon song... *Postman Pat* and *Okey Doke*, *Babar* and *Tintin*, *Fantasia*, *Grease*, *Mamma Mia*. *Ludvig*, a brilliant preschool cartoon using Leitmotifs from Beethoven for every character; *The Clangers*, teaching notation and music-powered space travel! Randy Newman's brilliant and moving *Toy Story* score, tracking every millennial's childhood and coming of age; Mozart's soaring vocal quartet, filling the Shawshank prisoners with hope and beauty. The little boy on YouTube who conducts Beethoven's 5th while his parents film him, he becoming frenzied in his excitement as the last movement approaches (hearing what the composer wanted us to hear). "Here comes it!" he cries, in pure ecstasy. My own kids showing just the same irrepressible delight as *Fantasia* portrays the climactic beauty of *The Firebird* or the adorable mushrooms dance to the *Nutcracker*, the terror of the *Rite of Spring* or *Sleeping Beauty*, sobbing nostalgia for *The Snowman*.

And if no one learnt the bugle, a feat of technical prowess that its simple sound belies, where would we be on Remembrance Day? *The Last Post*. Despite – or perhaps because of – its being in a major key, and it being infused with a stoic, jaunty nature, that solitary line of music makes us weep.

The Quartet's journey continues. Whilst our travels take us to the four corners of the globe, we are frequently invited back to our old haunts in the North-East, performing for the local music societies still going strong. We were all awarded Honorary Masters at Teesside University, now sited in the old Polytechnic where we had given our very first public concert, the ceremony being held in that other old haunt, the Town Hall. We work with Streetwise Opera there, a superb initiative offering participation in high-quality music to people who have experienced homelessness. The TYO (now called Tees Valley Youth Orchestra) recently celebrated its fiftieth anniversary with a reunion concert and party, but we were as far away as it's possible to be, performing that night in Sydney Opera House.

By all accounts it was a great night, with many of our old friends attending. We sent a video message from down-under. Edwin is no longer with us but his spirit was in every note resonating around the Town Hall, some of his favourite repertoire from the old days being reproduced lustily by our young counterparts in today's Youth Orchestra. Even now they are well aware of what was begun here; there's an energy you don't necessarily find in all such young performers. I sincerely hope they find their path is true and unfettered by political posturing and callous cost-cutting.

Even as the economic effects of seismic world events threaten lasting and tragic damage to the arts as a whole and music in particular, it should be our priority to preserve it for future generations and remember just what it means to us all.

Otherwise, as Churchill once said, what would we be fighting for?

> After orchestra we walked home in the rain and got chips. We had the most brilliant impro we've ever had with a fantastic ending with me leading. After that we had a great dance to African Sanctus. It's amazing!!!

Acknowledgements

I would like to thank those who have helped me during the writing of this book. It was a monster of a project to realise for me, a total novice.

For their encouragement and constructive criticism in the editing process: Adam Kuper, Helen Greathead, Caroline Grace-Cassidy, Karin Koberling-Whiteman, Andrew Ford, Paul Cassidy and Alan Thomas, who also proofread.

For their help jogging my memory: Lynda Perry, Angela Daly, Sally Beamish, Martin Roscoe, Eleanor Wilkinson, Sophie Harris and Ian Belton.

I would also like to thank my parents and siblings who encouraged our efforts from the beginning, along with the Belton and Robertson families. Thanks also to our families and to friends Tim and Anne Jeans, Rob Tooze, Lynda Perry and Jacksons Solicitors for their help in gathering the photo gallery, and to Luca Bonnano for his patient help in compiling it.

Huge thanks to Holly Cassidy and José Palma for their fabulous work on the cover. I feel I can embrace my younger self at last! Thanks also to Celia Cassidy for the trophy photography and to Holly for her help compiling the montages.

Thank you to Sarah Cresswell for her wonderful present-day photos used on the cover and About the Author.

Thanks to Fern Bushnell and the team at Matador for their patient help.

And mostly I thank my beloved family, Paul, Holly and Celia, who have spurred me on from start to finish, in this project as well as in life.

Related titles available at Matador

Get Beethoven! by Paul Cassidy

A comic book character is born, the youngest of sixteen, into a war-torn country. Facing extreme brutality at school and on the streets, not to mention the oppression of the Catholic Church, he finds music. Armed with a violin and a burning passion, he escapes the madness and sets off to pursue his dreams. *Get Beethoven!* is the inspirational story of Paul Cassidy's life. Overcoming adversity in his younger years, Paul recounts tragedy, joy, horror and humour. Informative and entertaining, the book charts his journey up to joining the Brodsky Quartet in 1982.

Got Beethoven by Paul Cassidy

Following on from Paul Cassidy's popular prequel, *Get Beethoven!*, *Got Beethoven* is a brutally honest and relentlessly entertaining account of what it's like to be in a band. All the fun, angst, rewards and toil are brought to life and given the authority that can only come from actually living the life. The quartet's unique fifty-year history and ground-breaking musical journey means that on the same page we can enjoy tales involving such diverse artists as Sting, Anne Sophie von Otter, Björk or Maria Joao Pires. Their global travels release strikingly diverse adventures from King's College Cambridge to Roskilde, Montreux to St James' Palace.

With something for everyone, Paul Cassidy's highly personal story manages to be factual and informative whilst remaining infectiously entertaining. Suitable for all readers, from autobiography lovers to those who just love a great story!